THE COMPLETE WOMAN

Books by Patricia Gundry

HEIRS TOGETHER

WOMEN BE FREE

THE ZONDERVAN FAMILY COOKBOOK

THE WIT AND WISDOM OF D. L. MOODY
(compiler and co-editor)

THE COMPLETE WOMAN

Being a Whole Person

PATRICIA GUNDRY

Zondervan Books
Zondervan Publishing House
Grand Rapids, Michigan

The Complete Woman
Copyright © 1981 by Patricia Gundry

Zondervan Books
are published by Zondervan Publishing House
1415 Lake Drive, S.E.
Grand Rapids, MI 49506

Library of Congress Cataloging-in-Publication Data

Gundry, Patricia.
   The complete woman / by Patricia Gundry.
      p.   cm.
   Reprint. Originally published: Garden City, N.Y. : Doubleday, 1981.
   Bibliography: p.
   ISBN 0-310-21801-2
   1. Bible.   O.T.   Proverbs XXXI,   10-31—Criticism, interpreta-
tion, etc.   2. Women—Religious life   I. Title.
   [BV4527.G86   1989]
   248.8'43–dc19   88-33684
                                                                              CIP

Permission to quote from the following sources is gratefully acknowledged:

Excerpt from "Are Women Human?" From *Unpopular Opinions*, copyright
© 1947 by Dorothy Sayers, by permission of the Trustees of the Estate of Miss
Sayers.

Choose Success, Claire Cox and Billy B. Sharp, Hawthorn Books, 1970.
Copyright © 1970 by Claire Cox and Billy B. Sharp.

Printed in the United States of America

89 90 91 92 93 94 95 / LP / 10 9 8 7 6 5 4 3 2 1

For the two most important
women in my life, my mother,
Frances Smith, and my daughter,
Ann Gundry

Contents

The Complete Woman

CHAPTER 1

Who Can Find Her?

Women are seeking. From where I sit I can see in my bookcase *The Fulfilled Woman, The Total Woman, Fascinating Womanhood,* and *The Feminine Principle.* All these books try to tell women how to find what they are seeking. They tell how to get what you want. Or how to want what you get, and convince yourself it is wonderful. And they all do it by telling women to be weak, submissive, even subservient.

They insist that God is on their side. In fact, that is their proof that their way is best, guaranteed. God is in it. And that's exactly where they are wrong. God does not require that women stifle themselves to please him. The position reflected in these popular books is the result of a distorted view of God and of what the Bible says about women.

I don't blame the women who wrote these books for telling their fellow women to limit themselves and get what they want by manipulation. They were trying to help fill a gap with the best they had at hand. How would they know otherwise? We have been taught their basic philosophy from pulpit, textbook, and media for so long that it was only a matter of time before someone figured out all the angles to make it pay and wrote it down. But it won't satisfy. Not for long, because it goes against the grain of what we are. We are human beings. And human beings, even female human beings, don't seem to enjoy slavery or demeaning positions. They are ultimately uncomfortable with hypocrisy and lies. As long as women believe that being less than they really are is the way to find whatever it is they are missing, they will still be seeking.

If you are seeking for that certain something, something maybe you can't even put a name to, then I think I have good news for you.

I will venture to say that what you are seeking is *wholeness*. You want to feel together, complete, harmonious within yourself and in relation to the rest of the world. This desire for wholeness may not surface as such in your mind. You may think instead that the problem is your job, or the man in your life, or the fact that there isn't one in your life. Or you may think it's your looks or lack of poise or self-confidence. But under it all there is the feeling that something is missing. You don't quite feel *fulfilled*; part of what you need is not there. You want the inner conviction and the outward manifestations of being in sync with the universe.

I am going to enter a plea and endeavor to prove that this completeness is available to women now. And that it is not attained by trying to find your "place" but *by being all that you are*, both as you are at this present moment and all you yet can be.

Before you look at yourself disparagingly and say, "That lets me out, I'm not at all satisfied with what I am," let me warn you that you probably do not know all that you are and know only a fraction of what you can be. We, as females, are trained almost from infancy to hold back what we are, to minimize it, freeze it out, cut it off, make it shrink and die. The process is so insidious and relentless that we come to accept it and then foist it off on our daughters. So don't say that to yourself. You don't know yet all you can be.

The Bible is full of strong women. You will have to look hard and long to find any who would match the kind of descriptions being peddled to us now as the ideal. But one is hardly even aware of these strong women because they are rarely preached or written about accurately. Some are mentioned occasionally for illustrative purposes, but even then usually in a distorted manner. We could go from book to book in the Bible and analyze the resources and actions of these strong women, and that would be profitable, but it isn't necessary to range so far and wide. There is one chapter in the Bible that says it all in microcosm. It's all right there. So I invite you to walk through that chapter with me and look first at that woman, and then at yourself.

Then I hope you will choose to reach down within yourself and welcome forth that person who is really you. When we are finished, I think you will be surprised at all you are that is good and fine that you were unaware of before. And I think you will see possibilities for what you can become that will be only the beginning of lifelong growth for you as a person.

The chapter is Proverbs 31, especially verses 10 through the end of the chapter.[1]

Misunderstandings about this woman

I sat in an auditorium a week ago listening to an intelligent, gifted woman speaker talk about the role of women in the home, and heard her make jokes about the woman in Proverbs 31. I wanted to jump to my feet and say, "But you don't really know her. You've got it all wrong, she's not what you think." The speaker, as so many others have done, viewed the woman of Proverbs 31 as some sort of impossible superwoman who neither slept nor rested.

Not long before that, I read a witty article in a major Christian magazine that took the same tack. The writer said the Proverbs 31 woman caused a lot of problems for other women. She said, "She makes me tired just to think of all she does."

Both of these women missed the point of the passage. This Proverbs woman is not an impossible paragon we are to labor to copy. This woman is an example of a *whole person*. She is a woman with no repressed parts, no neglected gifts, no thwarted abilities. She is whole. Her whole self works itself out in many different ways. Our wholeness may express itself in yet other ways. But we can learn about wholeness and how we can attain it by looking closely at all she was.

The strong woman

Proverbs 31:10 begins: *Who can find a virtuous woman?* (King James Version). The Jews call her, instead of the "virtuous woman," the "woman of valor." The Hebrew word translated so seemingly differently is one that has a composite meaning. It literally means "strong" or "valorous" and includes implications that this fundamental strength extends into the moral realm, that she is strong in many good ways. Our translators, perhaps thinking their readers might understand her better by the word "virtuous," left it at that. But it carries much more in meaning. This woman *is* strong. She is self-confident, a good worker, manager, and planner.

What would you call a woman like that? I have chosen to call her "the strong woman" in this book because it exemplifies the core of what she had to be to carry out all she was in all its variety. She had to be strong enough to be her own person. And even stronger to be her own person without pulling away from others and being uncaring toward them.

Advice from a royal mother

Proverbs 31 begins with the explanation *The words of king Lemuel, the prophecy that his mother taught him* (KJV). We do not know who Lemuel was and know nothing else about his mother than this portion reveals. Some say he may have been an Ishmaelite king with a Jewish mother. But whoever he was, he memorized his mother's words.

She teaches him that he should not give his strength to women. It seems strange for her to say that in the same passage that tells all about how to recognize the best woman of all, this strong woman. Her point is that he must not have relationships with the kind of women who would dissipate and deplete him. Such women would be those who take but do not give, weak women who drag others down to their level.

Lemuel's mother then warns him against drunkenness, another pitfall that has so often deflected kings from their best. And she exhorts him never to forget his true calling, but to help those in need and to execute justice. Then, having warned him away from the worst kind of woman, she tells him about the best kind. To help him remember it well, she constructs her instruction in the form of an acrostic poem.

Hebrew poetry did not usually rhyme, but was assembled in parallels of thought or as an acrostic. This one, paraphrased to fit the English alphabet, would look something like this as an acrostic in our own language:

A wife with strength of character who can find?
Better than jewels she is.
Caring well for their resources, her husband need never fear,
Doing him good and not evil all the days of her life.
Ever with wool and flax she works with willing hands.

From afar, like the merchant's ships, she brings food.
Getting up early, she assigns tasks and apportions supplies,
Her hands plant a vineyard she has found and bought.
In strength she girds herself and strengthens her arms.
Just as she takes pleasure in good-quality workmanship, she also
   provides well for daily needs.
Knowing how to use the spindle and distaff, she uses them.
Leaving her work, she reaches out to help those in need.
May winter come! She has her family well clothed.
Never forgetting her own needs, she clothes herself well also.
One man is known in the gates because of her, her husband.
Putting her skills to work, she manufactures products for sale.
Quiet strength and dignity clothe her, she does not fear the future.
Reaching out to others, she speaks with kindness and wisdom.
She manages her household well and does not waste her time.
Tongues of her children and husband bless and praise her.
Unlasting is beauty, deceitful is charm, but a woman who reveres
   the Lord will be praised.
Verbalize her acts and accomplishments in the gates of the city;
   they will speak adequately for her praise.

Fortunately for me, there aren't the same number of letters in the
Hebrew alphabet as in English. I don't know how I would have
fared with x and z.

This woman was definitely married. Please don't let that stand in
the way if you are single. The qualities she had are possessed by people without regard to their marital status. And you must remember,
too, that Lemuel was told to *get* this kind of woman, she couldn't
very well be married already to another man. So it has to show *qualities* this strong woman would have, not describe a pattern to imitate,
or a woman to copy exactly.

Who can find her?

Now, how would Lemuel be able to spot an unmarried woman
like this one? And how could he get to know a prospect well enough
to find out if she was a "strong" woman? I doubt that he could. At
least, not in person. You see, casual dating just wasn't the thing one

did then. In fact, dating at all wasn't *in*. He would have to learn about her from others.

This made it even more difficult. The kind of woman kings were prone to acquire was not this kind of woman. A king might take a wife because she was very beautiful, as a decorative toy for himself. Or, more likely, he married the daughter of a neighboring monarch for political reasons. These women were apt to be laden with the faults that came from such backgrounds. They could be expected to be idle, gossips, followers of intrigue, manipulators, and shallow. Who would even think to offer him a strong woman like this one?

It amuses me to know that, in some circles at least, this would not be an enviable reputation for a woman to have when hoping for a royal husband, or any husband. For this woman is not compliant or subservient, she is capable and efficient, shrewd and reasonable.

Lemuel would have to actively search for a woman like this. He would have to ask, and be willing to do some investigating about her. But it would be worth it. She would be rare, yes, but she would be of great value (her price is far above rubies) because she would be a whole person, a balanced person. That's not only the best kind of person to be, it's also the best kind of wife to have, even though a king might not think so, left to his own counsel.

Why she was so unusual

I don't think it was easy to be this kind of woman then. Israel's was a patriarchal society in which women were regarded primarily as possessions. We do not know exactly when this chapter in Proverbs was written, so we cannot determine the prevailing attitude toward women in Palestine at this time from other sources. But we do know that early in the history of the nation of Israel, women were subject to the kind of abuse recorded in Judges 19, where a man set his concubine (a legal though minor wife) out to feed the sexual appetites of the neighborhood. When their mistreatment resulted in her death, this man cut her into twelve pieces and sent her severed body to the twelve tribes of Israel in protest against the bad treatment his property had received. The outrage was not that she had been sent back by her father to a husband she did not want to live with and had run away from, nor the use he had put her to, but that she had been killed.

Later in Israel's history, in the New Testament period, women were divorced by their husbands over trivialities (the woman could not divorce her husband). A husband could even keep his wife's dowry for such offenses as going out of her house without a covering over her head. Women were considered to be inferior humans, and a threat to pure men because of woman's assumed seductive nature. They were not educated. Their ability to even be taught was questioned by many.

Yet, in such a society as this, there were strong, whole women. In spite of the obstacles, they existed.

In a culture that places one group of people firmly under the domination of another and excuses the oppression by claims that the disadvantaged group *is* actually inferior and the inferior status merely custodial, certain weaknesses and vices can be expected to flourish. Among those who have the upper hand, oppressiveness and self-righteous hypocrisy proliferate. Among the disadvantaged, inertia, listlessness, lack of a feeling of personal worth, pandering, and manipulation and deceit grow.

A woman reared in a culture that regards her as an inferior being, and restricts her activities and intellectual opportunities accordingly, has a tendency to take on one or more of the above timeless methods of the underdog to make her way in life. She adopts these slave tactics to get what she can, or just to manage to keep sane in her situation. It is not easy to throw off such conditioning and live a whole life.

I have to think that somewhere, someone gave these strong women a sense of their importance to God, a feeling of worth, and an example of whole-personhood to adopt. There had to be some beam of light for them to follow. It may have been a parent, or some other relative, or even a servant who had not bowed to conform to society's inferior expectations for him or her. Being a whole person begets other whole persons by example.

Why strong women are rare now

We live in a culture that is also patriarchal. It has some obvious improvements for us over that of ancient Israel; it also has some disadvantages. Women may have been viewed as inferior beings then, but they were valued for the very real assets they could bring to a household. Our contributions, as women, are little valued in our society. Whether they be the contributions of a mother or household worker, a teacher or businesswoman, the respect and salary afforded women's efforts are minimal.

In our society we are told we are not inferior persons but are treated as though we were. Educationally, we are led to believe we will have equal opportunities. In grammar schools there are many bright little girls learning along with the boys. But in high school the girls begin to fall away scholastically. They begin to respond to our society's message to women: "Don't try so hard, keep back, women should be passive." From high school onward, women's opportunities and aspirations decline at an alarming rate.

The effects our society's treatment of and attitudes toward women have on its women are in many ways similar to the effects ancient Israel's attitudes and treatment produced in its women. Lacking a personal identity of our own, we tend to submerge ourselves in the identities of others, such as husbands and children. Those of us who do not marry often feel even more at a loss for personal identity. The unmarried woman is treated as though part of her is missing, and she has no one whose identity she can assume or partake of.

We do not dream of what we might do with our abilities. We learn to be less and less, instead of more and more. We adopt the ways of the underdog, learning to manipulate and pretend in order to get what we want. We sell our selves to gain position and things. No, it's not so easy to be a whole person here and now, either.

But it can be done. There *are* whole women out there. You see them occasionally and you never forget them. I went to a seminar on women at Wheaton College in Illinois a few years ago. One speaker burned her image on my mind. She was electric. It was not so much what she said, though that was good. It was the very force of her presence, the conviction that she was "together."

She mentioned the pitiful lack of role models for girls, that they have so few women to look up to, learn from, and pattern themselves after. I thought as I sat there listening and watching her, *She knows the value of her own presence here for these college students.* The young women in that audience could remember her strength and confidence and believe that they, too, could keep on when being whole became difficult. They could believe that they, too, could become as she was.

Never underestimate the power of your own example, even if you think it isn't much. About two years ago I was asked to speak to a college class about biblical equality for women. The class was team-taught by a married couple. The woman, a psychologist, is a capable, confident woman, well educated and poised. After the class session she enthusiastically and repeatedly told me she was so glad I had come to speak. I must admit, I thought she was being overly kind. My speaking is not *that* great. I said, "Thank you, but I didn't feel my contribution deserved such praise." She said, "You don't understand, *I needed* to see you up there before the class talking about your own journey toward wholeness. You were a living encouragement to *me*. You affirmed me as a woman by your presence." I was surprised that this woman even needed affirming, that she could need the encouragement of a housewife-turned-writer. But she did, and I in some way supplied it.

Since then I have not been so flip about it when someone tells me that what I have said or written meant a lot to them. We never know what needs we may meet in another by being a living example of someone who is being real, or whole, or kind, or understanding. We contribute from the depths of who we are just by being that person to those who need the reassurance to go on being *their* own person in a stressful or uncertain time. *It is always worth being you and being whole, whoever and whatever you are.*

Scope of the book

We will look at what it was like to be a woman long ago when the book of Proverbs was written. But mostly we will look at what it is like to be a woman today, here and now.

I want to encourage you to be all you can be, and in that sense this will be an inspirational book. But more than inspiration, I want to share information that is practical and usable about *how.* Some of the information comes from things I have learned about myself by making mistakes and living through situations, some comes from observing others. Other information is from sources that have helped me reach out toward my own inner self, encouraging me forward to grow and become more me, and more confident and secure about being me.

This is a sharing book, from me to you. I want the best for you just as I want it for me.

Why a biblical orientation?

Why am I writing this in the framework of a chapter in the Bible telling about a "strong" woman? Why a biblical base for a book to help modern women find themselves and become who they are?

There are basically two reasons for my approach. The first is that I personally like and believe the Bible. It has always been an encouragement and guide to me. I really believe that God made women equal persons to men, that he loves us and wants us to be all that we are capable of. And I came to that conviction through studying the Bible myself. Since I feel the Bible is a good source for information about how to live my life and know about God, I like going to it for help with my identity as a woman. I think women with similar views of the Bible will relate to what it says on the subject in a positive and joyful way.

But there is another reason that this book is biblically based. Many women do not have the view of the Bible that I do. They see it as an interesting book, and perhaps as a book that tells about God, but little more. Even though it may not seem so to them, the Bible has an important part to play in their lives as women.

We all come from a culture that has based much of what it does and thinks on a religious heritage that has its roots in the Bible. We live with stereotypes and prohibitions that have been defended as biblical norms for women by our religious forebears. Today's woman lives with the cumulative results of centuries of biblical interpretation that restricted all women. Whether we want to agree with the interpretations that have been used to restrict women or not, we live with the results of those interpretations.

Culturally we are tied to the Bible in many ways. Whether we be Jewish, Protestant, Catholic, or undecided, we are affected by what people have thought the Bible said about women. It will be good for all of us to see what this portion says about what a woman can be— what a woman can be with God's complete approval and praise for so being.

I feel it will be a freeing experience for you to learn about the Proverbs 31 woman and relate that knowledge to your own life. She has a lot to say to us and for us.

CHAPTER 2

Her Value

She is far more precious than jewels. (Prov. 31:10)

Many women feel they are not valuable. Oh, they may know that others rely on them and even honor them periodically on Valentine's Day or Mother's Day or in National Secretaries' Week, but *day-to-day* treatment tells them another story.

The work of women is generally not highly valued in our society. Even obviously superior work is commonly worth less if it is done by a woman worker or creator. Pay is less, respect is less. And that attitude is nothing new. Anne Bradstreet wrote in 1642:

> . . . I am obnoxious to each carping tongue,
> Who sayes, my hand a needle better fits,
> A Poets Pen, all scorne, I should thus wrong;
> For such despight they cast on female wits:
> If what I doe prove well, it wo'nt advance,
> They'l say its stolne, or else, it was by chance.[1]

A few years ago, while writing a book about equality for women in the Church, I discovered a feeling of worthlessness in women that surprised me. I had noticed long before, both in myself and in others, evidence of an inferior self-image. But I had not realized the extent to which a feeling of inferiority permeates almost every woman's self-image. The contrast I noticed in women who were gaining a new understanding of God's opinion of them and their value to him startled me.

At the time I began work on my book there was almost nothing of its kind in print on the subject, almost no biblically solid voice disagreeing with the traditional position that women were to be subordinate in the Church. When news of my proposed book was shared with a few friends and they told others, I began gradually to get phone calls from women that went something like this: "I have heard that you think women can be equal with men and that the Bible supports your view. How can that be? I wonder if I could come over and talk about it with you?"

It takes about three hours to go through all of the key Bible passages and explain what is wrong with our traditional repressive interpretations and give other possible interpretations that do not violate good interpretative principles. Most women would be skeptical at first. They were eager to free themselves, but afraid to believe that adequate reasons actually existed. They were polite, but not anticipating solid believable answers. But about midway through those explaining sessions I would begin to notice a change in my questioners. The skepticism would fall away gradually. I would begin to see a new brightness in their faces, a new *hope*. I could see them thinking, *Maybe it is really true.* Then an increasing eagerness to listen, verbal agreement, an increasing intensity. Their minds seemed to come alive in a new way, as though they were free to really believe they could think for themselves.

When these women left, they walked with a new vigor, stood taller. I can only say that their faces shone. They, for the first time, *really believed* they were equal persons in God's estimation. They knew for the first time in their lives that all they had been told about subordinate positions, and about not doing good and fine things because it was not their place or role, that all these negative and restrictive teachings were false. They were ignited by what the Bible said about them, understood in a new light.

I began to watch for this change. It never failed to occur. Women come alive when they find out their true worth. A teacher who uses the finished book, *Woman Be Free!* in his sex roles and relationships class told me not long ago that he, too, sees the same transformation in his women students as they become aware of their equality before God.

But most women haven't heard this good news. They don't even know the extent to which they hold themselves back from their best work, their freest expression, their full creative potential. Most women do not know how valuable they are. They have been taught to value themselves as others do. And others value them for only *part* of what they are and can be, and only to the extent that is convenient for the people they serve.

Our strong woman was valuable because she was uniquely herself. She was multitalented and multifaceted. She was whole, together, she was balanced.

You are valuable to God because you are one of his human creations. You are as valuable to God female as you would be if you were male. Maybe more so. Perhaps the unique combination of your abilities and insights, personality and potential, added to the fact of your gender, fit you for a job or contribution that only a female person would be able to do in our time and place. I like to think that God made me female because he had some things that needed doing that the female experience and my assets would make possible.

Others may not value you as highly as you deserve. But God does. And you can. Your greatest value quotient will, however, be reached only as the balanced whole that you potentially are. You are not as valuable in a *practical* way when part of you is suppressed and misused or not used at all. You are still as valuable *as a person*, but part of what you are is not being used. Its value is hidden, not convertible currency. It cannot spread and add to the wealth of others. It cannot add to your own personal sense of worth hidden away in secret within you. Being whole means using all facets of yourself, leaving nothing that is you out in the cold to freeze and die.

It isn't always easy to be whole. Some people are threatened by wholeness in others—particularly in women. During certain periods of history, wholeness in women could be extremely costly for the woman daring to go as she must as a whole person.

Anne Hutchinson is a name from America's past. She was accused of heresy in colonial America and banished from her colony. Her heresy was identified as "antinomianism," that is, she was accused of wanting to live above the law, to be without God's instruction and rule. Whether that is a true appraisal of Anne Hutchinson's philosophy and reflects her theology is a debatable question. She may only have wanted to exercise her freedom as a Christian to go to God directly, sidestepping the parson and elders. Her flaw may have been to resist the power others wanted over her. But whatever her heresy or difference, she was banished for daring to express and live by her own conscience in religious matters. For her and her family, it meant leaving the protection of the settlements and going into the wilderness to live, where they were then massacred by Indians.

If Anne Hutchinson were alive today she would fare much better.

Her detractors would have to settle for trying to discredit her, perhaps put some pressure upon her employers to fire her or to fire her husband. There would be lies, innuendos, maybe even public humiliation. But probably not even that. It wouldn't cost as much now to differ with the religious powers.

During the witchcraft craze in Europe thousands of women died for daring to be a little different, for speaking out when others wanted them silent, sometimes for imagined slights. Knowing the dislike many people can rouse for a woman who is "uppity," "doesn't know her place," is "unfeminine," "brazen"—or any of the other derogatory terms for women who don't stifle when they're told to stifle—I am convinced that witchcraft was too often a handy accusation to use to punish women who insisted on being whole persons.

Being a woman who doesn't follow along sheeplike can be compared, in some respects, to being a slave who knows too much or is not subservient enough. If the slave bowed and scraped and kept his or her "place," they would be relatively safe from abuse. But if too much initiative or individuality was revealed, then the slave became a threat and a target.

But slavery is not here anymore. No one can own your body. Some people may try to by saddling you with obligations and restrictions that keep you working and in fear. But there are ways to escape that bondage. They do not own your body. And more than that, no one can own your mind. The cost of freedom is not so high anymore.

It's still not easy, though. Not for most women. It's not that there are obvious barriers to fling ourselves against. They seem to be invisible. We struggle against attitudes and conditioning, custom and training. There are laws and practices that hold us down, it is true, but more insidious than those are the attitudes within us that hold us back, and the attitudes in others that make them block our way out and up toward being all we can be. Often they think it is for our own good, that they are protecting us when in fact they are smothering us and taking away our own initiative and confidence.

Difficulties in being whole when married

I am married. There are lots of things I like about being married. But I remember the awful cold loneliness I experienced when I realized shortly after my marriage that I was no longer the same person in the eyes of many of my friends. It was as if I were now the possession of someone else, I no longer belonged to me.

The first thing I remember about this feeling, so new to me, was a trip to the bank to establish a joint account with my husband. The bank clerk said, "You will want to sign your name Mrs. Stanley Gundry, won't you?" And my husband answered for me, "Yes." I had a feeling of losing myself. *But I love my own name,* I thought, *it's me!* "No," I said, "I will sign it Patricia Gundry." But the feeling stayed. *My last name is gone, they were going to take away even my own first name. My identity will be entirely submerged in that of my husband.* We were students together in college, sharing library study time, discussing philosophical questions, sharing so much. Until we married. Then our ways split; mine was the lesser way.

I had enjoyed the friendship of many of my classmates who were young men. I don't mean dating, we were just good friends, we talked and joked and were relaxed with one another. Not more than a week or two went by before one of them said to me in a conversation, "All right, Patsy Smith, that's not right . . ." and caught himself. "I forgot that you're married, that's not the right name." This time the name loss wasn't what bothered me, it was the change in his relating to me after he caught himself. I wasn't his friend the same way anymore. I was someone else's woman. He would be careful and keep at a respectful distance. It was a subtle wall that rose between me and every other fellow I knew. And I did not erect the wall.

One of my husband's classmates from a previous college came by to see him not long after we were married. The young man looked at me with awestruck eyes. I kept feeling as if I were some possession he was envious of my husband for having acquired. *I was not a person to him, I was an object.*

I am sure my newly married experiences are not unique to me. Other women must have felt that awful loneliness too, that becoming some*thing* instead of staying *someone.* I now had a "place," a role. But it wasn't me, not all of me. Yet what I was didn't seem to matter to anyone anymore except me. I wondered what was wrong with me that I didn't fit in. Why was I so lost?

My husband probably didn't understand what I was experiencing at all. He had none of the same problems. I had friends at the dorm who continued to flirt with him as always. No one asked him to give up any part of himself. It was understood that I would drop out of school when there was no longer money for both of us to go. He had been raised to accept women as mysterious and puzzling. So when I tried to tell him I hated the institution of marriage, that I wanted our *relationship* with each other to be as it had always been, only closer, but I hated what *marriage* was doing to me, I'm sure he didn't understand what I was trying to tell him. It didn't bother him very much, however, because I was not to be totally understood, and he was busy going to school, planning for his future, working. While he had a full and promising life ahead, I was beginning to wonder about mine.

Many women give up more than a sense of self in marriage, more than an identity. They give up using abilities, growing intellectually, dreaming dreams and making them come true.

Some women give up their health. I knew a student's wife when my husband was in seminary who was literally losing her health serving her husband. She worked full-time to support him while he gave his whole attention to his studies. Not only that, but she also typed all his papers and saw to his other needs, as well as those of their apartment. He was accustomed to being served and accepted it as his due. She, so used to doing his bidding and putting her own well-being last, did not seem to see what her burning-the-candle-at-both-ends life was doing to her. They made quite a contrast together, she pale, thin, and tired and he vibrant, hale, and hearty. I have thought about her occasionally since those years and wondered if she is still alive. How she could keep that up indefinitely I can't imagine.

Some married women give up parts of themselves because their husbands are demanding, some because they are afraid their husbands will feel inferior if they cut loose and be all they long to be. Some have subtle games played with them that destroy their confidence over the years. Finally the light of hope goes out in their eyes. They become cowlike and plod along, waiting for death to free them.

Trivialization

Whether married or single, women are all subjected to the trivialization of their desires, abilities, and aspirations. Girls' sports aren't as important as boys' sports. Scholarships for women aren't as bountiful as those for men. A woman has a job "because she is waiting for a husband" or "has only herself to support." When neither explanation fits, the true financial need and ability of the woman worker are neatly forgotten.

One woman told about the trivialization of her work as a beginning writer in an interview with a writers' magazine. She said, "Well, I do know that it was important to me; and my then husband would say at parties, 'All I have to do is buy Judy some paper and pencils and she's happy. Isn't that terrific—it keeps her out of the stores—it keeps her away from the card games!' I was so angry at that kind of statement—that my efforts were taken so lightly."[2]

But she did one very important thing for herself that kept this discounting of her work from snuffing it out: she took her own self and desires seriously, even when others did not. She continued, "It was true that nothing was being published and that remained true for two and a half years. Nevertheless, I was working very hard and I was taking this seriously even if no one else was. You know that wasn't even criticism. That was just joking. And while it really hurt, he had never read anything that I had written. So it hurt in one way, but it didn't hurt in another because it was like I had this secret. I knew what I was doing and he didn't."[3]

Our whole society trivializes the work of women. The reasons for this attitude can be traced historically and sociologically, but it is more important for us to face the fact that it exists and come to grips with that fact in a concrete and decisive way than to analyze the root causes.

What is true of society at large is often true of society in its smallest units. Other family members usually do not view Mother's work as valuable compared to their own needs and work and the work of Father. But we do not have to reflect society's treatment of us. We can reeducate ourselves and gradually reeducate those around us to take our needs and contributions seriously.

Difficulties in being whole while single

If a single woman uses all her abilities, she is "compensating for not having a husband and children." If she is assertive and decisive, she is a woman "no man could get along with." A single woman is seen as someone with a piece missing. That piece is magically supplied when a husband is added to the picture. I've even heard sermons preached about men and women being two incomplete people, needing each other before either one is whole.

That's just not true. Even a half-hearted investigation of human experience, or of the Bible, or a reasonable assessment of the personalities and capabilities of men and women would reveal that people are people one by one. It takes one person to make a whole person. Individuals (male or female) may enjoy other persons and gain from a relationship with another and give something also, but each one is whole and complete by himself or herself. We are so created and, if allowed, will grow and flourish as individuals.

The notion that woman is incomplete without man is old. It goes back at least to theologians like Augustine, who wrote:

> The woman herself alone is not the image of God: whereas the man alone is the image of God as fully and completely as when the woman is joined with him.[4]

That was a neat invention to fit into a theological framework making man the center of the universe with woman firmly under him in every way. The Bible shows woman created equal to man with equal dominion over the earth:

> So God created man in His image; in the image of God He created him; male and female He created them. God blessed them; God said to them: Be fruitful and multiply; fill the earth and subdue it; bear rule over the fish of the sea; over the birds of the air and over every living, moving creature on earth. (Gen. 1:27,28)

A few verses later God expresses satisfaction with his creation:

> God saw that everything He had made was excellent indeed. (Gen. 1:31)

Surely God did not regret his equal creation of woman later and shorten her capabilities.

But unmarried women have reason to wonder if they are included. The single woman is treated like a social fifth wheel. Everyone wants to invite an eligible bachelor, I'm told, but it's a problem parceling out the eligible women. Then there's the term "old maid." All these attitudes add up to a message that you are somehow substandard if you are single and female. Either you are flawed and no one wants you, or you are bereft and widowed and surplus merchandise. Few encourage you to be all you can be. People seem to have a hard time seeing you as a full person apart from marriage or nonmarriage.

Self-valuing

We've been looking at a woman's value to others, how low it is and has been. But what about a woman's value to herself? Women are valued for parts of who and what they are, not often for all they are and can be. Do you value yourself accurately and fairly? Do you value all of your potential?

Women have given up (and still do give up) safety, security, even the respect of others to have the self-respect that comes from being all they knew themselves to be. But it is more than self-respect that motivates a woman to risk loss to gain herself. It is, I think, a hearkening to a God-given longing to use what one has been given. It could be called ambition if we looked at it only on the surface, but I don't think we can limit it to ambition. I believe God gives us abilities, talents, potentials, and that he also gives us the longing to discover and use them. It is, in a very real sense, the pain of ignoring this God-given drive that moves some women to go on against great odds to find and use their abilities.

Using one's resources, all of them, has been hard for many of our sisters in the past. It is becoming increasingly easy for us. I don't mean to say that it *is* easy, just relatively so. We can be encouraged. We are not in danger of being burned at the stake for stepping out of some "place" assigned to us by others. We may suffer misunderstanding, slander, and not a few other barbs, but in no way are we limited or burdened by the weights many of our foremothers had to lift off themselves.

And we have each other. Women have often found it hard to support other women because a woman's identity, even her safety, depended on alignment with a particular man. A woman could not afford to openly jeopardize her position with the key man in her life to support a sister who was stepping out or was forced out into the public arena. But women are learning. We are increasingly able to see one another in a light other than as rivals or competitors. We are learning to cheer one another on toward being whole and free as individuals even when the path a sister takes is not necessarily the one we would choose to follow.

A *valuable woman*. Could you use those words to describe yourself? To whom are you valuable? Why? What is your true potential value compared with your recognized value at this moment? To yourself and to others?

What are you potentially worth to your country, your church, your community, your friends and family, the world? Wouldn't it be an exciting process to spend the rest of your life discovering that potential and becoming it? Do you dare to dream of all you can be? Do you dare to take one tiny step forward into that freedom?

CHAPTER 3

Trustworthy

The heart of her husband trusts in her, and he will never lack profit.
(Prov. 31:11)

Since our Proverbs woman is the woman a particular man is encouraged to look for to fill the job description of wife, the virtues
and abilities talked about are within the framework of wifery. But
those virtues and abilities can be found in women regardless of marital status or age. They could be observed in a young girl, teenager,
wife, ex-wife, never-a-wife, and never-intending-to-be-a-wife. So if you
possess these virtues, own them with satisfaction whatever your mat-
rimonial or nonmatrimonial state. And if you would like to cultivate
them in yourself, you do not need a husband before you can begin.

The importance of trustworthiness then

A trustworthy wife was extremely important to our Proverbs man,
probably much more important than we can easily imagine. With
our generally uncomplicated view of life in times past and our stereo-
typical image of Bible women, we probably have little idea of what a
trustworthy woman meant to the average man.

Household management of that day involved more work and expertise and responsibility than most of us are accustomed to. It could
involve supervising many servants and large acreage. As manager, the
wife would carry the keys to the family storerooms and be in charge
of the accounting of household expenses. Even the physical well-
being of her extended household was in her hands, for part of her responsibility was treating the sick and injured.

Life was often uncertain then, and a man might be called away
from his home and properties for long periods of time to serve the

king or to go to war. There were religious duties that fell to men only and necessitated trips to the center of worship. A man needed desperately to have a wife who could be left in sole charge of all his possessions and personnel. He could not beg off duty to king and country by saying, "Sir, my wife is a cute little thing, but incompetent, and I can't trust her with making biscuits for breakfast, let alone managing the household. So I guess I can't come."

There was no Social Security then, no old age pension, no GI Bill, no veterans' benefits. If your wife let things go to ruin while you were gone, the loss could be irretrievable.

The importance of trustworthiness now

A man had to be practical about his choice of a wife. It seems strange to us, and unfeeling, to be so crass as to marry a woman in order to provide an heir to your property, to have a reliable manager for your household and business—solely to serve your own interests. We wonder, where was marriage for love? What about falling in love and marrying the beloved? There must have been an element of love and romance in many marriages, but the truth is they *had* to be practical. We haven't had to be.

And yet there is still a lot to be lost by untrustworthiness in a wife or husband. Since we emphasize love and romance, we too often forget the consequences of not being wise as well. How many divorces could have been prevented by giving careful attention to the attributes and qualifications of a prospective spouse *before* marriage? When I think of all the waste caused by divorce, the money, years of unhappiness, and the emotional cost of stress and disappointment, I wonder if we could perhaps use a little more attention to the practical side of marriage partner selection ourselves.

The unsung virtues

Trustworthiness is a compound virtue. It incorporates courage, intelligence, and capability. These component virtues are qualities that women are often penalized for possessing today.

A courageous woman is often portrayed as a masculinized woman. The popular media have trouble portraying women as real people. Women are so often presented as fearful, dependent, indecisive, and foolish. Occasionally you will see a real, courageous, together woman in a film or on TV. Interestingly enough, these women are usually atypical, that is, they are women somehow out of the mainstream of society. They may be minority women, those with uncommon backgrounds, or women from another time and place. Again, the effect is a statement that ordinary women, regular "normal" women, aren't like that. The message is that most women fit the stereotypes and therefore can be safely ignored. Things can continue as they have in the past.

Women themselves will sometimes stereotype all women as lacking some vital ingredient that would make them capable, trustworthy human beings. Yesterday I listened to a woman tell a television audience that if her son was wounded in battle she would not want some woman with *cramps* there trying to help him, she would want a *man*. To make it worse, several other women in the audience laughed at this insult. I was relieved and proud of my gender when another woman rose to counter this indictment of all women. She said, "I believe women are as courageous as men, possibly more so because we know how precious life really is."

Two stories of women's courage rise in my memory to meet and counter the effects of what I see and hear about us now. The first story is set on a country estate in India where a group of people gathered around an outdoor table are engaged in pleasant conversation. They are discussing courage, particularly whether women are as courageous by nature as men are.

Suddenly a woman at the table says softly to a nearby servant, "Bring a bowl of milk and place it yonder on the grass." All conversation stops as the guests' eyes widen in fear. The servant quickly brings milk and places it as directed. Slowly a cobra glides from beneath the table, the milk's scent attracting it away from its potential victims.

After the poisonous snake has been killed, the guests and their host turn to the woman. "But how did you know the snake was under the table?" they ask. She replies, "It was coiled about my leg."

I also remember reading a legend about a child stolen by a great predatory bird and rescued by a woman. The bird had swooped down and snatched an infant up from the cradle and carried it away in huge talons. The child was taken to the bird's nest at the top of a nearby mountain.

Strong men from the village set out to climb the mountain and try to save the child. But because of sheer cliffs and the fierce bird's attacks they were all beaten back and forced to admit defeat.

At last the child's mother was allowed to try. She alone was able to climb the mountain and retrieve the child alive. The story was told to illustrate a mother's love. I think it says much more. To me it says also that women are courageous, that they can do hard things and succeed where others think they cannot.

Not long ago I watched a series of programs on TV about the life of Lillie Langtry. I was impressed with her intelligence, courage, and capability. She was able to exercise those qualities and still be feminine (whatever that word actually means). I became so interested in her story that I made two trips to the library to get her biography.

Lillie was unjustly accused of many things purely because she dared to do the unusual. Clergymen tried to deport her from America, others wanted to ban her plays. (In case you don't know who she was, Lillie Langtry was a famous British actress of the Victorian and Edwardian eras.) The actions against her were often taken because of libelous stories and nothing more. She paid a price for doing unusual things and daring to be her own natural self in a society that was intolerant, snobbish, and artificial. But it seemed to be worth the trouble, to her, to do what she felt was right for her.

I am not saying that Lillie Langtry was in all ways a woman to model yourself after. I am saying that in the area of using her mind and abilities, she was. She did not need to stop and ask if what she wanted to do was acceptable to everyone around her. It was enough for her that it made good sense and was harmless to others.

Trustworthiness as qualification and means for growth

Being trustworthy and a woman may not mean much to the people who surround you. To them it may only mean they don't have to be suspicious of you or watch you too closely. Usually trustworthiness does not in itself earn a larger area of freedom or responsibility or authority for a woman, as it would normally for a man. A woman must, as a rule, put some effort into expanding her area of freedom and opportunity. Often she must help those around her accept her trustworthiness as a basis for more trust from them and more opportunity for her.

Mara's husband liked to keep a tight rein and reign over her. He wanted her to consult with him about any expenditure that amounted to more than one dollar. It can be said for him that he was also willing to do this with her about his own expenditures. He was happy to live a narrow, tight little life, or so he thought.

She at first went along with his smothering way of life. But eventually she saw that it was destroying her. She felt herself changing, becoming less and less of her own self, more and more an echo and shadow of him.

Finally Mara issued what he felt amounted to an ultimatum. She said she would, from then on, have a household allowance. He was not to question her use of a single penny of it. He was frightened. What if they went bankrupt? What if she made some foolish use of the money and they were in terrible straits before he realized it? She reminded him that he had always thought her to be a competent person and had never known her to make a really foolish purchase. She also reminded him that she had managed her life and money very well before meeting him.

For the first few months, Mara's husband was uncomfortable, to say the least. But after he saw that disaster was not going to fall on the household, he did a curious thing. He admitted to her that he liked her better now that he did not have all that control over her. He felt he was getting back the woman he had so admired before he married her and began narrowing her life and stifling her initiative.

Mara continued to make more freedom for herself in spite of his fears, never giving him reason to justify them. Her abilities are able to grow and find use now. If she had not insisted on using them, she would have not only allowed the death by degrees of her own personality and potential, but allowed the destruction of her husband's respect and admiration for her as well.

Husbands aren't the only ones who bind up trustworthy women. Employers who are paternalistic and dictatorial reduce benefits for themselves as well as their employees. Schools are notorious for their deadening of creativity and spontaneity among staff and students alike. Parents sometimes wrap themselves so tightly around their children that they cannot allow them to grow to full personhood ever, even as adults. In such cases you must not wait for others to give you permission to be your whole self, to use your assets, realize your potentialities. Such a situation calls for stepping out alone to use what you are: carefully, perhaps gradually, but courageously.

You will very likely meet opposition. There are two important points to remember when you do. The first is that it is unnecessary to create victims in order to free ourselves. We do not need to be cruel to others in order to be kind to ourselves. So think through what you do with this in mind, before you do it. The other important point is that those who hold the controls of your life now may very well insist that you *are* being cruel (or irrational, or foolish, or any number of other bad things) to them when you take steps to reduce their control over you and replace it with your own. Listen to your own wisdom, not their threats and accusations. They may even threaten you with the loss of their love. Jo Coudert had something to say about that in *Advice from a Failure* that I underlined a long time ago and have shared several times since then.

> There need be no insistence on the self at other people's expense. No aggressive maneuver is involved, but a standing still in the face of encroachment, a refusal to be manipulated by guilt or fancied obligation or fear of loss of the other. What is required, when under pressure to relinquish choice of action for the self, is the courage and the conviction to answer an implied threat of loss affirmatively with, "Yes, if you are willing to carry it that far, if you are willing to give me up if I don't do your bidding, then I, too, am willing to lose you.[1]

She goes on to say, in regard to employers:

> The most satisfactory relationship I have ever had with an employer was in a job I decided to be fired from rather than accede to being bullied. As it turned out, I was the only employee who was not bullied.[2]

Trusting yourself

There are others besides husbands who lose from being associated with women who are less than whole persons. I'm referring to dependent people who rely on us to care for them, protect them, and provide for them. Some of those people are children.

I know what my less-than-wholeness has cost my children. The times I caved in to pressure from others concerning my children and did not trust my own feelings, or my own solid convictions, are times when my children lost. I finally became confident enough of my own judgment, my own trustworthiness concerning my children, to refuse to give way before the well-intentioned insistence of other people. But for many years I allowed others from time to time to tell me what to do, when I knew better than they. I don't think this giving way before pressure is an uncommon thing in mothers. I see it often.

Nell wanted to breast-feed her baby. She was having a small problem with it and a large problem with her family about it. Her husband was just barely supportive. Her mother was sure Nell's breasts were too small, her mother-in-law didn't feel breast-feeding was a good idea at all.

I loaned Nell some literature on successful breast-feeding and tried to encourage her. That very evening her husband made a special trip to my house to return the books I had loaned her. With a great deal of intensity that he was trying unsuccessfully to hide he said, "She is finished with them. She won't be needing them, the doctor says she should stop." And she did.

I felt badly about it because I knew too well what had happened. My first child had been breast-fed for one month. She was colicky, so my doctor had said, "Cut her off without a drop." But wouldn't it be better to experiment first, and at least go slowly with a change, I wanted to know. No, he ordered a sudden and complete shift to formula.

As I sat crying and holding my baby close to my hurting breasts full of milk she could not have, it was not my physical discomfort that I was crying about. I was crying because I knew in my mother's heart that it was wrong for her and for me and that we were losing the closeness we could no longer share.

My second child was born a year later. The same doctor told me that since the children were so close together I should not even attempt to breast-feed this one. He said I would be so busy taking care of both of them that I would not be able to get the rest that was necessary for breast-feeding mothers.

With child number three I finally decided *I* would do what was best for me and my child, *no matter what*. So I resisted all negative pressures and contacted La Leche League[3] for information and moral support. Both mother and child did very well.

By the time number four came I was not listening to anything negative on the subject. I now knew my own opinions and feelings had been right, from the beginning.

When our children were small, my husband was pastor of a church in a farming valley in Washington. Because dairy farmers must work in the early evening, services at the church began later than they do in most urban areas. I found that taking the children to evening services guaranteed that they would be fussy and miserable the next day. But it was not acceptable for the pastor's wife to leave her children at home with a baby-sitter. It just wasn't done.

I weighed their own needs against my need to be acceptable to everyone and decided they should stay home. I hired a baby-sitter. The children were much happier, they got sick less often, and I was happier, too.

Of course, I was told in all seriousness that I was influencing my children adversely by not bringing them to church, whether they got anything good from it or not. But I finally was getting what my Arkansas ancestors would call "gumption." I guess it could also be called backbone. The important thing is that my children profited by my being able to be whole enough not to bow to social pressure on this matter.

In your case, it might not be your own children you are able to help or not help in this way. It might be children left in your care, it might be someone who is in your care because of a mental or physical handicap. But sometime someone is going to depend on all of us.

We women can be as confident of our well-made decisions as men are of theirs. We do not have to discount either our thinking ability or our abilities to put our conclusions into action.

Balancing trustworthiness

American Indians of the Pacific Northwest used to have potlatches. A potlatch was a feast, the high point of which was a sort of keeping-up-with-the-Joneses binge of destruction. Rich chieftains vied with each other to give away or destroy more and more valuable possessions.

Some women play potlatch with their lives. They live lives of self-sacrifice and self-destruction. Their trustworthiness and steadfastness cause them to do for others but not do for themselves. They often marry men who will guarantee them an increasingly narrow and miserable existence.

Women can be very self-destructive. We are taught to give to others. We are not taught when to stop and let others give to us. Many of us know how to give, but we do not yet know that the best kind of life, both for us and for those around us, is not giving but sharing. You, as a whole woman, may need to reeducate yourself to share and not to empty yourself out destructively for others.

God's gift to you of all you are was not meant to be squandered or thrown out. Treasure it.

Trustworthiness running free

What would happen if you took *your* own value system and lived it, using all the assets you have? What if you allowed yourself to express your courage in acts when needed? What would happen in your life and in the lives of those around you if you really used *all* the mind you have, took the lid off? What would happen if you asked yourself every day, "How can I use my abilities to their fullest today?" Would you be more self-confident? Would you feel better about your life and purpose on this earth at the end of every day? Could you handle the criticisms and wait for them to fade?

Wouldn't it be delicious to give it a beginning try?

Our culture says to us that only dull, unexciting, unattractive women possess these trustworthy virtues. You know the stereotypes. There is the spinster librarian, and the hardworking secretary who loves her boss from afar but never attracts him because she is so dull and lackluster. Then there is the abrasive, loud woman who gets things done, who is capable; but nobody is attracted to her either. Those stereotypes are fed to us from the cradle.

But, ladies, *it isn't so*. You *can* be bright, capable, courageous, and everything else that you possess and not be dull, drab, offensive, or carnivorous toward the male species.

Whole women are attractive women. Their faces shine, and not because they need a bit more powder on their noses. They shine from within, from knowing the satisfaction of a job well done, an ideal defended, from that hum of satisfaction that comes as a result of a good "together" feeling.

I think the German word *gestalt* explains it. *Gestalt* is supposedly not wholly translatable, which is good, because then you don't have to get it just exactly right. But I'm told it means a sense of completeness. It can be a complete transaction, a finished bit of emotional business, a good feeling at the end of the day when it all went together into a good whole. A whole woman experiences *gestalt,* and she shines.

CHAPTER 4

Beyond Manipulation

She does him good and not harm all the days of her life. (Prov. 31:12)

Women manipulate men. I've known that since I was a little girl. I always wondered why women are so tempted to do it. What makes them write manuals teaching manipulation? Why would women like Marabel Morgan or Helen Andelin justify it with Bible verses, case histories, and personal examples of their own approach to pragmatism in marriage?

I think they do it because they live in a double bind. Women are the underdogs in the family and society. So they gravitate toward survival methods common to underdogs, methods that are as old as the Fall.

Here's how it works: the underdog is afraid to approach her superior directly. Though direct approach is effective some of the time, too often it is not. When dealing with a superior power that is also unscrupulous and unfair, being direct is often dangerous. Underdogs learn to manipulate in order to get along—or survive.

Manipulation is ultimately dishonest and demeaning. Unfortunately, justifying dishonesty does not change its basic essence, especially in this situation. It remains dishonest.

Manipulation is demeaning both to the one doing it and to the unsuspecting victim. If you're a woman, your actions say to the man you victimize, "You aren't very bright, or honorable. If you were smart, you would see through my tricks. If you were honorable, they wouldn't be necessary."

This kind of scheming has a further disadvantage. It makes close, honest relationships between people impossible. The Proverbs woman did her husband good and not evil all the days of her life.

She did not manipulate him. This is probably only a small part of the good and not harm that she did him, but an important part.

That this woman refrained from deceptive dealings with her husband says a lot about her, though not necessarily a lot about him. We don't know whether her husband deserved the considerate treatment or not.

Some men seem to earn what they get in tricky dealings. But the harm of manipulation is not wiped out just because a man is such a stinker that those around him feel they must posture and plan their way around him. Doing good and not evil to the one who has power over you, or to whom you are bound, is important for *your own* self-respect and personal dignity.

One man in the Bible certainly deserved a conniving wife if anyone did. Nabal was husband to Abigail. (His name means "foolish," and he was aptly named.) Though she did not manipulate him, she did use *discretion,* in not trusting him with more than he could handle in an emergency.

Abigail received information from her servants that David, on the run from a jealous King Saul, had sent emissaries to Nabal for a contribution toward the provisioning of his armed force in hiding. Since David's soldiers had protected Nabal's herdsmen and treated them with respect and honesty, this was a reasonable request that should have been graciously granted.

But instead of giving David's men the provisions they requested, Nabal sent them away rudely. This breach of courtesy almost cost the lives of all his household. Abigail learned of her husband's action while he was engaged in a drinking bout.

She immediately sent food to David and followed quickly to intercede for her household's safety. In the best diplomatic manner, she cooled the fires of revenge and prevented disaster.

Did she tell Nabal some tall story the next day, or just keep the whole thing from him? She told him the truth. He was so shocked to learn what he had almost caused that he went into a decline and soon died. David, recognizing Abigail's abilities, proceeded to marry her.

It is not doing a man a favor to deceive him, even in seemingly loving ways, "for his own good." It is not *doing good and not harm.*

Husbands are only part of the manipulator's quarry. Any person we want something from, or who has the power to inconvenience us, can be a target.

Girls learn this tactic early in life. Julia was out with some of her friends when she was stopped for speeding. She began to cry. Tears splashed on the steering wheel. "I am *so sorry*," she said. "Someone was chasing my car and I had just gotten away from them and was afraid to go too slowly." The officer said the equivalent of Now, now, don't cry, and sent her on her way. After he drove away, she began to laugh. She laughed so hard even more tears fell. It had all been an act.

What's wrong with that? It was a lie. She was saying, I get what I want by deceiving people. I don't have to play fair, be a regular citizen. I am someone who is playing crooked games.

When I was a little girl, I used to wonder why women acted toward children or men the way they did, with their secrets and their condescending smiles and tricks. Why did they act as though I, a child, were part of the enemy? Why were men *different*, fair game? I think I know now. Women who manipulate don't feel good about themselves. They think that they will lose something if they are open and direct with men. They only practice on children, or maybe they find it easier to deal with children that way. But eventually children grow up and find out what Mother is doing, and they don't respect her as much after that.

We don't have to manipulate

It may *seem* necessary to manipulate. It may even be so second nature that some women will have difficulty unlearning the habit. But I'm convinced it is neither necessary nor right if one wants to be a whole person. There are several things you can do.

You can quit cold turkey. Simply refuse to do it anymore. Look for situations in which you are prone to manipulate and plan not to. If you catch yourself at it, stop and admit what you did. Say, "I have a bad habit I'm trying to break. That is not how I want to do that, I'll start again. Here is what I wanted to say." You do not have to admit all your past schemes and devious ways. Confession may be good for the soul, but laying out every such thing you have done to someone may so horrify them that they will be hurt by it. It does little good to do that.

You can try to associate with people who welcome honest dealings. If you are not married, you should consider this before marrying: does the man you are interested in encourage manipulation, or is he happy to have a person of equal worth level with him? Does he manipulate you? Does he come from a manipulating family?

I have a friend whose husband comes from such a family. She didn't realize that was actually happening until after she was married. It didn't seem to matter at first that they kept secrets from each other and "arranged" things so one or another member of the family wouldn't get mad or hurt. She thought her family had simply been different, more direct. But manipulation was the game, and it was not easy to live with a man who grew up playing it. He did not want to know the truth. He wanted to be protected from anything he did not like. He actually wanted a pretend wife, not a real person.

If you are already in such a situation, you will have to reeducate the man in your life, not yourself only. Begin by being genuine and honest. I'm not, by the way, advocating tactlessness, I'm talking about plain old openness and fair dealings.

I can tell you that it may be scary and very lonely at first. It isn't easy to face the consequences of openness when concealment has been a way of life for a long time. But the freeing and releasing of both yourself and the other person makes the change worth it.

Relationships can be renewed and grow closer than was ever possible before. You can respect yourself and the other person again. It may surprise you when you realize how much self-loathing you have accumulated from your own scheming and going along with the devious ways of others. When you free yourself from that, you will find you like yourself better, too.

Who pulls your strings?

In *Pulling Your Own Strings*, Wayne Dyer says he believes we should decide what we want to do and think and feel, that we can choose. And we should choose on the basis of what is best and right from our viewpoint, then follow through with our choices and act upon them. We will not be victims if we choose not to allow others to victimize us. He insists that we victimize ourselves by not "pulling our own strings." We let others pull them instead.

There is considerable pressure on women to let other people pull their strings for them. We are encouraged to believe that if we're not good little girls and compliant women, we'll turn out to be pushy, aggressive, and repulsive. But it is possible to be *assertive* without being abrasive. Being assertive means being able to stand up for yourself without putting others down. Many people alternate between being aggressive and being submissive. That is, they must either dominate or be dominated, they know no middle ground.

Assertiveness training has become a popular way to gain the skills many women and men need in dealing with conflicts and decisions in a nonsubmissive and nondomineering way. Two good books on the subject are *How to Be an Assertive (Not Aggressive) Woman in Life, in Love, and on the Job,* by Jean Baer (Signet), and *Effectiveness Training for Women,* by Linda Adams and Elinor Lenz (Wyden).

Reeducation

I've mentioned the need for reeducating yourself and others to allow you to be all you can be. It occurs to me that I should explain what I mean by reeducation.

There are certain turning points in anyone's life, corners that change direction for us. These incidents and insights are sometimes small things that make big differences in our future. A turning point in my life involved the concept of reeducation.

Several years ago I found myself in an uncomfortable situation. My husband, the pastor of a small rural church in the Pacific Northwest, was busy and preoccupied with his work. I was lonely and overworked, caring for three preschoolers and trying to be the perfect pastor's wife.

The people in the church were kind. But each one had his or her own idea about what I should do, and which meeting I should attend (preferably all of them), and how I should raise my children. I was trying very hard to do everything perfectly and please everyone. That, of course, is impossible, which I was fast finding out.

We had been spending our summer vacation time at Union College on the University of British Columbia campus in Vancouver, British Columbia, where my husband was working on his master's degree in theology. My turning point came one evening at a symposium held for the wives of summer session students.

It was a beautiful evening, with the sunset filling large windows overlooking Point Grey. Forming the panel were a psychologist, a sociologist, and a third speaker whose occupation I don't remember. We were to discuss the problems and stresses we experienced as clerical wives.

During the first hour little was accomplished. A few of the women commented about how much their church members loved them and how happy they were. But gradually we began to loosen up, and finally the truth came tumbling out. This woman was under tremendous pressure, that one was overworked.

The panel members had answers and information we could actually use. The answer that changed my life was *reeducation*. It was the good news, to me, that I could change people's expectations about what I should do and whether they had any say at all in what I did.

A panelist explained that whenever two people meet, they immediately begin to educate each other about what both are like, what they will allow and what they will not. This education is all on an unconscious level. But we soon understand that with some people we may not joke, or we must be careful not to ask certain things of them, because we somehow *know* it wouldn't fit with them. They have educated us to know that.

He said that we inevitably educate everyone in our lives as to how we are to be treated. Now, he said, if you do not like the way you are being treated, all you have to do is reeducate the people in your life to treat you the way you want to be treated.

His explanation was for me like water to a woman dying of thirst. I soaked it up with every bit of brain I had. He went on to say that reeducation does not involve confrontation or lecture, or telling anyone things will be different now. It merely involves sending different signals to those around you. You do not push, you merely firmly but gently resist incursions on your rights, or person, that you do not want. Gradually the people around you will relearn how you are to be treated and will no longer be surprised by your new behavior.

I went home with hope and put his instructions into practice. I had been going to every meeting of every kind that the women of the church could dream up. I felt I had to because I was the pastor's wife and it was expected of me, whether I had anything to offer to or receive from the meeting or not.

My first opportunity, or rather need, to reeducate one of our parishioners came within a week. Mrs. Miller (not her name) approached me after the Sunday morning service and told me there was to be a meeting at such and such a place and time. I said, as kindly and inoffensively as I could, "I won't be able to attend." She looked startled and snapped indignantly, "Why not?" Now, Mrs. Miller is kind and considerate, full of hospitality, and I can't imagine her answering anyone in that manner. But she did it to me, I suspect because she had become so accustomed to the idea that I was someone who could and should be told where she must go that it seemed an outrageous thing for me to do anything different. I ignored her testy question and repeated that I wouldn't be able to come.

I continued my low-key reeducation of everyone who tried to run my life for me, and it worked. Gradually, I detected a difference in the way I was being treated. I think they eventually admired me (some, a bit grudgingly) for being my own person. I have noticed, repeatedly, that people respect and admire someone who will not allow others to dominate them and control them, especially when the resistance is gracious and considerate in manner. People in your life may try to control you and even threaten to not like you unless you knuckle under. But when you don't, they eventually like you more, not less.

Occasionally now I realize that things have gotten out of control again, that I am doing too much for too many, or one of the children is becoming a tyrant of my, or others', time. Then, if I am hitting on all my cylinders, I remember the lesson I learned that sunset evening in Vancouver and embark on another reeducational effort. It is a non-pushy process. I quietly reeducate my audience. It works. Try it for yourself.

Women seem to manipulate when they are afraid they cannot get what they want or need by other means. Direct confrontation seems closed to them. And it is true that sometimes a direct approach will, with some people, simply bring out the worst in them. But manipulation is not the only alternative. Reeducation is an option that can be done quietly, with a minimum of confrontation and friction.

Doing good and not harm

Reeducating a demanding boss is a way of doing him or her good and not harm. It is not dishonest and it is not demeaning to either of you.

Husbands and men you care about should get the kind of respect and honor you would like for yourself. Do you enjoy being manipulated? I like to think that loving a man means, among other things, that I will not treat him as less important than I am. To treat a man as someone who needs the wool pulled over his eyes for his own good or for you to be able to get along with him doesn't say much for him or for the wool puller's taste in men either.

Beware of compensating

The woman who does good and not harm to the man in her life, or to her employer, does not need to do herself harm in the process. Women tend to be self-sacrificing in work and love relationships. They tend to take the small piece of cake in uneven situations.

It is important to understand that people who sacrifice this way often even the score later. We are not as selfless as we think when we give up things as a matter of practice in such relationships. When we consistently give more than we get in a relationship, we tend to *compensate*. We expect more or *take* more from the other person in little ways, or unconscious ways, to even the balance scale. If you doubt this happens, or doubt that you do it if you are one who is a self-sacrificer, observe yourself for a while and see if you can catch yourself at it. You may be surprised.

An example of this kind of compensation is the mother who gives up everything for her children, then expects the children to let her dominate their lives when they grow up. This mother uses guilt to get back her investment, her selfless service. Another example is the employee who works long hours and then takes things home from the office supply without paying for them. *The company owes it to me*, she thinks. *After all, I do a lot for them that I'm not paid for.*

The chronic self-sacrificer harms herself by not being fair about meeting her own needs and giving her life the importance it deserves. And the self-sacrifice is probably less kind and selfless than she thinks because of unconscious compensation.

Why not be open, honest, and fair to yourself? And why not be the same to the men in your life? If you need to make changes, reeducation is a way to do good and not harm, for all your life.

CHAPTER 5

Worker

She seeks wool and flax and works with willing hands. (Prov. 31:13)

The Hebrew text indicates a purposeful and pleasurable approach to her work rather than constant gathering and working.[1] Our woman enjoys her work. She plans what she will do (seek wool and flax), and once the raw materials are accumulated she takes pleasure in the work itself. In other words, this woman is not a passive follower who waits for others to plan for her or prod her into action. Instead, she takes actual pleasure in planning what she will do and then doing it.

I saw women work this way as a child on the farm. I remember the rows and rows of canned vegetables, fruits, jams, jellies, pickles, and relishes my mother's friends and relatives showed her proudly when she came to visit. And I remember the pleasure and anticipation of growing them in our garden, going out in the morning to hoe before it was too hot and admiring how the onions were doing, what a good crop of tomatoes we were going to have, then the flurry of activity when jars were checked for nicks in their rims and soaked in hot soapy water and scalded to be ready for the produce, then picking and shelling and sharing work among family members or friends to put up the fruits of the garden and orchard. And I remember the lasting satisfaction when it was done.

These were not subservient women who felt they had to have sex under the dining room table and dress in "costumes" to hold their men. They were vital, efficient, willing, and pleasurable workers. And they were valued and appreciated for who they were and what they could do, not for their decorative worth or usefulness as a toy. They did not see themselves as satellites of another person, a husband, but as individuals responsible for their own convictions and good work.

I'm afraid we're in danger of losing their kind. I don't want that to happen. I don't want them to be the last of a breed of women marching down through history, passing pride and pleasure in work from mother to daughter. I want them to live on in me and in my daughter, and in my sons, too, and then on from them to their children. But something has happened to us and work that makes these good strong workers an endangered species.

It all began many years ago with what we call the Industrial Revolution. The Industrial Revolution gave women a particularly rude and vicious swipe from which we have not yet recovered. And our modern technological explosion continues and compounds its effects.

Before the Industrial Revolution almost all manufacturing was in the form of cottage industry. Individuals, families, and large households with many servants or slaves manufactured a product or products for sale or trade. In addition, they produced much of what they needed as a family or household in the way of consumer goods and foodstuffs.

In this kind of an arrangement, being a woman was not a disadvantage when it came to working. One could do work for money and take care of one's children or supervise their care without leaving home. And a woman who had a skill or trade could find employment with another family or household if she had none of her own.

Even though, throughout most of history, women did not enjoy equality with men either religiously or politically, they did have the means to support themselves by producing a service or product. But woman's work changed radically when cottage industry was wiped out suddenly by the Industrial Revolution. Those who had made a living at home in the family business were now forced to work in factories, often necessitating a move to a large city to do so.

From this point onward woman's work became a torment to her. Now she must choose, if she could, whether to work at gainful employment or stay home to care for her children and other dependents. Most women did not have a choice in the matter. Starvation-level factory wages made it imperative for every able-bodied worker in every family to work long hours in order to survive.

Women alone, without families to share housing and food costs, were at the mercy of factory owners and supervisors, and many were forced into prostitution. One of the prime reasons prostitution flourished during the Victorian Era was because working women were so destitute that they often had to sell their bodies to avoid starvation.

Over a period of time a polarity began to develop. The working woman became more and more a symbol of immorality and vice. And the woman who had a husband or father rich enough to keep her out of the factory became more and more a symbol of a good woman, a lady. Before the Industrial Revolution and its profound changes on society, women had been generally regarded as somewhat loose and licentious by nature. But with the changes brought about by the shift in work for women, the ideal woman, even the *normal* woman, came to be regarded as an asexual, pure, idle, and decorative creature protected and kept in this lofty state by a man who went out to prostitutes for sex in order not to brutalize and destroy his pure lily at home.

It is this attitude about women from the Victorian Era, an attitude caused by social changes arising from the Industrial Revolution, that led to the Total Woman and Fascinating Womanhood mystique. This mystique is the logical result of the new view of woman as decoration and lapdog begun way back there. It has only been somewhat modified. Marabel Morgan has added "sizzle" to it by reintroducing sex into the picture. This is one big reason why her book sold so well. She found a way to satisfy the consciences of all those women who had been taught to be ladies and keep their dresses down and cater to men, but who, deep inside, wanted to feel sexy, too. Her book is a genius combination of Victorian upper-class mentality and something that mentality hadn't allowed, sexuality. Helen Andelin left the sex out and concentrated on the intricate and myriad ways to manipulate a man to get what you want. And because she left the sex out, her book didn't do as well as Marabel's, because, of course, women aren't sexless beings after all.

But neither are we the kind of creatures who will be satisfied to work at what our husbands tell us to, or spend all our time trying to please and manipulate a man. The Total Woman and Fascinating Womanhood message sounds good to many women at first because they have been taught the Victorian-lady ideal all their lives. It appears to all fit together neatly now.

But it doesn't really. And there are several reasons why it doesn't. One of those reasons is that it robs us of the joy of working the way the Proverbs woman did: planning it out, assembling and acquiring the raw materials, and then digging in with pleasure, and afterward feeling that great worker's satisfaction of seeing the fruits of one's labor well done.

Woman's work or man's work?

Now, so far in time from the actual removal of our good work from our own hands, we are told that work, other than household work and child care, is and has always been man's work. Not so, as Dorothy L. Sayers, in "Are Women Human?" (Inter-Varsity Press), says so well.

At this point, somebody is likely to say: "Yes, that is all very well. But it *is* the woman who is always trying to ape the man. She *is* the inferior being. You don't as a rule find the men trying to take the women's jobs away from them. They don't force their way into the household and turn women out of their rightful occupations." Of course they do not. They have done it already.

Let us accept the idea that women should stick to their own jobs—the jobs they did so well in the good old days before they started talking about votes and women's rights. Let us return to the Middle Ages and ask what we should get then in return for certain political and educational privileges which we should have to abandon.

It is a formidable list of jobs: the whole of the spinning industry, the whole of the dyeing industry, the whole catering industry and—which would not please Lady Astor, perhaps—the whole of the nation's brewing and distilling. All the preserving, pickling and bottling industry, all the bacon-curing. And (since in those days a man was often absent from home for months together on war or business) a very large share in the management of landed estates. Here are the women's jobs—and what has become of them? They are all being handled by men. It is all very well to say that woman's place is the home—but modern civilisation has taken all these pleasant and profitable activities out of the home, where the women looked after them, and handed them over to big industry, to be directed and organised by men at the head of large factories. Even the dairy-maid in her simple bonnet has gone, to be replaced by a male mechanic in charge of a mechanical milking plant.[2]

A major reason why those farm women from my childhood were so different from "total, fascinating" women is that they had not yet been robbed of their importance as workers. They knew their value and gained respect and self-worth from it. They also were more satisfied persons because of the natural pleasures and satisfactions they derived from their work.

Of course, there is no such thing as woman's work and man's work. There is only work, and whoever can do it should be able to do it. It's time we retook our lost position as proud, competent, good workers—even workers who can support themselves, who are not so dependent that they cannot make a living on their own.

Reclaiming the benefits of work

One thing we can do is learn to *honor* work. We can make changes in our own attitudes toward work. Does work represent personal satisfaction for you? Or is it only a way to keep body and soul together? If it is the latter, then maybe it is time you reevaluated your work. Is your work valuable? Is it necessary? Are you suited to the task? If you are not, why are you doing it? Can you do other work, prepare for other work if you have no choice now?

One of the problems with solitary work—and much of the work women now do is solitary—is that we view it as *interval*. We see it as only a means to get from here to there. If you see your work this way, take another look at it. Can you awaken yourself to the pleasure to be gained from doing it well? Can you vary your job to make it more pleasurable?

I personally think that, to be a willing worker, one has to get some pleasure from it, the more the better. Work *ought* to be pleasant. If it's not, do something else. Or if it has to be done and it's not pleasurable, find someone to share it with you. Women don't deserve to have all the dirty jobs.

I find when I can choose what I want to do, when I decide that I want the results of the job even though the process is not my favorite activity, that I can find satisfaction in doing the work. I can look forward to the end result and see each step as a building block to that end. I also find that if I *look* for pleasure and satisfying aspects to my work, I am more apt to find them.

It is advantageous to work with someone else who is a good

worker, who values work. There are people I enjoy working with because they are friendly and companionable. But even friendly people are not as good to work with as someone who is also a *willing* worker. Vita Blaus is a person like that. I love to work with her because she *enjoys* work. She never told me that she does, but I know it's true. She enjoys both the process and the satisfaction that comes from finishing the job.

Vita and I belong to a food co-op. I look forward to working co-op with her because she talks while she works (I love to talk, too), and she is an efficient, fast worker as well. I say efficient even though Vita and I have had our share of fiascoes measuring out things and having to do it over because we couldn't account for a pound of something and wasted a lot of time looking for it. But we enjoy the work, and part of the enjoyment is in sharing it.

Children who have parents who enjoy work and are willing to share work and enjoyment with them are fortunate. Some parents seem to take pleasure and pride in their own labors but will not work with their children in an enjoyable manner, or will not let them help at all.

I was fortunate to have parents who enjoyed my company when they worked. They praised me for working. And they passed on to me what must be generations and generations old, the feeling of living in harmony with all working things. Work was not some ordeal to be done with in a wild frenzy of last-minute effort. It was work when needed, rest after, and play, too. I felt that work belonged in my world, it was a part of the real world, not just something for poor people who could not afford to sit back and be served. I appreciate that legacy.

Writing this makes me realize that I need to put more effort into teaching my own children, who have so few opportunities to get it anywhere else, to value and enjoy work. A television set in the most prominent place in our living room calls them with the message "Sitting and watching is better than doing." It seduces them away from a participatory life-style into one of passive consumerism. I don't want to throw out the TV, but I should realize what it is doing and control it and counter its influence. (Since writing that I have moved it to the basement. Working has gone up and viewing gone down.)

Non-money work

There are several other benefits from all this manual labor that I would like to see reclaimed. There is the pleasure one gets from a necessary, though nonpaying, job well done: pride in workmanship, you could say. But it's more than that, it's knowing that you have made a contribution to your family, church, neighborhood, country; that you are pulling your weight and doing your share.

Even though it is important to receive the money we deserve for our labor, not all work should have a price tag on it. We should not deny ourselves the pleasure of doing our share to help or simply doing good, without pay.

I mentioned earlier that so much of woman's work has been removed to factories. Still more is denied her by modern technology. Much of the satisfaction my childhood's farm women received from their work came from knowing that it was needed. Their work was essential, and they were valued because it was.

Now much of that work can be done more easily and quickly by machines. This has caused a decrease in job satisfaction. It isn't as creatively satisfying to go to the market and pick up a dozen eggs as it is to hatch the chickens, feed them, raise them to laying size, hear them cackle and sing, pick up those eggs in your basket, admire the scenery on the way back to the house, and then have a few extra eggs to sell at the end of the week besides.

When you can buy the dozen eggs so easily it seems kind of ridiculous to go to all that trouble. It's the same with machines and gadgets. You are told on every side that they can do it better and faster and "everyone else has one." So you feel like a bit of a clod if you do it the old way.

Non-money work at home has thus been reduced in status and satisfaction. But we should salvage what we *can* use from the past.

It is important to regain that lost satisfaction. You need to search out ways to bring it back for yourself or increase it. There is a renewed interest now in cooking from scratch, baking bread, and quilting—all ways to regain some of that lost creative satisfaction women once received as part of their usual work at home. You might want to try your hand at one or more of those activities. When you design a quilt yourself, make each square, set it together, quilt it day by day until it finally lies there all fresh and new, your own creation smiles back at you. The pleasure of work done well continues each time you handle that quilt, placing it on the bed, covering your child, and washing it. It is an extension of you, a lasting evidence of your work.

Understanding relative values

Another benefit from manual labor is in knowing the true cost of anything. If you dig your own ditch, you know the cost in sweaty, dirty skin and tired muscles. If you pay someone money to dig it with a machine, the true cost is obscured by many factors. The price you pay represents a burden of money expended after being earned, by someone else perhaps. It also includes taxes taken out of that money before you even see it. It may also represent doing without something else because the money must be used for this. And perhaps it also represents having to give account to another person for the expenditure of that money.

Personal involvement in the project revises one's view of its cost. As someone has said, women oppose war more than men do because women are in a better position to know the true cost of a human life.

Valuing the work of others

Working with your own hands also creates a respect for all workers. I notice a disdain for those who do muscle work among some who work more with their minds than with their hands. People who don't know what it's like to do manual labor tend to devalue those who do. It may be subtle, but it's often there. That's a disadvantage for the one who feels superior. A narrow existence and experience tend to fold people in upon themselves; they lose the balance in judgment and decision-making ability that comes with knowing what life is like for a wide variety of people. This also seems to create a smallness of spirit. We become lopsided when we do not use all our resources, as we do also when we do not recognize the true resources of other people.

Being realistic about life

In college I worked at a large men's clothing store in Los Angeles. One of the temporary workers for an annual inventory was the daughter of one of the senior sales staff. This girl had been served all her life. She did not *do* manual labor, at least not willingly. I heard several accounts of her "work" that day and later. All who worked with her were repulsed by her attitude toward work.

She was unfortunate in that she had a mother who was a good and tireless worker, who had brought home money to meet all her daughter's needs, as had her father also; but the child had not been taught the pleasure and honor in work herself.

How would she manage in a tight spot requiring ingenuity or hard work? She will very likely at some time in her life need to work, but she will probably not enjoy it or be good at it. Also, those around her aren't going to enjoy working with her.

Not only had she been spoiled, she was handicapped as well.

Be willing and wise

It is easy for a willing worker to be exploited if she does not take care to be a wise worker as well.

You must value your work even when others downgrade it. By that I mean that you may be praised for your good work, but not "raised" because of it. In so many jobs women are the willing *workers* with supervision positions all reserved for men. Because of this, women tend to be naïve about the value of their work.

If others are paid for work with dollars and you are receiving mostly smiles, wake up. We do not need to comply with society's expectations for us. A woman's work is as valuable when she does it as when someone with a different hormone balance does it. Beware of complacently and quietly settling for what they want to give you. Insist on what you are worth. Some books to help you get up the courage and give you the techniques are *Getting Yours*, by Letty Cottin Pogrebin, *Everything a Woman Needs to Know to Get Paid What She's Worth*, by Caroline Bird, and *Effectiveness Training for Women*, by Linda Adams.

Which work are you most willing at?

Maybe you aren't such a willing worker. Maybe it's not because you don't like work or never learned to like it. Maybe you are in the wrong line of work.

How do you find out what line you should be in? One way is to ask yourself, "What do I like to do so much that I would do it even if they didn't pay me?" Why not do *that* for a living?

We often ignore our real abilities and desires workwise because we don't think of them as work. Putting them to use seems too much like play to us, and we remember our parents saying, "First we work, *then* we play." We feel we can't do that because it's not working. Look at it again. You can become accustomed to having fun working, it just takes practice.

One way to discover some of your hidden possibilities is to take out a sheet of paper and write all the things you would like to do, ridiculous or not. Write them all down. Let it sit awhile, then come back to it and ask yourself about each item, "Why not?" Rate each one as to how much you like the idea, then as to possibility. If you can't do it now, could you work toward it?

Another thing you can do is read the book *Wishcraft.* You may have guessed by now that I am a book lover. This book is easy to love. It is the very best one I have ever read on how to find out what you want to do and then actually do it. I can't recommend it highly enough.

Barbara Sher, the author of *Wishcraft,* knows what she's talking about. She says she came into the workaday world with the most unmarketable degree possible, a B.A. in anthropology. She shares her own experiences and then her expertise in helping other people find out what they really want to do and then how to successfully do it.

This isn't one of those inspirational pull-yourself-up-by-your-own-mental-bootstraps books. It's solid meat-and-potatoes practical. I'd tell you the bare bones of what it says, but I don't want you to have to make do on the bare bones of this one. I want you to get the whole animal. So please read the book if you're wanting to know how to find out where you want to go, and how to get there.

But whatever you do, don't deny yourself the pleasure and joy you can find in your work. Working well is historically a very womanly thing to do.

CHAPTER 6

A Bargain, a Bargain!

She is like the merchant's ships; she brings her food from afar. (Prov. 31:14)

What do you suppose that means, "she brings her food from afar"? It could mean a lot of things. Maybe she didn't serve the same old mush for dinner every night even though it was locally grown and that's about all there was. It might mean the lady had some variety on the table. Or it might mean that she spiced things up, added an ingredient from a distance that made a difference in a boring diet.

I tend to think it means she was a sharp buyer or trader for her household's foodstuffs. She probably did the other things, yes, but particularly she was a shrewd buyer, going out of her way to get more and better for her family with the same expenditure.

Why is this here in the Book of Proverbs' section about a special woman's qualities? What does being canny about food acquisition have to do with being a whole, balanced person? Well, she's a *practical* woman, first of all. She isn't so *nice* that food isn't one of her concerns. She knows the needs of her household and she knows that food is one of the most important. She is realistic enough to know that the best person to see to a task is the one who has the most at stake. She knows she is the one to see to the food acquisition.

I have three teenagers. They can all cook to a degree, some to a greater degree than others. But all have been sent to the market on occasion to do a substantial amount of shopping for food. They sometimes enjoy this a great deal. All those goodies that will taste so good and especially the ones Mom won't buy, or seems to forget to. They come home happy, anticipating good eating. And as the bags are unloaded, I am mentally counting the cost. They see the food and the taste, but only I know how the money will stretch. And that's because I am the one who must make it last till the end of the month. I am the one with the most at stake.

Now, my kids are conscientious about their shopping and I mentioned that they can cook, so it would be obvious that they aren't babes in the aisles. They have an idea about what is too expensive and what is all right. But they don't *care* about it the way I do. Because they don't have to. And besides that, I am more experienced in cutting corners and making things reach further.

The woman we have been reading about is not only practical and realistic about her family's needs, but cares about their needs. I think I can say that from the evidence. It is even more apparent later in the Proverbs chapter. She wants to do well by her family nutritionally. This woman does what she can to provide needed food and care for her family and, incidentally, for herself also.

It is one thing to be thrifty because you are stingy, and quite another to be thrifty because you want to get the best use from your money or want to care the best you possibly can for your dependents and yourself. This woman seems to be the caring one.

I keep wondering what it involved for her to bring her food from afar. Did she make arrangements with traveling merchants or caravan leaders to bring her certain things? Did she send her servants out into the countryside away from the city to buy food that might be cheaper or better than that brought to the bazaar? Or did she go along? I would like to know how she did it.

The modern equivalent: co-oping

I mentioned in the last chapter that I am a member of a food co-op. It is called the West End Co-op, although most of the people in it live on the east side of my city. I once asked someone who had been in it a long time, "Why the name?" She said the co-op originated in the West end of Chicago. I didn't think to ask her how it got to Wheaton, thirty miles away. But after being in a co-op for a while nothing seems too strange to believe.

Co-oping is fun, maddening, tiring, educational, and you can freeze at it in the winter and melt in the summer. (How would you like to divide up potatoes in an unheated garage in the middle of a Chicago-style winter—potatoes for a couple of hundred people?) But most of all, co-oping saves you money. And it will also buy you things you can afford from the co-op but not in the store. When raisins were going out of sight in retail stores we were buying them for ninety-nine cents a pound through the co-op. Nuts would be too expensive to put in cookies if not for our wholesale prices.

This co-op isn't a large one. It's all volunteer labor. That means the cost is low and sometimes the mix-ups are large. We regularly have a few pounds of flour, or pounds of something, or box of that, lost. Usually, after a lot of searching around and checking, the missing pieces are found. It will turn out that they were lost through miscounting or misplacing or transposed numbers, just people errors. But sometimes it all remains a great mystery, like the eight pounds of flour I never found. One hot August afternoon I was dividing up three hundred pounds of flour for a subgroup. I was also carrying on a conversation with those beside me who were weighing spices and brown sugar. That day we had only plastic bags that held not much more than about five pounds of flour each. So I dipped out of my big hundred-pound sacks into those small plastic bags balanced on a baby scale, to weigh out a lot of those bags. After I had accumulated several, some kind soul began to distribute them to the large grocery bags with members' names on them. Alas, and poor me, when I got down to the final order, eight pounds of flour were missing. We then collected all the distributed bags and recounted. We compared scales. We refigured. I got hotter and tireder and hungrier. No luck. We did it all again. We never found the eight pounds. I even called everyone who had taken their orders home early to have them re-weigh their flour. It is possible for sacks to be short in weight from the mill. But the particular company we had bought the flour from usually overfilled their sacks and had more flour in them than they were supposed to have. And eight pounds is more than the stingy ones run under.

I think any group of people could start their own co-op on a small scale and expand if and when they wanted to. Actually a lot of people do this sort of thing informally and don't even realize it is co-oping. Such as when your neighbor says, "I'm going up to Michigan over the weekend and I'll bring you back a bushel of apples if you like." A co-op just gets more people together who want apples, and sends a van, and pays the gas money. Or if they get enough orders, they may be able to locate a farmer who will deliver the apples in his truck.

Our group buys produce from a company in our area that acts as a wholesaler for co-ops. There are enough in a large metropolitan area like this to make it pay. Some co-ops send their own members to the produce markets for wholesale purchases on a rotating basis. Others go directly to farmers in season and contract for a certain amount of produce at an agreed-upon price or for the price current on the wholesale market at the time the items are ripe.

We buy from several different wholesalers on a need basis. When we decide, for instance, that we want to order from a company that sells nuts and dried fruits, we make up an order, send it in, and send our people to pick it up on the determined date. We order only when we have enough need for those products to make it worth our doing it. Since both nuts and dried fruits store well in the freezer, we buy for several months at a time.

Actually, belonging to a co-op helps make a freezer more than just a convenience. It takes several dollars a month to supply energy to a freezer, and without a substantial savings on what you put into it, it becomes a luxury item. Not that it is entirely that, because convenience is worth dollars and cents, too. Not having to go out to eat or to the market because there are raw materials in the freezer to make a meal in a tight spot definitely saves money.

I freeze flour to keep it fresh between flour orders. I usually order at least twenty pounds at a time, or even more. If you freeze your flour you can afford to invest in several kinds without the likelihood that you will let some get stale before you get around to using it all up. It's fun to make different kinds of variety breads. With flour in the freezer you can be sure you have fresh materials on hand whenever the inclination to bake strikes you. Dry granular baking yeast freezes well, too, and is much cheaper by the pound than it is in those little packets in the market.

Many specialty items are available to us through cooperative buying. One company sells to health food stores. We can buy everything from vitamins to tofu from them. I buy wheat germ five or ten pounds at a time and freeze it until I am going to use it, keeping a small amount in the refrigerator for current use.

I find I use more high-nutrition foods like wheat germ and soy flour when I can get them cheaper and in larger, fresher amounts. It's easy to get into the habit of putting a little in baked things as an added nutritional bonus. And you might even find yourself changing a recipe or two to improve the food value and coming out with a whole new invention that tastes better, too.

If you are interested in taking advantage of wholesale buying and don't have access to a co-op, why not see if you can find a few friends and neighbors to go together on an experimental basis for one purchase and see what happens.

Do-it-yourself wholesale buying

There are three ways that I know of to do this. One is to order from wholesalers directly. Another is to buy from outlets. The third is to take judicious advantage of sales in your own area.

You may be able to scout out wholesalers near you by checking the Yellow Pages in your phone book. Often wholesalers will also sell to the general public. You may be able to get a few friends together to buy in bulk if that is necessary in order to get wholesale prices. It's amazing how much information about the ins and outs of bargain buying in your area you can accumulate if you put your mind to it. Ask friends and acquaintances if they know of wholesalers or special breaks for employees or members organizations that you may be eligible for. Get a copy of *The Wholesale-by-Mail Catalog*, by Lowell Miller (St. Martin's Press).

Another way to run your own personal co-op is to buy from outlets. Some areas seem to be especially favored by companies for outlet locations. About ten miles from here is a street with outlets strung through three different towns. It is particularly well endowed with bakery outlets. Pepperidge Farm, Sara Lee, and Butternut are all represented. I can take a drive over there once every couple of months and keep us in "day-old" (actually three days old) bread and all the goodies I will not buy from the market because they cost so much. Sara Lee love is even lovelier when it is less expensive.

Even the outlets have specials. Sometimes because of a bigger goof at the factory or an experimental product that is not being marketed yet you can get bargains that make you go home feeling very competent and good about being "like the merchant's ships."

Large catalog houses like Sears and Penneys also have outlets for their overstock and last season's catalog remainders. We have a Sears outlet near us, and I have become so spoiled by my bargains there that I hate to pay retail for any item of clothing. Savings are from about 20 percent on up. I once bought a $25 jacket for $2.99. It had been assembled with the lining in one sleeve twisted a whole turn, so you couldn't even get your arm through it without real effort. I pointed out the reason it had not sold and the manager reduced it to my rock-bottom price. When I got home it took me all of twenty minutes to remove the cuff on the sleeve and sew it back after straightening out the lining.

You might try asking the manager of your area catalog store where the nearest company outlet is. Or you could write to the main offices and ask for a list of all the company's outlets. Better yet, buy one of the directories for outlets available at most bookstores. I have *Save on Shopping Directory*, by Iris Ellis (Caroline House), a national directory with offerings listed state by state, and *The Good Buy Book*, by Annie Moldafsky (Rand McNally), with outlet listings for Illinois, Indiana, Michigan, Minnesota, Ohio, and Wisconsin. These are outlets for legitimate manufacturers and distributors. They aren't discount stores. They sell damaged merchandise, overstock, discontinued lines, remainders, and remnants.

With a copy of one of these directories your next vacation can combine pleasure with super shopping. You can sample the wares of those that are along your way and maybe even plan to go to an area that has a rich supply of them.

Another way to be your own wholesaler is to keep a home supermarket. In a magazine interview[1] Dr. Heinz Biesdorf, consumer economist for Cornell University, told how to accumulate an inventory of food and supplies, all bought at bargain prices.

He buys sale items in quantity and stores them until he needs them. A few shelves in a closet, a special cupboard, even the area under a bed can house your purchases. If space is limited, be inventive and look for space not being used. For example, a small table can conceal several cases of food by the addition of a tablecloth with a long skirt. And then you won't have to vacuum under it either.

The article states: "You can start with as little as $2 for those eight cans of soup on special. . . . Arrange the items in categories, just as a store would. This way you can tell at a glance which supplies are low, and be on the lookout for specials to replace them. Remember, this is a cumulative process that doesn't require a big investment. This system allows you to become what grocers refer to as a 'cherry picker'—the kind of shopper who *only* buys items on special. Planning meals around weekly meat, fish and poultry specials completes the process. Combining your home supermarket with the weekly specials, *you never pay full price.*"

Being a smart shopper

Being a smart shopper is not merely searching for reduced prices. An item on sale isn't a bargain if it doesn't fill the *actual* need you have. A bargain isn't a bargain if it isn't a bargain for *you*. That blouse which looks so cute may not go with a thing you have.

My dear mother came from a childhood where money was scarce, and clothing was, too. As a teenager, she worked in a canning factory to earn money for clothes. But even then so little money had to do so much that it was hard for her to be comfortable buying the clothes she wanted. She agonized over her purchases. And after she had finally made a choice, she wondered on the way home if she had made the *right* choice. She was afraid it hadn't been the absolute best use of her money.

She has never completely gotten over this. When I was a teenager I had lots of odds and ends in my closet that Mom had bought for me on sale. The buy was always a great saving. But it frequently didn't match up with anything else I had. So I often complained that I had nothing to wear, and my mother would be puzzled as to how that could be because she had bought me this thing or that and it looked good. But a checked blouse and a flowered skirt did not always combine well.

Do you, like my mother, take your past anxieties along when you go shopping? Do you buy to fill your needs from long ago, or those you have now? It might be worth thinking about that one. It could save you money and provide much more buying satisfaction for you, too.

Is *someone* going along, making choices for you? Some women don't receive full satisfaction from shopping because they take another person with them on shopping trips. It can be someone actually present, or an invisible person in their own conscience who says, "Are you sure that this is the best buy? Do you really need it?" The invisible person may be a parent, a husband, a sister, or someone else who, in the past or even now, tries to tell you what you want or should want when you spend money. Listening to that voice can impair your judgment and take away the satisfaction you should get from doing your own good job shopping. You should neither auto-matically obey that shopping adviser from within nor automatically go the opposite direction and reject everything the adviser would rec-ommend. What you need to do is realize that you have been intimi-dated in the past, and then consciously and decisively make *your* own choice on the basis of your standards and desires.

If you shop with other people, how do they affect your buying? Are they impatient? I hate to go shopping with some people because they are always in a hurry. They seem to have been born itchy. If you ponder a few seconds too long for their taste they are visibly im-patient—often verbally so, too. Leave them at home. Either go alone or go with someone more compatible. But beware the companion who encourages more free spending than you are comfortable with. Some people are catalysts to excess. You find yourself being outra-geous with them. They bring out the bohemian in you. This may be fine in some situations, but when spending money it can be very ex-pensive.

Shopping with children is a whole 'nother ball game. The best ad-vice is usually "Don't." Children have a way of needing to go to the bathroom at the worst times and in the worst places. And the younger ones have the disadvantage of not being able to hold it if you can't immediately get them to the proper receptacle.

They also get hungry and thirsty. But most of all, they get bored and tired. Shopping with children seems to bring out the beast in many women. I have seen really vicious verbal, and even physical, at-tacks on children by their mothers in large shopping centers. I think those women would be horrified if they knew how they look, what they are actually doing. I certainly hope they would be.

It is worth the extra money to hire a sitter, trade with another mother, or get some better arrangement for children other than drag-ging them along.

There is another kind of shopping trip that children *are* good on. That is the just-for-fun trip. But you don't find many bargains on those.

Comparing investment and return

There is another side to saving money by bringing your food from afar. It is possible to be such a clever shopper that your time is wasted. You need to compare the advantages gained in pursuit of savings and better merchandise with what it costs you in time and energy. If you shoot a whole morning going from market to market finding all the specials, burning up a lot of expensive gas in the process, you may be spending too much for what you gain.

There are several factors to take into account. What is your time worth? That may sound rather irrelevant because many people do not get paid for their time, or wouldn't be on a day they do their shopping. But it's not just a dollars-and-cents value that should be placed on your time. What is your time worth to you, personally? Would *you* be better off spending your time doing something else? I see a lot of weary women in the market who I think would be better off getting their hair done, or lying down with their feet up, or reading a good book. Do you need something else more than saving money at this moment? Why not go after it?

Women are pretty bad about putting themselves last when it comes to special treats and kindnesses. We need to look at ourselves lovingly and care for ourselves, too. So does this saving and searching rob you of more valuable pursuits? If so, it really isn't a bargain.

Another thing to watch out for is being so runaround-conscious that you end up being frazzled and disorganized. I have come home from forays to find that I had goofed up several other things that needed my attention that day. I had been so busy that I either forgot all about them or ended up so tired that I couldn't do them at all, or at least couldn't do them well.

And bear in mind that maybe saving money isn't the main value for you to pursue in shopping every time. Maybe you need the time out away from the house, the office, or the dorm. Maybe shopping would be a good and mending thing for you to do because you need a change of pace, a new place to go for an hour or two or all day, a place where no one is going to ask you for a drink of water, a favor, advice, or an assignment.

There are fringe benefits to shopping and bargain hunting that you can also enjoy. You learn. You may make new friends and acquaintances. You can see new places. Make shopping a pleasure for you.

Ah, but it *can* be tiring, and can give you a royal headache. Don't forget to eat when you are shopping. I find that is the worst problem

I have. I forget to eat, or I put it off and then get tired and miserable. Hunger probably causes the majority of shopping headaches.

If you don't want to stop and eat a regular meal at mealtime, at
least snack as you go along. That's much better than nothing. Food
is especially important when shopping with children (and dare I say
such a sexist thing as it is also important when shopping with some
men?). Children really wilt when they get hungry. Since shopping is
tiring, which doesn't help the average child's disposition, the least
you can do is keep their tummies full. It's surprising how much better children will behave away from home if you feed them, water
them, and take them to the bathroom thirty minutes later.

Some men get very bearish when hungry (some women, too). So if
you want a pleasant shopping companion, rule number one is: Feed
the bears. Pleasant shopping rule number two is: Do your own deciding. Rule number three is: Have a good time. And if you can save
money also, that's even better.

CHAPTER 7

Thinking Ahead

She rises while it is yet night, and gives food to her household, even a portion to her maidens; (Prov. 31:15)

I can see why some people aren't too eager to copy this woman. They think she is a workaholic—that she serves everyone, never asking anything for herself. Fortunately, that isn't the only way to look at the information beginning this chapter.

She isn't getting up while it is yet night because she is a workaholic but because she is a good planner. She doesn't just let life happen, she makes it happen the way she wants it to. And she wants to take care of the basic needs and plans first thing. This woman likes to get the day off to a good start. There are lots of ways of doing this besides getting up before every one else in the house and fixing breakfast for them.

The Proverbs woman didn't have electricity. She probably went to bed at a very reasonable hour. It's hard for us to imagine what it's like without electric lights until we go camping out in the wilds. Even then, most people have bright kerosene lights to extend the daylight hours for them. But long ago, when this woman lived, campers would have had only a campfire. And where she lived, in a town or city, they had the hearth fire and oil lamps. Their lamps were small clay receptacles that produced very little light, only a single small flame to push back the darkness.

So many passages in the Bible talk about darkness contrasted to light, the night to the day. It talks about eagerly waiting for the morning. The night was much longer and darker for them than it is for us. So this woman's getting up early did not necessarily rob her of any rest or sleep. The important thing here is that she doesn't wait for the sun to waken her.

She didn't have an alarm clock or a clock radio to wake her to music. She had to awaken herself with her inner clock unless she had a servant who would have been up already who could wake her. My point is that this woman had purpose and planning in the necessary things in her life—like feeding her dependents. She had the vitality and purpose that wake a woman early to go about her work with enjoyment and satisfaction. She didn't chase the day all day because she began late. She marched with it in partnership.

The part that says she gives a portion to her maidens can mean either that she apportioned food to them or that she laid out the day's portion of work for them early in the morning so they could begin their tasks without waiting for her direction. She was either a good provider for her employees or a good manager of her hired labor. Perhaps she was both.

This portion has something to say to modern women. So many of us are prone to simply let life happen. It appears to us that so many things in our lives are out of our control, that we had best drift with the tide jellyfish-like. Since we are also taught at an early age to be followers, not leaders, to be compliant, not assertive, to be passive instead of active, this kind of planning and action passes most of us by. We have been told that *feminine* women aren't good managers.

But that kind of training produces an out-of-balance human being. Most women aren't made of a puttylike substance. The brainpower, ingenuity, and determination are there but they are hiding, afraid to come out. If we use all the resources we have to problem-solve and plan and carry out those plans, we are afraid we will step out of some protected place. We are afraid we will not be loved and respected anymore. It's a nameless fear, a subtle one, but all the more tenacious for being underground. It is hard to grasp it around the neck and throw it from us, because we aren't just sure what its boundaries are. We are afraid we won't know where decisiveness and competence end and where being pushy and domineering begin. Those two latter terms are fear words used to keep women from using their resources.

A balanced, whole woman is also a competent woman. She need lose none of her womanliness, her winsomeness, her attractiveness. It is a lie that women are not able to be strong without being offensive. We are able to be capable *and* normal. Indeed, being capable *is normal*. Not being all we are capable of being is what's abnormal. We settle for the perversion of our natures when we agree to let only part of what we are live and grow.

It is possible to take charge of your life and live decisively and efficiently to a larger extent than you may think. There are so many situations women find themselves in that make them think there is nothing they can do to change things. They feel trapped. In fact, feeling trapped is probably the number one problem of the majority of women.

You may feel trapped in a family situation. As a teenager you feel that if you can just stick it out until you grow up and get out on your own, all will be fine. Or you think that you can marry out of your situation. You will find someone who really loves you and love will conquer the problems you live with now. You look for a Prince Charming to rescue you.

Women look for rescuers all their lives. And usually those rescuers don't come. If they do, they often turn out to bring a different kind of prison, a different kind of feeling trapped.

We believe in fairy tales. We think that we will live happily ever after if the right things happen to us. But we don't realize that *we* can make things happen in our own lives. We have learned to be passive; we must learn to be active in our own behalf.

"The place to begin is where you are" is a good motto. Our Proverbs woman began her day in an efficient, well-ordered way. She began where she was, with the resources she had for *this* day. That is where you should begin.

It may be possible for you to quickly change your situation drastically for your betterment, or it may not. But you can almost certainly change it for the better in some ways. Do not neglect the little things that give satisfaction. Give your life meaning a day at a time. Organize and live reasonably *today*. And make tomorrow another reasonable today when it comes. You only need to live a day at a time if that is as much as you can plan with confidence that you will be able to carry it out. There may be situations and times in which even planning and doing reasonably with your life for a whole day is too much. Then do it an hour at a time. You can be your own person for a minute at a time if that is necessary.

Ask yourself some questions: What do I want to be like? What can I do today to be like the real me I am and want to be? What can I do today to make my work more meaningful and satisfying to me? How can I take charge of my work and responsibilities instead of their taking charge of me?

More questions for you either now or later when you want to get into it: What do I want right now? And what do I want in the long-range future? Am I doing what I need to do to help myself in both cases? Or am I neglecting the present in the hope that the future will somehow be better? Is that a reasonable and satisfying way to live? Beware the Pie in the Sky syndrome. You can spend your whole life hoping that tomorrow will be better, but never living in today. Tomorrow never comes. It is always replaced by another today. Live reasonably today, each day, and your tomorrows *will* be good.

Are you sacrificing your future to a shortsighted fling now? Have you thought about where your present course of action will land you in six months? In a year? In five years? Where will it leave you in ten? Are you sure it's worth it?

How to set and achieve all your goals

Earlier in this book I talked about a turning point in my own life when I learned about reeducating people to treat me the way I wanted to be treated. I want to share another turning point with you from my own life in hope that you will be able to reach out and choose for yourself.

I was a child with an inquisitive mind. I loved to learn about almost everything. I enjoyed all kinds of things. When people asked me what I would like to do when I grew up I could never make up my mind. I didn't know that some of those questions were merely academic because many people in my life wouldn't expect me to *be* anything. They expected that the relationships in my life would take up all my resources and that I would be married to a house as well as a husband and that *work* would be only a stopgap before marriage.

But I didn't know that then, and I mused about what I would be someday. I decided I would be a farmer, go to agricultural college and farm the Arkansas hills scientifically, raising sleek fat cattle on green pastures. I would own my own farm and my own tractor and my domain would be a vital, peaceful, flourishing haven. My cousin Chris and I spent long evening hours talking about our dreams and what we might like to do *someday*. We shared our thoughts, our hopes, and our ambitions.

Then my parents moved me away from the Ozarks, and farming began to fade from my horizon. I saw the problems I would encounter. How would I get my land? How would I get the money for college? Nursing now seemed to be a good thing to go into. I loved biology, and if I hadn't been growing up in a time when girls weren't encouraged to become doctors, I would have set my mind for that. But nursing sounded challenging, and interesting and altruistic. Of course, I didn't really know what nursing would actually be like. Probably most young people who choose a medical career do not know what it will be like, that it is not as clean and neat, as upbeat, as they think.

But when I realized that I would probably have to live in a city and be confined to a big antiseptic-smelling hospital day after day, my country-girl heart rebelled. I couldn't stand the thought of years of that. So nursing began to fade, too.

My problem was worse than that: I liked so many things, had so many interests, that giving all of them up for just one was more than I could bear. I kept trying to figure out how to find the *one* that was the best one, the most interesting, most perfect career for me. I never found it.

I went to college, got married, then stopped college and began having babies. Soon I was so busy that anything besides housework and child care was just more work, and impossible. But I never gave up the idea that someday I would do something more. What, I didn't know.

Chris and I did not see each other for years. Then one summer he and I happened to be in the Ozarks again at the same time (my parents had finally returned to the area). As we sat on the porch talking about those meaningless things that people who have been close in the past but haven't seen each other for too long are prone to waste the precious moments with, he looked at me with the old twinkle in his eye and said, "Patsy, have you decided what you want to be when you grow up?" I said, "No, have you?" He said, "No, me neither."

I had produced four children and was occupied day and night, it seemed, with caring for them and doing all the things my husband's jobs and pursuits demanded of me as well. But as my children grew older I began to realize that the time would come when I could salvage time for "what I wanted to be when I grew up." My problems in trying to figure out what that would be were exactly the same as when I was a child. There were too many good ones to narrow it down to only one.

Then I stumbled upon a book. I was browsing in the library when I came across a book with such an outrageous title that I couldn't resist checking it out to see what it had in it and who would claim so much for a book. It was called *Choose Success: How to Set and Achieve All Your Goals*. The author was listed, Billy B. Sharp with Claire Cox. *Not a very humble title*, I thought, *probably one of those books that claim a lot and deliver precious little*.

But I read it with growing enthusiasm. Its basic content was simple. It sounded as though it would actually do exactly what the title claimed. It changed my life.

It told me that I did not have to choose only one thing to do with my life. I did not have to limit myself to one job or career. I found there were ways to determine what I wanted to do now, and in the future. And there were techniques to achieve what I decided to do.

There were questions to ask myself to determine my real values, find out what I wanted as opposed to what I had *thought* I wanted (often what others thought I should want). I was to do things like write down all the places I would like to live, every imaginable thing I would like to do. Then there were ways of narrowing these down to a starting place.

I was to choose the one thing I wanted to do first. Nothing need be tossed out, everything was a possible option. If I want to, I can have twenty different careers and jobs. I am not stuck with only one. I only need to determine what I want to give my main effort to *first*, or *now*.

I chose writing. I had always wanted to write, even from childhood. Teachers had praised me for my writing and I had even tried to write for publication once. When my first and only article was rejected the first time out, I put it in a drawer and tried to forget the whole thing. But I couldn't forget it, I kept thinking about it. It wouldn't go away. So I determined that would be first. I would pursue writing until I decided to do a different job.

That set me free. I reasoned that no matter what I did in the future, writing would be a good skill. If I decided to go into nurse-midwifery (another top choice at the time) I could write about my experiences. Wherever my choice of paths leads me, I can document it and create fiction or nonfiction from my experiences.

When I came to my turning point I was still very busy caring for my children and home, but I could see space for something extra just over the hill. My youngest was in kindergarten. Half a day was mine. I used the rest of *Choose Success* to set and achieve my writing goals.

I've done about everything to get a copy of that book for myself. I couldn't find it in the bookstores, so I wrote to the publisher. It was out of print. I even called the author. He didn't have any copies stashed away that he would sell me. There is one copy in our public library that I am afraid will wear out, it's getting a little dog-eared (probably from all the people I have recommended it to).

There are seven basic steps involved in setting goals after determining your values and wants. (The values section is so long and involved I find it impossible to condense here, but I highly recommend that you read *Wishcraft,* by Barbara Sher, which I have already encouraged you to do, for that.) Those seven steps from *Choose Success* follow (some italics are mine):[1]

1. "*Your goal must be conceivable to you* . . . this does not necessarily imply that you have to know every step of the way. But you must be able to conceptualize the goal so that it is understandable to you and then identify clearly what the first step or two would be."

2. "*Your goal must be believable to you.* . . . You have to believe that you can reach the goal. If you say that you want to become a millionaire, then you have to be able to believe that you can do it. If this is unbelievable to you, then you should drop the goal or revise it; perhaps it would be more realistic for you to say you would like to have $50,000 in the bank."

3. "*Your goal has to be achievable for you.* . . . If you say you want to be a history professor at a major university in three years when you have not yet even finished high school, you are not being realistic. But if you say you intend to go to college and graduate school and to prepare to be a professor, you have set an achievable goal."

4. "*Your goal should be stated without an alternative.* Our research has shown that if a person says he wants to do one thing *or* another—giving himself an alternative—he seldom gets beyond the 'or.' He does neither. This is one of the most common traps that ensnare people in goal establishment. . . . Flexibility does not imply that a person must have two goals in mind at all times (though it

does imply the ability to keep the mind open to alternative courses if the need arises). . . . One criticism of this guideline has been that it leaves no room for maneuvering, that it is inflexible. That is not the case; even though you may set out for one goal, you can stop at any point and drop it for a new one. But when you change, you again state your goal without an alternative. It is also possible to accomplish one thing and to go on to something else, thus providing another kind of flexibility."

5. "*Your goal must be stated so that its achievement is measurable in time.* . . . It is common to err in goal-setting by saying, 'I'm going to study more this week.' That is not the way to state an objective or be motivated to action. Rather, you should say, 'I'm going to study history this week by reading three chapters in the book *The American History Series No. 2.*' You do not merely say, 'I'm going to read more'; you state exactly what you are going to read and how long you plan to take to read it."

6. "*Your goal should be something that you really want to do.* . . . Whatever your ambition, it should be one that you *want* to fulfill rather than something you feel you should do. We are taught to be basically 'should' people. One of our greatest difficulties lies in convincing people that when they say, 'I want to finish my term paper in English this week,' they often are not setting a goal they want to reach but one they feel compelled to achieve."

7. "*Your goal should be restated if it includes the involvement of anyone else.* Or you may prefer to get the permission of the other person or persons to be included in your goal." This guideline avoids making goals that are doomed to fail because they involve the work and inclinations of others. Also, it is unfair to others to include them in goals without asking their permission.

The means for achieving the goal you establish are simple and brief. First, determine the first step toward your goal. Then take that step. If you were successful, and your goal remains the same, determine the next step and take it.

After each step toward a goal, evaluation needs to be made of the original goal and of the success of the step just taken. If you were unsuccessful, perhaps you can modify your method and try again, or you may want to change your goal and then determine what the first step to it will be.

It works.

I said I chose writing as my first long-term goal. I wanted to state it specifically, so I aimed for publishing an article in a magazine within two years and a book within five. I determined that the intermediate goal was to learn more about writing. My first step was to go to the public library to check out books on writing.

I read them. At first there was so much information that I could not assimilate it all. It was like learning to drive a car. You can pay attention to what one foot is doing, or even both, but to keep an eye on the road and turn the corner or shift too is too much to do all at once.

Gradually it made more sense. I achieved my goals and went on to more. I have been writing for five and a half years now. This is my fourth book. There have been many articles.

I want to keep on writing for now. Someday I may want to change that goal to another one. I'll wait happily until I do because I know that I'm not only a writer, I'm many things, and I can change course when I want to.

The principles in that outrageously (but accurately) titled book will work for you. You can choose goals and achieve them where you are, now.

Another encouragement for me to find out what I wanted to do and really do it was a magazine story about a man who had made a list of, I believe, twenty-five things he wanted to do in his lifetime. The list was written when he was fifteen years old. He was in his thirties or forties when the piece was written and he had already done many of the things and was in the process of doing another. His ambitions included living with a group of natives far away from civilization and climbing a certain high mountain. I can't remember all of them, but they were varied and some quite unusual. They were the dreams of his heart. And he was doing them.

I thought, *Why not me, too? Why not write down all the things I would like to do and then set out to do them one at a time?*

Most people are afraid to find out what they really want. And if they know, they are often afraid to go for it. I decided not to be that way. You do not have to be that way either.

You can be capable, competent, a good planner. You can set goals for your day, for your near future, and for the long term. Why not bite off a manageable chunk and begin.

CHAPTER 8

The Investor

She considers a field and buys it; with the fruit of her hands she plants a vineyard. (Prov. 31:16)

We've talked about investments before: investing your time and energies, saving money, investing in cans of soup. We looked at one factor in investing in the last chapter: planning reasonably and realistically.

Planning for financial security and increase is an important kind of planning that women need to educate themselves about. Our Proverbs woman is not only eager to put her money to work and try a new enterprise, she is thinking ahead in order to meet her and her family's future needs. I wonder if she also invests as she does because she enjoys doing something positive and creative, because buying and planting a field makes her feel good.

I suppose this undertaking of the Proverbs woman interests me and pleases me partly because of my farm background and my own early dreams of farming. Who knows, I may do it yet.

First she *considers* a field. This information may be wasted on those who don't know that fields differ. She didn't buy just any old field, or consult her local real estate broker and take his or her advice. She considered the field itself. Not every soil or location will grow good grapes. Not every location would be suitable for her particular needs.

Having considered the field, she makes up her mind. It isn't a pipe dream, not she *might* buy a field *someday*. No, she does it. This isn't a foolhardy, impetuous, or impulse buy. She's careful, but she's also decisive.

She buys it. This woman doesn't have to have assistance in making up her mind, and she is able to buy it herself. I considered buying the house next door to us several years ago. I thought I would call a bank and ask for information about the availability of loans, interest rates, and down-payment requirements. This would be only a fact-finding call. I needed to know if it was practical to pursue the matter further.

I asked for someone in the loan department. I had hardly asked my first question when I was interrupted and asked patronizingly, "Excuse me, have you talked to your hubby about this?" I was taken aback and really didn't know how to respond to that question. Whatever had it to do with the information I was asking for? Was it any of his business? I think I stuttered something about, of course, but I was just gathering information. The man said, "Well, you talk it over with your husband and then you can come in *together* to talk about it."

I hung up the phone and became very angry. It was like a cold slap in the face, the proverbial wet fish. I had picked up the phone a rational adult. Now I felt like a child who had been out of "place." Then I wished intensely for sudden riches so I could take all my new money to someone else's bank.

We, as women, have to be aware there is an attitude abroad about us and money that is demeaning and insulting and thwarts our plans—if we let it. That prevalent attitude should not be allowed to influence our own attitude about us and money. And it should not be allowed to succeed in keeping us from the financial success we need to achieve and can achieve.

Women need money. They need money for several reasons. First of all we need it for the same reasons men need money, to eat and be clothed and have a place to live, to receive an education. People tend to forget this. Women are raised to believe otherwise. *If you are a good girl, some nice man will marry you and all will be well.* That is the message girls get about money. Money isn't even mentioned in the message; it is hidden, but implied, that money will follow. Or that it won't be necessary. The saying that lovers believe they can live on love isn't far off. They do think that. Especially girl lovers.

And it isn't that we are dumb or silly, empty-headed things either. It's because we are raised to think that to talk and think about money in a clear-eyed, rational way is to be crass, mercenary, and definitely unfeminine. Do you realize that there is no male equivalent of the term "gold digger"? It is a derogatory term that applies only to females who are out to get money out of men. Yet the other choice for many young (and not so young) women is to do without, because they are not trained to think of their own financial security and future. Someone else will take care of that, someone who loves them. Maybe.

We are taught to be unrealistic about our financial futures. When I was a college student having to pinch my pennies, I worked with more than one young woman who spent all she made on clothes and makeup. These girls were often better dressed than their supervisors at work. They had no interest or inclination to salt any of that money away for investment or future use. They were going to get married someday and their husbands would provide for them then. But as Estelle Fuchs says in *The Second Season:*

> What is true, however, is that often in marriages women have no property or money in their own names, or even in joint accounts with their husbands. And in these cases, at times of divorce a woman can find herself financially stranded, having been totally dependent on her husband. This is a curious situation in the modern world—the eventuality of divorce in many societies has led people to devise customs to protect women in this regard. Moslems and Hebrews allowed women to keep their dowries; bride price was often returned; even in contemporary Greece where there is a dowry custom still, the law states that if the dowry has not been signed over to the husband, which is not the usual case, at divorce the woman retains rights to that dowry and can take it with her.[1]

The woman in Proverbs may have been using her own money to buy that field; in fact, that is probably the case. She could have been investing her own dowry money, or the increase from her previous investments of the dowry. A man had the right to keep the increase from his wife's dowry later in Jewish history; whether men generally did so or not, I have not discovered. But her original money and possessions remained hers.

In the not too distant past, British and American fathers secured marriage contracts for their daughters stating what amount of money and property would be settled on the woman in case of widowhood, divorce, or desertion. These contracts were necessary because of discriminatory laws regarding property ownership for married women.

Under British common law, upon which most of the laws in the United States are based, a woman ceased to exist legally at marriage. She became, under the law, a part of her husband. As such, her property became his. Unless separate documents were drawn up to make exceptions to this arrangement, the marriage ceremony gave the husband possession of all his wife owned, or ever would own.

Women have gained a measure of freedom from the one-sided laws of the past, but we are not all the way out of the dilemma created by those laws. We still have a remnant of discriminatory laws. Yet even where marriage laws have been equalized, attitudes have not always followed suit. We still believe that Daddy and husband will take care of us financially.

The days of premarital contracts initiated by Daddy are gone. But we act as though they were not. The days of insoluble marriage are gone, so the questionable security it provided for woman is gone also. *Anyone* can be divorced. You may think that it could not happen to you. It can. And anyone can be widowed. To that you cannot be indifferent. It is not a lack of love for and trust in a man to be concerned about your own welfare if he were no longer with you.

If it is realistic to believe we *may* need to support ourselves someday, it is also realistic to prepare for the possibility. Educating yourself about money and investments makes good sense, no matter what you think about working wives, femininity, or marriage. It's living in the real world to be realistic about the future and money.

But provision for the future isn't the only reason for being interested in investing. There is the pure pleasure of doing well by yourself, of having the power to care for yourself. The joy of accomplishment is a reason to invest, too. Money isn't crass, not unless you are crass to start with. If you aren't, don't worry. If you are, start to work on your sensitivity and wholeness, don't toss out your investments.

Why should men be the only ones who know the satisfaction of closing a business deal? Why should they be the only ones who get the fun of analyzing the market, or the field, and buying it? And why should they be the only ones who can plant that field and harvest those grapes? I don't know a single good reason why women should not be right in there enjoying and succeeding, too.

Investments in people

But, you know, money and property aren't the only investments a woman can have. We have investments in ourselves, and in others.

Relationships with those around us are investments in our future and in theirs. I often think of the foolishness in being rude or unkind to children. It seems strange to me that arrogant adults forget that someday they will be old (if they are lucky), and those children they are mistreating will be the adults who have something to give to or withhold from the very ones who have set them such a bad example. It pays to be kind to kids; someday you may need one for a friend.

But beyond the purely selfish or just plain good-sense reasons for treating children right, there is the contribution you make to their future.

It is true that people become like those they are with most. We rub off on other people like chalk. We may not make them a *lot* like us, or *exactly* like us, but we make a definite contribution. Over years of interaction with others and involvement in their lives, the investment we have made in them, whether conscious or not, will pay its dividends. We can invest in their futures in a way that will pay good interest and be tax-free.

It is possible to help the children in your life skip some of the misery you have experienced, simply by refraining from passing your own bad habits on to them. But beware of punishing them for the bad habits they learn from you as the means to inhibit the transfer. That won't work very well. Example is the best teacher. Changing *yourself* to be more like the person you hope your child will be able to be is the best way to help make it come true.

Parents are far from the only people who influence children, who invest in their futures. Anyone who has contact with a child contributes to the data bank of experiences and perceptions that child carries. Out of that data bank are formed conclusions about personal worth, potential, what others are worth, what is good, what is right, what is fun. Any contact you have with a child can make a difference.

I was moved about a lot as a child. It all began when I was six years old. We left rural Arkansas for California defense work during the Second World War. Adequate housing was very hard to get there and so we moved from place to place when something better became available.

It was rough being the new kid. I was kicked, pushed, made fun of, harassed. Sometimes I felt I wasn't worth much since so many of my peers seemed convinced of it. And there were adults who didn't do much to dispel the notion.

But there were oases in my desert. Some were fleeting encounters with adults who by their unaffected respect for me, or joy in me, as a *person* (who just happened to be a child) lifted me up to have confidence that I was not an ugly duckling after all. Others were my teachers for a term, or however long we stayed in that place. In the second grade my teacher was Miss Montana. Wherever you are, Miss Montana, you made a difference. I felt good about me that year, and I thank you.

I can look back into my childhood past, before those travels, and see other lights. My parents made tremendous investments in my future during the first five years of my life. On the farm we lived a life into which I fitted very well. I tagged along wherever either one of them went without ever thinking that I was in the way. I believed I was the central person in their lives and that they were very pleased to have me with them. I still think they were. My grandmothers made similar investments in my future. My grandfather Smith carved popguns and squirt guns and whistles for me. I always felt it was because he thought I was someone he wanted to do something special for. I couldn't imagine him making things for me because he thought he owed it to me, or *should*. He was the patriarch of my father's family, others did *his* bidding and pleasure. I was honored.

Then there was Aunt Agnes. When she came home on vacation from schoolteaching to visit my grandparents, there was always a surprise for me in her suitcase. I was sure I was her special pet. To her I owe in large measure my love of books. Whatever writing I do, my aunt Anges has a part in it. The treasures she gave me were often beautifully illustrated picture books. I never lost my early love for those stories and books.

There were many others who invested in my future. Their confidence in me and assessment of me as something worthwhile, someone fine, carried me through bad times. They were lights to keep me going in dark places.

You never know what your contribution will mean to some child now or later. Make it a good one. I remember the importance of those brief meetings of the eye or few words I gathered from caring adults long ago when I see a child who I know is bending under a load. I try never to be blind to his or her need. I give them what I can, to hold on to. I will never know the dividends it will pay for them, or the loss if I do not do it. But I can know that in some case it might make all the difference. It's a good investment.

Personal involvement

I've been talking about investments in people. You really can't invest well in people by remote control. You can't hire a professional to care for you. You have to do it personally.

Being personally involved in your investments is important no matter what kind they are. Our Proverbs woman was involved in her investments at every stage. She knew what was going on. Not only did she assess the value of the land, make her own decisions based on her own perceptions, pay for it herself; she also planted the vineyard. Now, I don't think this necessarily means the woman got out there and did the whole thing herself without any help. She undoubtedly had servants, because the previous verse talks about her "maidens." She was such a good manager, I'd be surprised if maidens were the only help she had. But she doesn't seem to be afraid to get her hands dirty, she seems to even enjoy it.

It's important to know all the steps toward completion of the tasks you set for your hired workers. It's not so easy to successfully supervise work you don't know too much about. It's not only a poor use of your money because of the waste and inefficiency that is bound to result, but it's also a poor use of your human resources as well. Respect and allegiance from your workers are essential for a well-running household, farm, or business. To gain and keep that respect, supervisory personnel (you) needs to be competent and knowledgeable about the job and personally involved in it.

Educate yourself about money

Perhaps you have been concerned about the gaps in your money knowledge. You would like to take a more reasonable and responsible part in providing for your needs and future. Where do you begin?

You can learn about money several ways. There is the formal, direct method—take classes. And there is the casual, easygoing method —read books. And some fortunate people in certain lines of work get to learn on the job.

Money education is easy to come by just now. It probably has something to do with the pinch imposed by inflation and the growing awareness that personal responsibility for one's own finances is the only way to get anywhere in today's monetary situation.

Junior colleges have courses on personal money management and investments. Seminars on these subjects are offered at the college near me several times a year. You could enroll in similar classes as a start.

If that doesn't appeal, or isn't practical for you, try the book method. You can go to the library, which will probably snow you under when you see all the books on everything from how to make a million dollars in real estate and how to succeed on the stock market to budgeting for the family. Just browse. If something looks interesting, check it out and see what it has to offer. Some of the books will be useless to you. Either you won't understand what they are talking about or they will seem boring or ridiculous. But somewhere in the stacks will be a few that give you information you can digest and begin your education with.

Perhaps better than a trip to the library would be a trip to the bookstore to browse. Several money books for the non–financially minded are available in paperback now. There are even quite a few written specifically for women. You might want to take a peek into some of the following, either in the library or in a paperback edition at the bookstore. *The Joy of Money*, by Paula Nelson, was one I enjoyed myself. *The Only Investment Guide You'll Ever Need*, by Andrew Tobias, has a lot of good information. Don't let the title deceive you: the author says it wasn't his idea, that the book won't do everything but it *will* help. It is interesting reading and practical. Then there's *What Every Woman Should Know About Finances*, by Fred A. Lumb, and *A Woman's Book of Money*, by Sylvia Auerbach.

These are all books written for the common Jane. They won't tell you everything you ever want to know about money, but you will be able to use much of what they say now. If you would like to get into some of the background of why money means what it does for and to women, try Phyllis Chesler and Emily Jane Goodman's *Women, Money and Power.*

What money?

I can hear you thinking: *What good is it going to do me to learn about investments? I haven't GOT any money to invest.* Okay, I'll buy that. Do you *ever* get any money, for *anything?* Then you have money. It's just that you don't have any extra, right? If the problem is that you really don't have any at all, then you can put your mind to the task of trying to get some. Even a little is a beginning.

Starting small is no reason not to start. A few years ago I read an intriguing account of a young man who, when he was ten years old, at the hobby age, decided on a money hobby. He said he noticed that money was interesting and a good thing to have in many cases and he said to himself, *Why not a money hobby?* So he set out to treat it like any other hobby. He read about it, asked questions, collected it.

Since collecting money involves getting more of it, he studied different ways for a kid to make some by working. He got one job, then when he heard of another that paid more, he took that. Then he studied ways to make money multiply. One of the interesting things I personally have learned about money, which he found out early, was that money makes money, it reproduces itself.

So he invested. This went on at a leisurely pace, just like any other hobby, as he was growing up. While in his teens he finally cracked the million-dollar mark. He said it was embarrassing to have to have his parents sign business papers for him because he was legally a minor, but that he made his million without undue difficulty.

The newspaper account I read of this young man was not trying to tell anyone how to make a million dollars. He said that making and having money was relatively easy in this country, that you just had to know about it and use a few simple principles. For example, spending money is not the way to have money. He said that if you take your original money and never spend the profit, but reinvest it, it will keep on growing.

That story so intrigued me that I decided to have a money hobby, too. I started with eight dollars I received from a craft item I had made and sold at a gift shop. That eight dollars was invested in more craft supplies. My profits from those paid for some old bentwood chairs a school was selling. I resold them (at a profit) to women who were eager to refinish them for their homes.

From time to time I made a little bit of money at one thing or another. Once I experimented with propagating chrysanthemums and sold my extra plants at a flea market. I never spent any of my money-hobby money, that was my one rule. If I had to borrow from it, I paid it back.

Finally I had enough to buy a little stock on the stock market. It doubled. Boy, did I feel successful! My money-hobby funds now stand at about three thousand dollars.

Now, I didn't tell you this to prove how rich I'm getting or how smart I am at making money. I'm neither. It's to prove that even with almost nothing to start with, you can invest, and it can grow. Begin now to learn about investing and use what little you have. Start where you are to change things, don't wait for a new day or a golden opportunity. Use your ingenuity.

You don't have to be a wizard to invest. I know a woman in her seventies who lives comfortably on her stock interest. She inherited a group of stocks from her father when she was about forty years old. She says she reads *Forbes* magazine and has a broker she has confidence in. She says you can gradually gain an understanding of the stock market that will help you know safe investments from marginal ones. She is conservative, but she makes money. She has no formal financial training whatever.

Real estate is another area where women can invest to good advantage. Paula Nelson tells about a woman who got started in real estate without intending to. In her book *The Joy of Money*, Paula tells about Pat Martin's financial turning point. At that time it was difficult to find apartment owners who would rent to people with children or pets. Pat, with a two-year-old and no shelter, was intensely searching, with no luck.

She said, "This came as a rude awakening to me, that in looking for a place to live, as basic a thing as can be, you are dependent on someone else, you're at their mercy. If you had a child or dog in those days—I think it has changed a great deal since—you were entirely dependent on someone else's understanding attitude.

"And I made up my mind then that I would never in my life become dependent on anyone else for anything. So I determined that several things were necessary.

"First, we had to have a roof over our heads. I had a job at the time, but my income was barely enough to keep body and soul together, or so it seemed. Then I discovered that actually I had money to spend on other things, that I just had to rearrange my values a little."[2]

Pat used a small inheritance she had received and combined it with a loan from her mother to make the down payment on an apartment building. She wanted to be in a position to do something about both her own needs for housing and those of others who had children or dogs. From that beginning, Pat bought other houses and is now the owner of a large amount of real estate. She used the resources she had, even though they were small, to help herself. Then, learning more about investments, she continued to make them wisely.

Some women sell real estate part time because they have other obligations or work that makes full-time involvement difficult. But even with part-time work in selling, they are able to use their profits to buy houses for rentals. Once it is rented, the rental fee pays for the house. They gradually add to their investment property in this way.

It is often possible to be an investor even though at first you would not think so, considering your circumstances. But take another look around you. Call forth your resources and use your imagination. If you educate yourself about the ways of money and investments you can become a wise and successful investor with your money.

And in thinking about investments, don't forget to look around you at the lives your life touches. Invest your human resources in the future of others, and make dividends for them.

Everyone has resources. It's what you do with them that counts.

CHAPTER 9

Physical Strength

She girds her loins with strength, and makes her arms strong. (Prov. 31:17)

In Bible times, soldiers girded themselves up for battle and strengthened their arms. This woman is as fit as a boot camp graduate. She isn't afraid to treat her body with respect and prepare it to serve her well.

I have noticed that art from the past portrays men of all ages with well-muscled bodies. One could assume that artists simply preferred to sculpt or paint well-built men. Actually, in an age when bodies were used from childhood to *work*, muscular men were the norm. A man did not have to lift weights to look like a Greek statue, he just had to be a Greek who worked. There were no cars or elevators and few laborsaving devices. As a result, people were forced to use their bodies as they were engineered to be used. Only rich people could afford to be flabby.

Though women of the time must also have been more active by necessity than many of us are, this woman does not seem to have been satisfied to gain bodily strength accidentally, she was purposefully strong. There is a contrast here between the strong woman and the kind of woman King Lemuel would be likely to come across in the palaces he frequented. Women of the royal court would not have to work or be strong. They girded themselves with costly clothing, not so practical a thing as strength. They were decorative, she was practical. They were not sturdy, she could be relied upon. They might be dissipated or at least deteriorated physically by their idle existence, she only became stronger from hers.

A woman who consciously strengthens herself has been rare for a long time in our culture. The Victorian image of the idle, frail, helpless female has done a great disservice to us who have inherited her legacy. It hasn't been feminine to be strong. And it still isn't to a large extent. I can't help thinking of the contrast between this strong Proverbs woman and the women who take advice that tells them to have their husbands open jars of food, saying they are too weak to do it themselves. And I wonder how Victorian preachers handled this passage in Proverbs when they spoke to the ladies who wore tight corsets that made them prone to fainting spells.

"Virtue," in the Elizabethan Era, could mean strength, but came to mean chastity and purity in the Victorian Era—quite a switch. So the "virtuous woman" fit right in with the Victorian feminine ideal —as long as you didn't read the whole passage very carefully.

I would like to think we have grown beyond the social games of the Victorian Era. But I wonder if we really have. When girls cannot play sports because it "isn't ladylike" and women are excluded from health clubs except at hours when men don't find it convenient to come, then we can't have come far enough yet.

Fortunately we do not have to act Victorian, or pretend weakness and manipulate men that way. I do not have to be weak when it is fashionable. And I don't *want* to be weak. It's a good feeling to be strong. You last longer that way, too.

Actually, I feel good about the way fitness for both men and women has become more popular in the last few years. Maybe it means we are coming to terms with our technological society and beginning to realize that our bodies are resources we can no longer afford to take for granted, that we must *make* use of them. Perhaps we are able, at last, to put machines into their proper place.

What shape are you in?

Have you noticed how terrible people look in those three-way mirrors in clothing store dressing rooms? Isn't it demoralizing to go out after a long winter, looking forward to buying yourself something new and spring-y, maybe a bathing suit, then stripping down in front of one of those mirrors, to be brought face to face with your huge and flabby self? (I used to come home and feel discouraged about it for several days. But now I have it figured out. The mirrors and especially the fluorescent lighting in most stores bring out the worst in all of us.)

But what kind of shape *are* you in, even in good light? Have you looked at yourself coolly and calmly lately? Try it. Go take off everything, or almost everything, and take a look. Do you like what you see?

It's hard to face the fact that our physical well-being is in our own hands. We inherit a certain body build, true, but what we do with that raw material is up to us. We do not have to boil this down to fat and skinny. I'm not talking about that basically, though we need to touch on the subject later in the chapter. I'm talking more about basic fitness.

What are you doing with the body you have? It's the only one you'll get. Would you treat your car that way? Put the wrong kind of gasoline in it? Never get a tune-up for it? Forget the antifreeze? Never vacuum out the interior?

Why do people neglect and mistreat the only possession they can't replace? There are probably lots of reasons, all the way from traumatic to trivial. But I think one reason is that we don't have to buy it, so we have trouble realizing its true value. We always have it with us, so we don't know what it's like to do without one. And our bodies work so well, even when we mistreat them, that we find it hard to take them seriously until it's too late to repair the damage.

But no matter what the cause for neglecting or misusing our bodies, it is a waste of our resources. It is taking a part of ourselves and not using it to its fullest. More than that, not treating our bodies with respect means that whatever else we do right, we always run the risk of being cut short in our endeavors by illness, disability, or just plain foggy, sluggish thinking and action.

It isn't smart to misuse your body. It's dumb. Some people seem to think it's righteously self-sacrificial not to pay attention to their bodies. They don't get enough sleep, eat right, or exercise. They think self-sacrifice is an admirable trait. But there is another name for it that isn't pretty. It's called *masochism*, the joy of treating yourself badly.

I remember reading something written by Phyllis McGinley, which I can't find, or I would quote it exactly. As I remember it, her family was having a conversation about what they each wanted to be, or which saint they would choose to be, if they could. One child surprised them by saying she would choose to be a martyr saint. When asked why, she replied, "It's the easiest thing to be. You only have to work at it once, and everyone thinks you are wonderful from then on."

Being a martyr on purpose is a selfish act, not a noble one. It means trying to get attention by hurting yourself, trying to get others to serve or bow to you because of your sacrifice or misery. Beware of playing the martyr with your body, whether to impress someone else or to impress yourself.

Strength for balance

Suppose you have taken stock and you find either that a few minor repairs are needed or that a complete remodeling job is called for. Why not embark on it? What do you have to lose besides your inertia? You don't have to groan and get sore or be miserable to make physical changes. Laurence E. Morehouse and Leonard Gross, the authors of *Maximum Performance*, say that if you hurt yourself or make yourself sore in acquiring fitness, you are doing it wrong. They say you don't need to hurt to make progress, that that is an "old coaches' tale" and has been shown to be false by modern research into how the body works and conditions.

A strong healthy body balances the strong healthy mind our Proverbs woman has. It is possible to have a live, vital mind within a body that is weighted by disease or disablement; I know people who have such minds. But usually that is not the case. Healthy bodies go with well-being on all levels because we are *one organism*. We are not body as one part of our being, and mind or spirit as another separate compartmented resource. We are so interrelated and interwoven that you cannot draw a dividing line. When your head hurts, you can't think straight. When you are hungry, you drop things, and bump into corners, and become grouchy.

Things that affect our bodies influence our minds as well. Because this is so, taking care of our bodies, making them strong, fits us for maximum performance in all areas. It gives us the winning edge, whether it is in sports, enjoying life, or accomplishing what we want to with our lives.

Why not decide to begin with one thing that you want to improve or strengthen? You can use the goal-setting and -acquiring skills we talked about in Chapter 7 to make that change.

Be careful about making physical changes on too large a scale at one time. It is easy to make a list of all the things you want to do and decide to do them. But *doing* them all at once—that's *hard*. Instead, why not give yourself the satisfaction of many smaller victories and successes rather than trying to hinge everything on one master plan. But do pick one thing to begin with. No matter what your need, you can begin somewhere.

Incidentally, if you are a teenager and think you look terrible, let me caution you. You may be too hard on yourself. Find someone you can trust (not necessarily your best friend) for an objective assessment and ask that person if *she* thinks you are in as bad shape as you think you are. I say this because I remember what it was like to look in the mirror and see only the bad news, never the good news. Teens, perhaps more than the rest of humanity, tend to look entirely to see what is *wrong* with them. You can *always* see flaws others will not see. You may simply need more confidence about your looks, or minor improvements. *Nobody* is perfect.

But if there is something that does need improving, that can be improved, make a goal, a realistic one. And take the first step.

If you are in a situation that seems hopeless for making a real physical improvement, you may actually have the greatest opportunity of all. Bonnie Prudden, the fitness expert, says that even if you are in a bed or wheelchair and are so weak that you cannot lift your arms, you can begin to rebuild your body. She recommends squeezing a rubber ball to strengthen your hand. Eventually you will be able to raise your arm a little just from the strength you gain from ball squeezing. Any raising can be repeated until it eventually strengthens you further. By going slowly, at your own speed, you can, as others have done, rebuild your strength completely.

When I was born my mother was kept in bed for two weeks. She said she was so weak when she got up at the end of that time that she could hardly walk. After the birth of all four of my children I was up walking around within eight hours and left the hospital at the end of three days or sooner. The difference? Doctors had finally realized that lying in bed motionless makes one weaker instead of helping one recover strength, as had been supposed.

You can gain back strength by using your body, by gradually rebuilding, at your own pace. And if it's new strength you want, greater than you have ever had before, you can do that, too.

Finding a way that works for you

When you begin your own strengthening program, take care to tailor it to your *own* needs and wants. We are all different. True, we have a lot in common, and that helps us to be able to identify with and understand each other. But each of us still needs to find her own way to do things. It's not true that what worked for Sue will necessarily work for you. When you find out what you want to do, then discover your own way to do it.

We need to be able to enjoy our own particular way of becoming strong and fit and having fun even if our friends and relatives don't enjoy it too. You must be able to choose your own way without having to have it validated by someone else. You must go on beyond having to have permission, silent or otherwise, to do things the way you like. If you like to walk, and your husband or friend doesn't, don't let that take walking away from you. You can walk alone, with a dog, or with another friend. But walk, and enjoy it.

You may find you do best in a group. The YMCA or YWCA, health clubs, jogging clubs, exercise groups, or neighbors who get together to exercise or run may be your thing. Or you may be a solo strengthener, or a combination. Experiment until you find an arrangement you enjoy and can either stick to or can keep coming back to if you drop out for a while.

Educational TV usually has exercise or fitness programs. And there are also exercise records and books available. I have particularly enjoyed doing the exercises in Marjorie Craig's *21-Day Shape-up Program*. The exercises not only do the job, but do it gently and without discomfort.

The fat quotient

I said I would talk about weight a little. I don't want to spend too much space on it, though, because I don't think fat is the main problem with women who are overweight. Fat is the result of the problem, not the problem itself. I think dieting and being miserable to lose weight is a wasted effort if you do not find out from yourself first why you are overweight.

It's like this: if you are a way you don't want to be, but you are that way anyway, there must be a reason. If you find out the reason, then you can decide whether there is greater reward for you in being a middleweight or a heavyweight. It's the hidden agenda again. We eat too much *because*. We need to find out that because.

If you ask yourself why, and then listen for the answer, eventually it will come to you. Maybe not right away, but I think it will come. I asked myself that question a few years ago when I could not seem to take off pounds I wanted to lose. The answer that came back to me was that I was overweight because I was afraid I would be skinny.

When I was a little girl I looked like a colt, all legs. During all those moves from school to school I repeatedly heard the singsong taunts "Skinny, Skinny, two by four, couldn't get through the kitchen door." As a teenager I tried to gain weight, but I could never eat enough to do it. Well-rounded cousins laughed at my skimpy plate as they piled theirs high at family gatherings.

Not until I got married, began cooking for myself, and got pregnant did I gain any weight. For the first time in my life I could actually hold enough to add pounds, a few too many, it turned out. After the baby I took the extra off. But later, at a time when I was under tremendous stress, it came back and wouldn't leave.

I had just had my fourth child and endured a house remodeling begun soon after his birth (the church decided to add to the parsonage *after* the baby came instead of before). Within a few months we moved across the country and I found myself trying to care for an eight-month-old teething baby and three other young children who were longing for their old home, and to cook and clean at my parents' home while my mother recuperated from surgery. Overworked, and without enough sleep, I ate when I was tired instead of resting. The pounds gradually stacked up.

When my life finally settled down, I found that I couldn't take the weight off. It seemed to come off a little, and then go right back on. It was a mystery to me. So I asked myself the question: Why? One day the answer came to me: *I'm afraid to be slender. Bad things happened to me when I was. I might even become skinny and not be able to gain it back.*

I had exercised faithfully all during that last pregnancy and kept in tip-top shape so I wouldn't have to lose weight and spend a long time shaping up afterward. But soon after the baby was born, when I was back in shape and looking good, trouble began for me. Later, unconsciously, I was afraid to look the way I wanted to, afraid trouble would come to me again.

Knowing what was at the base of my fear and my fat helped me look at the situation reasonably and convince myself that my situation was different now, that what I feared would not happen. I could then decide consciously to lose weight and know that I would not trip myself up *unconsciously*.

An important factor in reaching the weight level you want and maintaining it is not allowing yourself to feel guilty or inadequate as a person because you are overweight. Our society is not kind to overweight people. They are joked about, discriminated against, and treated as though they are self-indulgent, lack self-control, and are gluttons. None of these attitudes and treatments help a person lose weight, but they do make her feel mighty bad about herself. Don't internalize your society's misconceptions. Don't assume any of these things are true about you. And don't feel guilty about being fatter than you want to be. Try to understand why. Then do what you can, in a rational way, to change that a day at a time.

You may find that you can do it on your own, or you may want to join with others in an organization such as Weight Watchers, Overeaters Anonymous, or TOPS where a mutual support system is an added benefit.

I think many women are overweight because they don't feel good about themselves. Or they are afraid to lose the fat because somehow it is security to them. Being a whole woman who is free to use and develop all she is and can be will help a woman in this situation because it will increase her own feeling of personal worth. When you are freer to be *you* (and happier about being you), I think you will also be freer to lose what you do not want to carry around on your body.

Food

A lot of women aren't strong and healthy because they just don't eat right. They may or may not feed their families right, or eat right when they are at home with their parents or share cooking with a roommate. But when it comes to their own nutritional needs, they act as though they were made of some substance that doesn't need replenishing.

You must provide the building blocks for body repair and maintenance if you want to feel good. You can't make something out of nothing.

Are you a leftovers container? Did you eat what the family wouldn't eat last night for your lunch today? Was it a little lopsided nutritionally?

Or, worse yet, are you a bite-and-run eater? Women who have jobs outside the home often make do with "coffee and," the "and" being sweet. Then they eat one relatively good meal a day in the evening. That really won't keep a person in shape forever. The homemaker or retired woman has her own version of bite and run. It's a little like being a secret nipper. What you do is eat whatever sweet thing you like a lot, just a little, for breakfast along with a glass of milk or cup of coffee or tea. You make a silent promise to yourself that later when you get time you will eat a better breakfast. At about ten o'clock you get to feeling hungry, but you are in the middle of something or too uninterested to cook anything. So you have another couple of those chocolate chip cookies (my downfall) and another glass of milk, and go right back to work or whatever you were doing.

You can keep this going all day if you time it just right. You will never feel too bad or eat much at any one time. But, cumulatively, you have a hideous diet, especially if you do it several days running.

And you wonder why you don't feel so good? Or why you get headaches?

Think about it. What *do* you eat? Is that any way to gird yourself with strength?

It isn't hard to come by a nutritional education. But don't make the mistake of trying to learn by reading the ads in women's magazines or watching the food commercials on TV. If you let them brainwash you, you will be in almost as sorry a shape after your "education" as you were before. Go to your trusty library or bookstore if you want to get some update on your food-for-fitness knowledge. I was always a fan of the late Adelle Davis. I especially liked her book *Let's Eat Right to Keep Fit* for its basic good-sense eating written in an interesting style.

Remember, you are what you eat.

Sleep

Some people have claimed the Proverbs woman didn't get much sleep because in the King James Version of the Bible it says her candle didn't go out at night. We'll look at that later, but I think she slept plenty. She wasn't superhuman, and she seems so sensible and creative and realistic that she would have needed normal sleep to keep that way.

Sometimes women have to miss sleep—especially mothers. I would like to start a trend as of this moment in the direction of training fathers to share the getting up in the middle of the night.

Bottle-fed babies can be fed and changed by either parent and feedings can be alternated between them throughout the night. Breast-fed babies can be fed by Mom (even lying in bed) and Dad can do the getting up and walking the floor with tummy aches and changing diapers and putting the little one back in bed. It works very well this way. And it's only fair. I'm for fairness.

And if you do miss sleep, try to make it up. I have read that it isn't necessary to make up sleep you have missed, just get a good night's sleep the next night and it will make up the deficit. But that is often easier said than done. And I'm not convinced it works, anyway. I feel better if I nap or half-nap to make up some of what I've lost.

I remember the sleeping habits of some of my dorm mates in college. The first year, students would play fast and loose with their health. They ate atrociously (the food in the dining hall made this very easy to do) and missed sleep constantly. They were usually able to get away with this regimen for the first year. The good health their mothers had carefully contributed to all those growing-up years was holding out. They were living on stored resources.

But the second year, things went downhill. The same living habits they could stand the first year brought sickness during the second. They had colds, and infections, and troubles of one sort or another. They *looked* worse. The healthy glow was replaced with pasty skin, or acne, or just a blah, dragged-out look.

Unfortunately young women often go directly from such living to marriage and pregnancy. Then they really pay for their years of borderline living. At the very time they need their best health, many are in their worst condition.

Fellow women, let's use some sense about sleep. And food. Strengthen your mind—be *realistic* about your physical needs and capabilities. And then strengthen your body. It can be your best friend. You should be its best friend, too. You're inseparable.

CHAPTER 10

Quality

She sees that her merchandise is profitable; her lamp does not go out at night; (Prov. 31:18)

Buyers of Palestinian antiquities can always find one inexpensive item in plentiful supply. The little clay lamps that were found in every home are dug up regularly. These flashlights and night-lights of the past are small and do not hold a large amount of oil. The lazy or careless woman was likely to have her lamp burn out before the night was over.

Our Proverbs woman was careful about such details. She saw that the lamp was full each evening. She was prepared for needs in the night.

The lamp was not lit so she could work far into the night (as would seem to be the case from the King James Version rendering of "candle") but so that she could give immediate attention to any needs that arose in the dark of night. Her time knew no light switch to flick on when the child awoke frightened, no flashlight to shine in dark corners. If there was a noise in some far part of the house, a lamp carried there could search out the cause; someone at the door, the face could be seen.

I remember the dark, starless nights of my childhood. We lived far out in the country away from the city glow that faintly lights even suburban nights. There was no electricity, so no light could be left on, however small. I can remember placing my hand in front of my face and not being able to see it at all. Nights like that needed a lamp like our strong woman's, one that could be relied on, burning on with its small flickering light, just in case it would be needed.

Quality merchandise

The first part of verse 18, "she sees that her merchandise is profitable" is interpreted variously in different translations. The King James Version says: "She perceiveth that her merchandise is good." The Jerusalem Bible says: "She finds her labor well worth while." I get the combined impression that this woman does good work, is reliable, and that it pays.

I enjoy seeing such good results from quality work. So much of what women do now is discounted. We often feel that what we do is "not profitable." And so much of what we do is not seen as "good" by others. Some of this negative image of our work undoubtedly comes as a result of the lost skills taken away from women at the Industrial Revolution. We have so little we can do that someone cannot buy somewhere else.

A woman needs to be able to hold a product in her hand that she has made and take joy from its creation. She needs to be able to know that it is good. Beyond knowing that she does a good job, she needs to see that it is profitable as well. It does not help her feeling of worth to be told, "Honey, why don't you save yourself the trouble and buy it next time. It costs as much to make it as it does to buy it already made."

Value your own work

It really helps if others value your work. But, realistically, that is not always possible. Sometimes you find that you are, at least for the moment, stuck in a place where you are not going to get any praise or recognition from others for your work.

But if other people do not value your work, you can value it yourself. You can do a quality job for *you*, for the sense of satisfaction you experience from knowing that it is good.

You should be realistic about your work's value. What will the real loss be if you do it poorly? Does someone depend on it? Would they lose if it was poorly done?

Another value your work may have is that of preparing you for other work. Your present work can be a stepping-stone of experience leading you to something you want to do in the future. As such, it is valuable to you.

Quality in perspective

"What's worth doing is worth doing well" and "What's *not* worth doing is *not* worth doing well" are both true.

It's important to recognize the need for quality work because of what it means to us personally and to our sense of worth, and because of what it means to others and to the needs that are to be filled by our quality work. But it is also important to have perspective about work. Not everything is worth your thousand-dollar job.

Some people never get much done because *everything* they do is so meticulously done that they just never get around to doing much. They have no comparative faculty for determining what has priority for quality work. Dealing with someone like that on a job must be maddening.

On a trip I once observed one such babe in the woods. An extreme case she was. I won't mention the name of the fast-food chain she worked for because, if I were them, I wouldn't want anyone to know I had hired a worker so unsuited for the job.

There was quite a long line for the food, as it was lunch hour and the establishment was located on a main highway. So as I stood waiting I had a chance to watch Sylvia (that's my name for her, all you Sylvias please forgive me) at work. Her job was to make milk shakes in paper containers, cap them with a plastic lid, and keep the spills wiped up.

She was so careful of each step that the other parts of the job kept running ahead of her. The drips seemed to bother her the most. She could not stand those drips that fell off the spindle of the milk-shake machine. So, rather than wipe them up with the cloth she had, which was clumsy and broke her pace, she began neatly to wipe each one up immediately with her forefinger, which she quickly licked. That finger was then used to pick up the plastic lid and run around the rim to snap it down.

I stood transfixed with disbelief. Sylvia was dispensing a touch of saliva to every customer who had the misfortune of having a craving for a chocolate shake that day. As I stood there watching in fascination and horror, I began to speculate about Sylvia's health. She was bone-thin, and since her uniform was about two sizes too big, it made her look positively gaunt. I wondered if she had tuberculosis, the disease my mother always feared in eating places and homes where people were nasty, as she put it (meaning they weren't so clean in the kitchen).

Sylvia's devotion to detail was running her ragged. Try as she must, even with her licking shortcut, things did not come out even. She grew more and more exasperated before my eyes. Finally I could make out the silent words she was mouthing: "I'm going to quit! I'm going to quit!"

As we ate I told my family about my interesting view. They all got mad at me, especially the one with the milk shake. "Well," I said, "she was only doing the chocolate shakes, yours is vanilla." "Oh, thanks!" said my suddenly full son.

I wondered if I should tell the manager what she was doing. It was so busy in there, I was sure he hadn't seen her. A sign outside said HELP WANTED, so I figured she must be a new trainee. I mentioned it to him gently, saying perhaps he would want to know so he could tell her not to lick her finger and then put the lids on with it. He was properly shocked and said he would.

The problem with Sylvia, it seems to me (among other things perhaps), was that she was so devoted to the small picture (the drips) that she could not get the hang of the big picture. She was such a perfectionist that she couldn't balance her work.

It's possible to be like that in ways that aren't so obvious. It's good to have a time away from your work and responsibilities periodically to see them in perspective, to ask yourself, *Am I using my resources to best advantage? Do I know what is really important and spend more on that, or am I bogged down in small details that "aren't worth doing well"?*

Mothers are prey to this, I know from experience. Children have a way of needing things. They need a drink of water, a story, a hug, attention, to be taught basic human skills, to be kept from killing each other. One gets to just jumping from demand to demand, eventually neglecting the real human needs of both the children and the mother. Time away, just a few hours, helps and will restore the perspective.

Quantity versus quality

I've noticed that mass production often works against quality. How often have you heard of a big company buying out a small company known for its quality product? Then do you notice that the quality product goes down in quality? Often conglomerates are not as committed to keeping the good name as they are to making a profit.

When you find something that has that ring of quality you want to clasp it to you as a great find. You hope it never changes. And when it does, it seems like a sad loss. When I worked at Desmonds, a large men's clothing store in Los Angeles, during college, one of the cashiers went out every payday and bought a certain kind of chocolates for us all. They were "indescribably delicious." But the candy company stopped dipping them by hand, and soon they didn't taste like heaven anymore. Something was missing. Over and over, it seems to happen, mass breeds mediocrity.

Mass media grind out TV shows for adults that insult the intelligence of twelve-year-olds with simplistic plots and silliness. Mass transit too often means packing everyone together in substandard quarters for uncomfortable rides. We seem to be infected with the tendency to destroy anything that we do in large quantity. Why? Other countries don't all do this, do they? Seems I have heard of old-established companies on the European continent and in Britain that still take pride in doing things as well as ever, even though they produce in large amounts. And Japan manages to maintain both mass production and quality.

Perhaps our problem is that, as a country of individualists, we lose our initiative and sense of responsibility when we are hidden in a crowd. Some of us forget our own personal integrity when we merge with a large concern. Maybe it is the same mentality that says it's all right to steal from a large company because "they will never miss it." Anything that is big becomes impersonal.

But *personal* integrity is important to the *person*. It is important to others, yes, but even more so to the individual possessing or not possessing it. It was important for the Proverbs woman to perceive that her merchandise was good and profitable because she needed to know it for herself. She needed to be a whole, balanced person, for her own self-respect and honor.

"Honor" should not be a trite word. We each need our personal honor. We need to be able to respect ourselves, to *love* ourselves in the best sense of the word. To do quality work, and take pleasure in the knowledge that it is good and profitable, is something we should not deny ourselves.

Quality versus quantity in one's personal life

We've been looking at quality in workmanship. Quality isn't something that should show only in one's products, material things, or workmanship. Quality in personal relationships and personal involvements is even more important.

It is too easy to be a volunteer doing little deeds of kindness on a broad scale, but never touch another human being in a meaningful way. One can be a hospital volunteer and sell things in the gift shop or pass out papers and magazines and never reach out to one of those hurting and frightened people. One can bake cakes and sell hot dogs and take up collections for blind children, and never see a blind child or really care about one either. It is involvement on a mass scale, but not on a quality scale.

Do you give quantity time to your friends and family as a substitute for quality time? How do you relate? Is it quality? Or is it surface, game playing, not touching?

You not only give more to others with quality relating, you get more back. And you feel better about yourself, too. Sure, it can be painful, one becomes more vulnerable. But more joy gets in, too, and more satisfaction.

Spreading oneself too thin

At meals, Walt Disney's mother passed buttered bread to Walt and his brother upside down. Their father didn't like her "wasting" money on butter. So he insisted on very little on his sons' bread. Her solution was to butter thickly when he wasn't looking and pass it to them upside down. Father was none the wiser, the sons well buttered.

We sometimes spread ourselves so thin, like Father's butter, that it is almost worse than none at all. It is so easy to become overbusy. Now is the first time, or maybe I should say the worst time, in history that our reach can so far outdistance our grasp. In the past, not so long ago either, it was not possible to do so much in a day. One could not travel far by horse and buggy, so long shopping trips in addition to other work and play were not possible. People could not be always hurrying from one activity to another. The length of time it took to make the transition from one place to another gave them some time to recoup, to distill their experiences into their own selves.

But now we can run around until we are so exhausted we hardly remember what we did all day or all week. The time goes so quickly in the busy-busy life-style that whole days are lost in the process. "Is this Friday already?" Long ago, there was so little hurry, it didn't even matter what day it was most of the time. When someone hurried then, there was a good reason. The hay would get wet if you didn't get it into the barn before the storm. The invader would get you if you didn't hide in the cave quickly.

Now we hurry just because we hurry. We are "on the go." The result is that many of us are spread so thin that we can do almost no quality work.

The woman we are looking at in this book is not some slow, lazy creature. She is an energetic ambitious woman, but she is one who can go slowly enough to produce quality work and quality relating to others.

She knows that life is more than how fast you can get through it.

CHAPTER 11

Home Skills

She puts her hands to the distaff; she manipulates the spindle; (Prov. 31:19)

No one wants to dry the dishes. When I was a little girl I would always rather *wash* the dishes. Washing was the prestige job. You didn't have to wait for someone to hand you the plate or place it in the rinse water. Instead, someone had to wait for you. My children felt the same way. By the time they could do a good job drying the dishes, they were above it, they wanted to wash them (before they could do a good job at that).

But the dishes of the world must be dried. (Yes, I know air-drying them is more efficient and sanitary, but I can make my point better this way, and besides, a lot of people dry them anyway.) There are necessary yet humble tasks that someone has to do.

The woman in Proverbs had no spinning wheel to make thread for cloth. In her day it was made with a simple hand spindle. Doughnut-shaped weights on sticks were rotated to form the thread. It must have been a boring job to spin enough thread or yarn to weave cloth. But it was an absolutely essential one if people were to be clothed with anything other than animal skins.

This woman is a possible future queen, yet she works at this simple unassuming job. She is not above "drying the dishes."

Proficiency in such a basic skill would reveal practical girlhood training. She had not been reared to be idle and totally dependent.

This sort of spinning could be done at odd moments and also while the spinner was engaged in other activities. I have seen pictures in *National Geographic* of shepherdesses in the East spinning with similar apparatus while they watch over their sheep.

A woman could spin to provide for the clothing of her family, or if she spun beyond her needs, for sale and profit. It was a simple skill, but a marketable one.

Honorable work

I suspect spinning was not a high-status job back then. There are jobs like that now, many of which are done by women. And often the status attached to a job has nothing to do with the work itself. Working in an office has more status to many people than working at home does. But the differences between the two do not always justify the higher status for the office.

What's more noble or exciting about stapling pieces of paper together or typing on a typewriter than making a kitchen clean and neat? I can't see any superiority in the office myself. Now, if the office job allows more creative expression and more contact with other people, making you feel you are part of the adult world again, then the appeal is understandable. But the work itself—that's a different matter. An awful lot of office work is just plain boring, more boring than cleaning the kitchen.

Some of the higher status for outside work probably comes from the prestige awarded the outside-the-home job by others. It may also come from the fact that we get dressed up to go out and at home we often dress like tramps to do the housework. But probably the biggest reason is that we get paid money to go out and work and we don't get paid for work at home. In our money-oriented society, things you don't get paid for aren't valuable. We have nothing to show for our time but the clean kitchen, which will not last, and nobody will notice anyway.

So it is not the job itself that makes us feel good about our work, not entirely, it's a variety of subtle factors. It helps to know that. We can reeducate ourselves to some extent to be realistic about our work, to value it more fairly for its *actual* contribution rather than its commonly perceived worth. We can raise our work status for ourselves. If we value it, we make a beginning toward a higher valuation of both us and our work by others as well.

Basic skills

I have heard of women who grew up like happy weeds, waited on hand and foot, and then went out into the world to seek their fortune and did not fare like the first two little pigs, but straightaway learned to cook and clean and care for all the little details that other girls were taught while growing up. I have heard about them but I haven't seen any. I *have* been witness to a few devastated by such an upbringing, and I know what the small holes in my own training have cost me in convenience and confidence.

Nancy was a southern belle. She was raised by a wealthy mother with servants. She could not cook, or mend, or clean when she went North to college. She married Tom, a student at MIT, when the ink on her diploma was barely dry.

They laughed about her cooking and didn't mind too much when things got a little messy. This was back in the fifties, and she stayed home to raise their expanding family while he got a job as a research scientist at an aerospace facility.

I was the teenager next door who baby-sat for her, toilet-trained the three-year-old who "just wouldn't train" (her rich grandma sent me two dollars in appreciation), cleaned her windows, washed her clothes sometimes, and was generally a hand of all work.

I really liked Nancy, but I was continually surprised that I had more horse sense about how to run a house and care for small children than she did. She was just as smart as I was, if not more so. The difference was that I had received basic training, and she had not. I saw her misery in trying to cope with three children and not knowing how to do simple things she had not mastered after years of living on her own and being married.

To this day I can remember the irony of baby BM* dried on the satin bedspread in her daughter's room. It seemed to stand for the kind of life she was trying to lead but failing in. The satin was what she had grown up with, the baby BM was what she had to deal with now.

She could, I think, have hired some grown woman to teach her the basics of cleaning, organizing her work, mending, all the things poor women have to know. It probably never occurred to her to do something like that. She probably thought she would get the hang of it eventually on her own—how could such simple tasks be so difficult?

But the skills women learn to manage a household and do all the things that need doing are not so insignificant after all. And the

* BM meaning, in nurses' lingo, bowel movement or human feces.

skills aren't so easy to come by either. I remember trying to iron without making more wrinkles than I erased. It took a long time. And I also remember watching my mother peel fruit for canning and wishing for her ease and speed while I hacked away and left almost as much apple on the peel as on the core. I thought of that not long ago as several of us were peeling apples together to freeze. My husband and sons were working with me. They said, "How do you do it so fast?" I said, "Practice, lots of practice." And I remembered watching my mother with the same awe.

Having three sons to send out into the world, I determined they should receive the same basic education as my daughter. I told them they must be able to be self-sufficient, that I didn't want them to have to marry in self-defense to keep from starving to death. My efforts took better with some of them than with others. But I still maintain that *everyone* needs to be able to know the basic human survival skills. There is no "woman's" work. All work is work, human work and honorable for all.

If you do not have the basic skills, the humble abilities so undervalued in the marketplace but so important to know, why not set out to educate yourself? You could pay or barter with someone to teach you. You can usually find someone who knows something you want to learn who will accept something you have or can teach in return. Actually, you can learn a lot for free by being a good watcher and question asker.

I will admit here that I became a skill stealer long ago. I first started when I went for a week-long visit with my Missouri cousins and began watching my aunt Ila. Ila is the most efficient person I know. I was thirteen years old and thought that our ways at home were the only way anybody did anything. I was fascinated to learn that they were done differently at the Epps' and they worked very well, too.

I began admiring my aunt's ways of doing her work. She seemed always to come out even, not more work than there was day, yet she got a lot done. And she didn't hurry or get in a tizzy either. But there was no wasted effort. So I began to observe quietly and analyze how she did it. That visit with my aunt began an interest in efficiency that stuck with me.

Ever after, I have tried to catch whatever gems of knowledge other women dropped inadvertently as they worked when I was in their homes.

My aunt Alta was another efficiency expert, but I could never catch her at it. She worked slowly, talked slowly, and usually had all her work done already when I was there, so I could never learn her secrets.

Eva Dow taught me a better way to wash dishes. She stacked them all neatly beside the sink before she began. I liked her method.

Pat Lindsey Galceran was simple and direct about her work, the most realistic worker I think I have ever known. Before she married we were students living in the same dorm together. Neither of us was very well endowed with cash, so we avoided unnecessary expenditures. A skirt of hers that buttoned up the front had lost a couple of buttons. Rather than buy a whole new set of buttons she simply replaced the lost ones with others not quite the same shape and color. When one of the fellows asked her why she had different kinds of buttons on her skirt, she replied, "I didn't have any that matched." That was it. Simple problem, simple solution.

She was never late. I almost always was. She knew her capacity and was realistic about what she needed to do. I watched her work in her home later and found the same sensible direct approach.

I learned skills I needed from all these women. Do you have any unpaid mentors? Can you locate more to learn from?

Marketable skills

When I was about to marry, one of the middle-aged women in my home church told me that, feeling she would always be better off with a marketable skill, she had not married until her schooling was finished. She urged me to do the same. She was right to encourage me to complete my schooling, though at the time I felt it was impossible because my money was used up and I did not think I could stay in school anyway.

Not that marriage is wrong before one is out of college. That is unreasonable for many people. But a woman does need a marketable skill, of that I am convinced. We have too long believed that all we needed to do was to be good wives and mothers and leave the supporting to our husbands. It doesn't work out that way for too many women. Without warning, they suddenly find themselves displaced by younger women, or through the death or disablement of their husbands.

For purely practical reasons, quite apart from any joy one gets from a skill that is also marketable, women *need* to be able to support themselves. And they need to learn a skill or trade that will support them above the poverty level. It is true that there are jobs women can get without a skill. But the pay is rotten. And there is little, if any, hope for advancement. Aim for a way to support yourself at a level at which you can be safe and comfortable.

If you feel you have already goofed here, taking stock and doing something about it now is better than later or never. If you are just starting out, you can begin now to gain the means to support yourself. Whether you ever use it or not, you need it. It is like an investment in your future, and in the future of those who may one day depend on you for their own futures.

Learn the basic skills, because they are important. Learn a marketable skill, because it may be absolutely essential one day. Simple things, wisely used, build fine and beautiful things, including lives.

CHAPTER 12

Sharing

She opens her palm to the poor and reaches out her hands to the needy. (Prov. 31:20)

Little children get a bad start at sharing because it is usually forced upon them. A disgruntled two-year-old malevolently eyeing the child he has been forced to share his favorite toy with is a common sight.

Mothers, being conscientious about starting out early to teach manners and morals, make the mistake of thinking that you can teach children to share by *making* them do it. But I've read that two-year-olds do not understand sharing because they can't yet comprehend the concepts behind it; to force it is worse than useless. It gives them the wrong idea about why we do it and the wrong feelings about it.

Even if one can understand sharing, the best way to become a sharer is to learn by example, not by force. Sharing with others encourages them to share with others, too. Not that a little encouragement isn't sometimes appropriate. But pressure is out. It's out because the result is not *sharing*, it's a coerced parting from one's goods in order to give them to another.

Sharing needs to come out of a full heart, not a guilty conscience. I guess that is why, or one reason why, I hate those ads with the pitiful child on them begging for my money. I am repelled by people who want me to respond from a feeling of guilt, guilt because my child does not look like that or have a similar terrible story to tell.

I want to share because I choose to, not because you force me to or make me uncomfortable if I don't. The justification for coercive giving is probably that it *works*. Guilt can often motivate us to part with our money. But that's just another form of coercion, and the result is no more sharing than the coerced two-year-old's experience.

Hand to hand

I love the way this woman shared—hand to hand. She did not hire someone to share for her. She did not keep safely uninvolved with those she helped by choosing persons far away who would not bother her when she would rather not think about them, who would not show up on her doorstep with tears and say, "Miss, my husband has just beaten me, and I have nowhere to go, will you help me?"

Pseudo-sharing is very neat. You can feel good without investing any emotion or inconvenience. It is antiseptic, prepackaged, mass-market sharing. Of course, you don't know if the person you're supposedly helping was the best one for you to help. You don't even know if your dollars got to *any* person who needed them. They may have gone to "administrative costs," and in some organizations "administrative costs" are very high.

I know a woman who has been a missionary in Kenya for several years. We asked her about a particularly well known religiously oriented relief organization, one that is highly recommended by several church leaders. She laughed. "Well," she said, "not much of that trickles down to the Africans who need it. It is all siphoned off a little here and a little there, so that by the time it gets out to the native in the bush, there is almost none left." She said if one wanted to make sure money actually helped the natives, it should be sent directly to missionaries one knew well enough to trust, with instructions on how it was to be used.

I live in a city that is highly populated by people who are concerned about sharing and helping others. They have discussion groups about Third World hunger and the oppressed, and this is good. But what troubles me is that they have for so long been accustomed to giving and sharing at a distance that they cannot perceive needs they could meet hand to hand.

Examples: I know a college professor who is concerned about world hunger and his own responsibility toward the needy to the extent that he is considering selling his home and moving into a smaller one so he can give more money. It is a painful, troubling

problem to him that he cannot help those who are suffering around
the world.

Another man is an executive who has, in his world travels, seen
much that troubles him also. They are both *genuinely* concerned, yet
when the matter of helping people who had real needs in their own
city was brought up to them, they were not interested. It seemed impossible to them that there could be a problem here, because they
see no beggars on the street, no rampant disease. So they, good men
that they are, are blind to needs around them because they have not
focused on helping hand to hand.

This problem is very common.

I was in a hospital, much to my dislike, several times in one year, a
couple of years ago. I learned several things there. One of them was
that you do not have to go far to find people with real needs.

I also discovered that there was a shortage of religious reading material in the hospital's lending library cart. This is especially ironic
because Wheaton, Illinois, sometimes jokingly called the New Jerusalem, is the home of several religious organizations and at least two
Christian publishing houses. Christian books should flow like water
here. But none had flowed to the hospital. No one had been looking
close enough to home for needs.

A trip to the local welfare office is very educational for people who
have never needed to go there. I will never forget the anguish I saw
on the faces of the people waiting in the hall for disdainful and slow
county employees to see them. Discouragement and defeat, pain and
loss, were written on face after face. I wanted to go to each one and
ask them what was wrong, at least hear their stories.

When I think of all our large, beautiful churches with huge paid
staffs and expensive pipe organs, I see those faces. And I remember
the drives to raise money for the organ, or the multimillion-dollar
building program one church in town is beginning. I can see all
those religious hands that drop neatly sealed envelopes in the offering plates on Sunday morning held out to the people at the welfare
office, to the teenager in trouble, or the battered wife instead.

And I wonder, *if, if it could be hand to hand* instead of imper-
sonally, distantly done, would we even need the welfare workers
with their bureaucratic mistakes that can mean a mother does not
get money for her child when the child needs it? And would those
desperate people then *believe* what was said in the church services

they are sometimes invited to but do not have clothes nice enough to attend in?

I conclude that remote-control giving isn't really sharing at all much of the time. It is conscience-soothing, nothing more.

Sharing is reaching out with an open hand. That hand may or may not contain something of monetary value. It probably won't contain money. At least not at first, not until you have reached out as one human being to another in friendship and caring. To really share, you must reach out your *hand*, not a present to make the one with the trouble go away and not bother you anymore.

Sharing should not impoverish or demean either the giver or the receiver. I always liked "The Andy Griffith Show" on TV because the characters understood so well the need to not demean others. People were regarded as equal beings, each one entitled to his or her own self-respect and personal dignity. Children were not to be put down and made fun of. No one was. Sharing is like that. It must not tarnish the sense of dignity and self-worth of the one receiving it. I think that is why our Proverbs woman reaches out her hand. She doesn't just contribute to United Charities and feel good all Christmas about it. She touches, as one person to another.

Finding needs

Charity begins at home is the saying. It is so often not true. That is why we need the saying, I suppose, to remind us that that is where it begins if it is *real* charity. Otherwise it is something else. It is not sharing but getting something for ourselves at a cost to those who know us best, those at home.

I've known a few who were well known for their charity outside in the big wide world, but at home there was hardly any at all. Phil is a respected teacher at a religious institution. His students love him, almost worship him. Because he gives all his resources to his job, there are none left over for his family. His own children cannot count on either his attention when he is with them, or more often, even his physical presence.

Phil wants to be important. To him work comes first. He thinks he loves his family. They know otherwise. They know he loves the attention and prestige he gets from his fans. His children are in the process of rejecting his religious faith, because the love he talks about at work is not present in his personal life.

Eli was a priest in Israel. He devoted himself to his work. His sons, however, grew up to use the priest's office as an opportunity for gain, personal pleasure, and sexual conquest. I've always wondered how they got that way. Did Eli's love for his work and his parishioners not extend to his family? Did he neglect his own sons' training in right living? Where did his charity begin?

Real sharing must have a short arm before it has a long one. We must be able to reach out to those in our nearest surroundings before we can reach farther. First we must be able to reach the family, then the neighborhood, the town, or city, and on to the surrounding area, the country, the world.

You do not have to go far to find someone who needs some sharing. Why not reach out to those you can *really* reach before attempting to help those farther off? Why not do the simple thing that will really help before throwing your money to the winds, hoping it will fall on those who need it far away?

Kinds of help

I like to think that help can be given to strangers instantly. The phrase "Have a good day" seems kind of silly to me, I must admit, but those who say it are on the right track. They are reaching out to others to share a good wish, however impersonal it may sound.

I am a Southerner at heart. I began my human journey in the Ozark mountains. Back there, no one would say "Have a good day" and leave it at that. They would ask you how your dog is, or more likely tell you it is a good-looking dog, or that your little girl is smart or pretty. They would make small talk with you in a ritual that says, "I'm human, you're human, we're all right." Northerners miss something by their brusqueness. We can all use a little of what the psychologists call "stroking." It is sharing on a small and casual scale. But it's good.

Then there is the perceptive listener and looker who cares enough to notice when someone is hurting. Just sharing time and space in a meaningful way by listening to the trouble and problems of another is sharing. Sometimes that is all the help one needs, a good listener to bounce one's thoughts against. Someone who cares enough to *re-*

ally listen, not feel they have to have answers or advice—just empathy.

Help and sharing can come in the form of work. Even a small amount of work can be very helpful at the right time. Mothers of new babies know how important a good assistant can be. Unfortunately not everyone knows what is appropriate and useful assistance. One friend was urged to go out to dinner the evening of the day she came home from the hospital with her three-day-old infant. That wasn't a very helpful offer. The very best help I ever had with a new baby newly home was when I lived in Whittier, California.

The women of our church scheduled helpers to be with a new mother all day and evening for the first day or two after she came home. One woman came over at suppertime and said, "I am a child person." She had brought small toys as presents for my two young children, who had just received new competition for my attention. My helper gave them their presents, fed them, and played with them. She was a welcome help.

Another woman came and tidied up and did whatever I asked her to do. She was meticulous in the kitchen and scrubbed my dish drainer cleaner than it had been in a long time.

The next morning the third woman came, and she was a cleaner. I have since that time longed to have her services again. She said, "I'm not much of a cook. I don't even *like* to cook. My husband is a caterer, fortunately, and he loves to cook, so he does a lot. But I love to clean. I really enjoy cleaning house." And she did. She hummed and whistled and moved all my furniture and cleaned from top to bottom. I enjoyed that happy sound so much.

Now, there are a lot of people I would be embarrassed to have find the dust under and behind things in my house, but not this one. She enjoyed her work so much, I felt good about having enough dirt to make it worth her while. Oh, how I wish she were here today—could I ever make her happy!

Those women helped me at a time when I really needed it. I had two preschoolers and my husband was a student with a job as well. He could not help me. My mother was seventeen hundred miles away. I don't think I could have bought better help anywhere even if I had had the money to hire it.

It is sharing to help someone find a job, more help than merely giving them money. As black people said during their efforts for civil rights, "We don't want the shirt off your back, we want a good job so we can buy our own shirt." That goes back to preserving the personal dignity of those we help. We must be willing to invest enough attention and caring in helping to be able to see the best way to do it, the best way for us *and* the best way for the person who needs the help.

Sometimes less is more. Helping people in ways they do not want, or more than they are comfortable with, is not the best help. You must be willing to listen to know what they are telling you, to understand what they are like, to know them.

Helping those who don't need help

As a pastor's wife I learned that the adage "Twenty percent of the people take 80 percent of your time" is correct. And, surprisingly, it is not the 20 percent who have the greatest need either. It is the 20 percent who want the most attention.

There are attention addicts just as there are chocolate addicts. In the case of attention addicts, other people are necessary to the habit. Chocolate addicts just make themselves feel bad. Beware attention addicts. They will try to make you think they *need* help, but they really don't want help, they want your time.

One girl called me to tell me she was suicidal. She called in the middle of the night. I had never met her, and took her seriously. I spent a long time talking to her and she "got better." She then called me regularly to talk about her troubles for hours at a time.

Quite by accident, I discovered she had a whole stable of listeners. Another pastor mentioned that a girl with a lot of problems had been calling him. We began to compare notes and ask questions and found she was telling variations of her story to several people. When I told her that I knew she was doing this, she decided she didn't need to talk after all.

Since that time I have met several others like my caller. They all have this in common, *they do not want solutions.* If they ask for advice, they will not take it. Or, more usually, they will say, "Yes, but . . ." and tell you how it will not work, or they are afraid to try, or they can't. And then they will repeat their whole long story to you again. Your time is of no value to them. They will apologize for keeping you on the phone for two hours, but they will not hang up.

Another variation on this is the person who *needs a little help*. She needs someone to watch her child a minute. She needs a ride. She needs you to take her somewhere. Or she needs to borrow your things. The difference between this person and an ordinary friend who gives and takes with you is that you soon get the impression that you are being had. It isn't always obvious just how, but inside you know it. It may be that when *you* need something, she is just not able to do it. *Usually* not able to do it. Or when she does, it turns out badly—always.

Disengage yourself. That isn't helping.

Then there are those who ask you to do something harmful to yourself or your things. Beware them, too. Just because someone has the rudeness to ask a personal question does not mean you are rude if you refuse to answer. Just because someone has the gall to ask to borrow your best dress doesn't mean you have to lend it.

I knew a couple in college who were so conscientious that they felt they could not refuse to lend to a relative who was obviously bumming off them. The husband's best (and only) suit was loaned and slept in on a drunken spree by the relative. They still felt they had no other choice. And I still think they were being suckered and made no positive impression for good on him at all. He just knew where the easy mark in the family was.

Save your help for those who need it.

Don't help if you can't help

As I have mentioned, I was in the hospital about two years ago. Now, I am not a hospital person. I had always been interested in biology and medicine, curious about science. I liked reading about diseases and cures and such. That is, until it was me. Then I was terrified.

I had to have double surgery. But I had never even imagined something like that happening to *me*. I was petrified. The counseling nurse from the recovery room came in the night before to see me. When I told her how scared I was, she said, "You must believe that God can bring you through it safely." I said, "Oh, I believe he *can*, I just don't know if he *wants* to or not!"

To make it worse, I had to lie around and rest for a week before going into the hospital. With nothing to think about except my possible demise, I was a silent basket case. One day as I was lying there mentally shaking, I received a phone call from the church I was then a member of.

A super-cheery voice said, "I understand you just recently had surgery." "No," I said. Before I could say more, she rejoiced, "Wonderful! You didn't need it after all!" "No," I said, "it's next week." "Oh." Need I say that that call did *not* help me.

Then a neighbor woman decided to come over and talk to me about three days before I went to the hospital. She had always seemed like a very kind, *extremely* kind woman. I am now suspicious of all women who are extremely kind.

She said she wanted to tell me what a hysterectomy was like. She had had one, and she wanted me to know what it was like so I wouldn't worry. She thought it would be worse to have a gallbladder out at the same time (which was what I had to look forward to), but she didn't know about that.

So she proceeded to tell me, in great detail, her own personal version of the misery and pain after her operation. All very sweetly, of course. I looked at my husband. He looked at me. We tried to change the subject. No way. She went on and on with her horror story. Then she wished me well and said she was sure I would come through it all right.

One of her main themes was the debilitating effect it had on her. She said she was so weak, she wasn't allowed to lift a teacup. That eventually became a family joke during my recovery. But at the time, her visit was a cruel extra burden on me. It was *no* help.

If you can't help with your help, stay home. Don't call. Please!

May I say to you, I survived, as you see. And was not only lifting teacups very soon, but up and walking all over the hospital in a few days, and home in less than a week. So if you are reading this in a similar situation, don't listen to them, listen to me. I was scared, and I made it. And I am in good shape. Just a little lighter.

You need to share

You may ask what sharing and reaching out to others has to do with being a whole person as a woman. What does it have to do with being a balanced person?

If you are able to share, really share, out of an abundance of love and a good feeling about it inside, it shows that you not only feel good about yourself, you feel good about others also.

A person all wrapped up in himself or herself makes a very small bundle. If you can't reach out and share, you need to be freed inside. It shows that you aren't confident enough about yourself yet. Maybe you need to love you more, so you can then be free to love others more. Maybe you need to be more generous with yourself so you will be full enough of receiving that you can let some spill over for others.

Being whole means feeling good about yourself. It also means having enough inside to have some extra to give.

CHAPTER 13

Making Provision

She does not fear the snow for her household, for they are clothed with scarlet. (Prov. 31:21)

There is some question whether the word "scarlet" here refers to color or quality; probably it refers to quality. Scarlet clothing was *better* clothing. The Septuagint version of the Old Testament says "double" here instead of "scarlet." Hebrew words were written with only consonants. The reader supplied the vowels. In Hebrew, the word "double" has the same consonants as the word "scarlet." Different vowels are used in the Septuagint to produce the word "double," meaning the clothing was warm enough for cold weather.

Whatever the word is, either way you take it, it all adds up to making provision for the physical needs of her household ahead of time. She foresaw the winter and did not wait for it to strike before providing clothing suitable to keep her household warm and healthy.

We, who are likely to buy most of our clothing ready made, and if not that, at least buy the materials for it ready woven and dyed, don't completely identify with her preparedness. We might look ahead to next season and buy warm winter clothing when it goes on sale in January. It involves guessing what sizes we will need, and if the people involved will actually wear it if we buy it. And of course, coming up with the money at that time of year. Then we have the problem of where to store it in the intervening months.

The Proverbs woman had a different set of problems to provide scarlet or double clothing for her household. One commentary says that this would have been wool clothing. Wool must be obtained in the spring, when sheep are sheared. It involved either having one's own sheep or buying the wool already sheared. One could buy cloth,

too, I imagine, but it would have been much more reasonable to produce it at home.

Not only did the projected clothing needs of the family and servants need to be anticipated in the spring, but enough raw materials
had to be assembled and cleaned, the thread spun, and cloth woven.
Workers for all these tasks must also be available for the jobs. A wise
woman probably had a storeroom of wool and spun thread she added
to constantly as she was able to take workers from slack jobs to
spend a little time spinning or weaving.

Working with raw materials from scratch takes much more dili-
gence and vigilance than going out to buy it all on sale, or even at
regular prices. When I was a small child, and then again later when
I was older, I lived on a farm where many items were made by hand.
My grandfather made our chairs. This involved planning ahead.
Tree bark was used to weave the seats. This weaving needed to be
done at a time of year when the bark from a particular tree was
available at a pliable stage. But the wood for the frame of the chair
had to be seasoned wood, that is, it had to be thoroughly dry. So one
had to begin long before the chair was needed to prepare for its man-
ufacture.

People on farms used the winter for manufacturing articles they
would need in the future. When no crops could be produced, imple-
ments were repaired, fences mended, new objects made. Farm
women spent the winter sewing, knitting, quilting, and laying up for
the needs ahead.

In summer the needs of the coming winter were anticipated. Hay
was brought into barns and layered in haystacks. Crops were planted,
cultivated, and harvested. Women worked in their gardens, canned,
and cured for the winter. Whether in winter or summer, those living
close to the soil have to be always thinking of the needs of the future.

It was like that long ago, for all but the most rich and pampered
women. Our wise woman was not one of those. Even if she became
rich, she would still be realistic about tomorrow. She would not be
vulnerable. She would be prepared. Recently I read an excerpt from
a book about being prepared financially for monetary collapse. The
writer claimed that one should have a year's supply of food stored in
case of national disaster or financial collapse in this country. He is a
Mormon and has applied the Mormon good sense about pre-

paredness in this area to his financial theories. It occurred to me while reading his recommendations that many people would think it strange and rather eccentric to store a whole year's worth of food in one's basement. And that made me realize how far we have come in one generation.

A generation ago that would not have been considered eccentric at all. We were not far removed from the pioneering days of this country when drought or disaster could mean death for isolated families who did not have food provisioned ahead. They were risking their lives to not have both food and clothing stored for emergencies.

We have become so dependent upon the supermarket and clothing stores that we have forgotten, if we even knew, that *we* ultimately are responsible for our own survival and care. And we are responsible for the protection and feeding of our dependents, too. It is easy to think that our government will step in in an emergency and send help and supplies. But we forget that governments are only made up of people, and people make mistakes. Governments fail, deteriorate, and goof. We are being unrealistic to suppose that the government can care for everyone, provide for everyone, in all situations. We are really *it*.

The difference between faith and foolishness

Many years ago I read a book called *April Snow*. That book made a fadeless impression on me. It is the poignant story of a woman married to a foolish and cruel man. The title comes from the Swedish saying that if it snows in April there will be a new baby in the family that year. Sigrid, the main character, sees a lot of April snows.

The author's portrayal of Sigrid's husband, Peter, is one of the most indicting revelations of character I have ever read. The man justifies all his carelessness and laziness by claiming that God will provide. He is the epitome of the religious person who uses his religiosity as a cloak to cover his own inner meanness.

Peter will not provide for his family. He will not even go out on the fishing boats with the other men on their annual trip to harvest fish for the winter. He has an excuse to put it off and says, "God will provide." Sigrid, whom he has at least had the foresight to trick into marrying him, must do the providing. She goes out with the fishermen to bring in the winter's fish.

The reader sees almost nothing good about Peter. His "faith" is shown for what it is for him, nothing but self-justification. But there are many people who justify lack of forethought by their own misconceptions about what faith is.

Faith is not pretending the real world is not out there. It is not pretending that winter will not come, that cold will not freeze because God will not let it reach you. Faith is believing God, not closing your eyes to reality. Reality is seeing the world as it is. A realistic response is to use your own resources, mental and otherwise, to prepare for your needs. The faith comes in the form of believing that God will not abandon you. He will not necessarily drop provisions from heaven. He has been known to do that, but that may not be the method he uses with you.

It has been my experience that God helps us use our own resources to solve our problems. Or he supplies a missing ingredient so that we can. It doesn't really make sense, does it, that God would create the world, including your body and mind, and then resort to magic to solve your problems and provide for your needs. I like to think that our minds are part of his good provision. We can think ahead to plan for our needs and fill them before they are needed.

That is not to say that we must have provided for absolutely every possible contingency before we embark on a new venture. Balance requires that we look at reasonable risks and provide for them as best we can. Then, if we are convinced this is the way we want to go or are supposed to go or must go, then we go. Wise provision does not eliminate risk, but it does minimize it. It does what it can. And usually it works.

Sharing the load

One of the nice things about the Proverbs woman is that she did her share. I still do not think she was an overworked overachiever who never took a coffee break. But she did carry her end of the ladder.

It seems to me that a man would be awfully glad to get a woman like that. Now, I am sure that some men, like Peter in *April Snow*, would want such a woman so he could loaf and take advantage of her. I have the feeling our Proverbs woman would not take too kindly to that kind of man. She might even be smart enough to see him coming and "be out to lunch" when he came around.

But a good man would really be glad to get a woman like this. He could rest easy at night, not wondering if there would be money enough to buy the children's school clothes at the end of August. He wouldn't be hit with the sudden need for four pairs of snow boots at the first snowfall. Our Proverbs woman would have already spun the thread, made the clothes, *and* the snow boots, or had one of her servants do it.

We run into problems right away, don't we? No child of mine would wear a snow boot I made. And how can you work all winter preparing school clothes when you don't know what your teenagers will wear next September? They don't even know in August what they will wear in September. Our life-style is so different from the Proverbs woman's we must not think we can simply yank a thing or two from her bag of tricks and zap them into our lives. We can extract the principles she lived by and apply them to our situations, even though we can't copy her exactly.

We can copy her foresight and preparedness. That will work with a few modifications. If money is what we are going to need come snowfall, we can find ways to get some and sock it away for then. We can be our own credit card company and pay ourselves a little each month, *before* those school clothes are needed, instead of waiting until after and paying Master Charge 18 percent interest plus buying all those postage stamps it takes to mail in the payments.

We can have a money cupboard we add to during the winter and at spare moments. It may not be quite the same as spinning the cloth through the months, but the result will be the same. When next winter comes, our households will be clothed with scarlet.

If you look around you at your home and your family (or your own personal needs if you have no family to provide for), you may be able to see still other needs that can be projected ahead and provided for.

If you have any ground space at all, you can grow some food. An area four feet square or the equivalent can grow a sizable amount of food. It doesn't matter whether you are a gardener or not. You can mulch garden with almost no work. Go to the library and look for Ruth Stout's books on mulch gardening. I have two of her books,

How to Have a Green Thumb Without an Aching Back and *The Ruth Stout No-Work Garden Book.*

It's real simple. You use grass clippings, straw, hay, almost anything vegetable, to cover the ground deep enough to keep weeds from growing. Then you dig a little hole and plant your tomato plants or whatever, and snug the mulch around it, and that's all. Water evaporates slowly from mulched soil, so you rarely have to water it. If you tuck your potato peelings and such under the mulch, they will decompose and quietly become food for the earthworms, and ultimately fertilizer.

You can plan ahead in the fall and pick your growing spot then. Cover it with several inches of leaves, say nine inches to a foot. Next spring the soil will be soft underneath the leaves and you can pull back the mulch enough to plant seeds and plants without digging up the whole plot.

You can even use an old piece of rug for mulch. Place the rug over the ground you want to use. Cut holes where you want to plant. Rain will soak right through the rug (unless you use a nonporous one like kitchen carpeting) and you will be able to walk in your rug garden immediately afterward and not get muddy.

Back to sharing the load. A man who has a woman who is dependent upon him for all provision has a heavy load to carry. Many men seem to sag a little under that load. It has not always been so. Before the Industrial Revolution, women contributed a large share of the household provisions. On farms this is still usually true. But our society has largely bought the belief that women must be passive consumers and men must be aggressive providers.

We have an uncomfortable arrangement. It not only drives men and women apart, making each contribute only part of what they are, but it also makes for an unwieldy way to live. Women are thwarted; men—some men at least—overworked and weary. Couldn't we share the load?

Rather than buy the personality-splitting idea that men are providers, women are nurturers, why can't we both be fully human and share both? Men are nurturers, too. They need to learn to express their full humanity. Women need to be free from the burden of being sole nurturer for the family and society. And women need to be free to use all their abilities and resources.

It may not be *easy* to change, because when people are accustomed to doing something a certain way they are often uncomfortable with change, even change to a better way. For this reason, we need to be gentle and kind about making changes. We can talk to the men in our lives about equalizing our relationships and equalizing work loads and emotion loads. Go slowly if speed seems destructive or unwise. Look ahead in that regard, too.

Balanced provision

The ancient world appreciated color. Women wore jewelry and trinkets. The black chador of Islam was not there then to drab Eastern woman's life. Nor was the Mao suit of China. Long ago, colorful clothing was desired.

It was possible to dye wool and linen with herbal mixtures to obtain different colors. But natural vegetable dye tends to produce muted colors. The port city of Tyre was famous for its purple dye made from a sea mollusk. To have your family and household dressed in scarlet might signify more than warmth from the cold. It could also involve providing good-quality, attractive clothes for one's household.

The way your family (and employees) look, the way they are clothed, is important for more reasons than keeping out the cold. We need a balance between purely practical reasons for clothing and reasons that provide more benefit for the spirit than the body.

We live in a world that says, "I can tell something about you by how you look." Children have to go out into that world to school and play. It is sometimes hard for adults to realize that at school their children move in a different world from the one they know at home.

Clothing that is attractive and current is important for the child's feeling of belonging. It helps to look good and not to look *different*. Everybody wants to feel unique, but not odd. To children, clothing is an important part of not feeling odd. They are not as genteel as adults about clothing. Children (not yours perhaps, but somebody's) will make fun of others who wear clothing that is far out of step with the going thing. It ought not to be that way, but, realistically, you must take it into account when clothing your family.

Are you providing for the emotional needs of your household while providing for their clothing needs? My daughter tells me that many girls who go to high school feeling they do not look as well dressed as the average lose self-confidence. They tend to gravitate toward the one group of students who will accept them socially, those who also are low in confidence, the pot smokers, the "burnouts," as they are called here.

She says that feeling good about yourself in a large city high school very much involves how you look. Again, it should not be that way. But you must be aware of the way it is in order to help your family and yourself.

Household provision

The strong woman's household did not consist of only family members. She had servants, probably slaves or long-term servants, living in the family residence. She may have had many such employees. These people, men, women, and their children, were dependent upon her for their needs, too. A hired servant might require certain clothing and wages as part of the terms of employment. A bondservant had to make do with what he or she was allowed.

I have a piece of paper, passed down in my family, that troubles me. It is a contract for the rental of a human being for a year. The man's name is George. He was hired from his owner by my great-grandfather B. McCord Roberts. One of the conditions of the contract is that the renter provide a suit of winter clothes and two pairs of shoes for the slave. The man who owned George did not want his property to be so ill clothed that he might become sick.

I cringe at the knowledge that anyone ever owned anyone else. That my ancestors rented a person, played a part in slavery, bothers me too. But the fact is that I may very well be descended from slaves also. Slavery has been around for thousands of years. In ancient times it did not depend upon being from a certain ethnic or racial group, it depended upon who won the war, or who was impoverished, or where the famine had been. My white skin doesn't exempt me from a slave heritage.

The provision for George's clothing seems so bare-bones commercial. But the reason for the crassness of it all was that George was valuable to his owner. He did not intend to leave his clothing to chance or the goodwill of the renter. Wouldn't it be a step forward if more employers were as realistic about the basic needs of their employees?

Are you realistic about the real needs of those who work for you? Do you look at your employees as actual people with real needs, needs that your wages and provision either meet or do not meet? Are your employees dressed in scarlet?

When you are making provision for your household, do you provide for those who work for you? Many of you are employers, or you will be in the future. You should face the truth of your own hold over the lives of your employees. They should not have to put pressure on you or look elsewhere for a fair return for their labors. You should make adequate provision for them. The balanced, whole person is able to regard others in the same light, as whole persons with similar human needs.

Do not *assume* that those who work for you already have their needs met, or that they do not need what you do, or that they need no more than you do. When my husband was a pastor, I got to know a lot of other pastors' families. I don't imagine it is too different for other religious employees. It is easy for the congregation or organization to forget that they hold your family's purse strings. They forget that you do not have the accumulated furniture, equity in a house, and savings they have because the pastor's family may have spent years in school and in low-paying pastorates before coming to their employ. Many such workers are ashamed to mention their needs. They should not have to.

Businesses are often run at the expense of lower-level employees. It is not right for upper-level management to live in luxury while workers live in difficult circumstances in order to subsidize that luxury. Look well to the needs of your *whole* household.

CHAPTER 14

Personal Appearance

She makes herself coverings, her clothing is fine linen and purple. (Prov. 31:22)

The more I read and think about this woman, the more I like her. She really *is* balanced. I don't see her always taking the smallest piece of her favorite cake and giving the biggest one to someone else. Not only does she clothe her household well, she clothes herself well, too.

And, ah! she doesn't make excuses for it. She just does it. I am wary of women who have to have a *reason* for everything that is fun or feels good. People who have to justify every nice thing they do for themselves make me feel a little uncomfortable. I guess I suspect they think I am an uncontrolled hedonist or *unspiritual* because I don't mind doing it simply because I like it. I don't have to have a justification to be good to me.

When I start talking about clothing, I feel there must be all kinds of hidden meanings and backgrounds to what women do and think about clothing for themselves. I know clothing has meanings for me that would be hidden to me if I hadn't been curious about why I do the things I do and ferreted the whys out of my own mind.

I don't loan my clothes. Never have been able to do it that I can remember, not without being uncomfortable anyway. I remember my mother's chagrin when, as a teenager, I would not let her borrow my blouses. I'd say, and mean, "I'll give it to you if you want to wear it that badly." She would look at me as though she had produced some mysterious mutant that she could not understand, and say, "No, that's all right, I'll wear mine."

She grew up in a family of nine children (seven girls). I imagine they traded and handed down clothes until it was hard to remember who was first owner. Me, I was one of two, and the other was a boy. We didn't have much conflict over clothes.

I suspect my fear of loaning and borrowing clothing may come partly from my borrowing Delores Logan's dress when I was about eleven years old and tearing a three-cornered hole in it on barbed wire. I was visiting with her and staying overnight, as I remember it. She had a pretty dress that she offered to let me wear. I did, and in some wandering over the farm I got hung on a fence. I was so horrified, I thought it was ruined (maybe it was, I don't remember her wearing it again after that).

Another reason for my possessiveness about my clothes may come from the fact that I was always a little hard for my mother to fit. I was tall and thin. She had a habit of making her own dress patterns. It worked fine for her, but my homemade clothes always had large sleeve holes. I tended to look extremely hungry in my dresses. When something came along that I actually looked good in and liked, I didn't want to risk it by loaning it out.

There must be many hidden agendas about clothing. Have you ever noticed that you tend to feel ugly when you wear something you don't like? And that a bright color that pleases you lifts your spirits? I have taken to wearing the brightest thing I have (bright, not wild) when I feel the dullest. It seems to bring me up more to its level.

What do clothes mean to you? And do you do right by yourself clotheswise, or are you less than considerate of you? Do you work in the raggedest things you have when you are home? Would you rather dress better? Why not do it? Have you let your best things, or favorites, hang in the closet until they were out of style because you were afraid if you wore them too much they might get worn out, or get ruined from a spot?

I realized I was doing that not long ago. It probably came from the lean years when I had no money for clothing. I had to make the things I liked last and last. Not that I wear most of my clothes out anyway, but I could have enjoyed my favorites more by wearing them more. I have determined to stop that. I really do not need a lot of old clothes, out of style, too good to throw away and not wearable either, waiting for me to do something with them.

The hidden things clothes mean are so tied up with the obvious that one has to approach clothing from several directions. I read *The Woman's Dress for Success Book*, by John T. Molloy, and found it interesting and helpful. At the time I read it, I was doing some speaking here and there, and on a subject that was not always accepted immediately by everyone in my audiences. Equality for women in the Church sounds fine to some groups, but among some conservatives mentioning it is like waving a red flag. They sense danger there because they have been traditionally taught that women *cannot* be allowed leadership and teaching positions in the Church.

I had a light blue suit and multicolored paisley blouse that I had taken to wearing every time I spoke. When I read Molloy's book I was encouraged to find that blue makes people look more believable. I thought, *I'll stick to my preachin' suit!* because believability was certainly what I needed with those skeptics in my audiences. I also read that paisley ties are women's favorites (in his first book, *Dress for Success*, for men), so I reasoned that my paisley blouse might function like a tie for me. My favorite outfit was making me more believable and likable to my skeptical female audiences. At least I thought it might help, and that in itself helped me.

After reading Molloy's books I have become more aware of the clothing businesspeople wear. And I can see that it is true: clothes do make a statement about the wearer. You might as well have your clothes say good things about you as bad. They can precondition people to anticipate either that you are businesslike and competent or that you are frivolous and a loafer. Why not at least give yourself all the help you can by dressing with an awareness of the messages clothing gives.

I used to think that paying attention to clothing was a bit vain and empty-headed. My tomboy heart wasn't interested in anything except comfort. And then, of course, there were those dresses that made me look so thin. That may have had something to do with it, too. And I still think that paying too much attention to clothing is a bad habit. But so is paying no attention at all to clothes. They do have something to say about you.

A couple of years ago I was in the habit of wearing sneakers all the time, except for obvious dress-up occasions. Living across the street from the grammar school, I was at various times room mother and library volunteer. I was seen over there a lot for a few years.

One day my fifth-grade son said, "Mom, don't take this wrong, but could you not wear those shoes when you come to school?" I said, "Do they look bad?" He said, "Well, no, but I wish you would wear some better ones." So from then on I did, and realized that he had been embarrassed when his mom came to his school wearing what seemed to him, or maybe to his friends, like non-mom-at-school attire. It wasn't a big thing, but it got me to thinking, *What does what I look like say about my child?* Then I extended it to *What does what I look like say about my husband, my employer?* How I look does not only reflect on me, it reflects on everyone I represent.

Oh, I know that there comes a time in a child's life, around teen trauma time, when the fact that they even *have* parents is an embarrassment. But really, how good a representative are you for your family? Could you improve on it with a little effort?

I also began to notice how employees represented their employers. I don't wonder that some women do not get promoted, or men either for that matter, when I see how they dress at work. I'm not referring to things like suits and ties and obviously expensive outfits versus casual and inexpensive clothing. I'm talking about neatness, clean hair, clean shoes, and appropriateness. There are casual jobs and noncasual jobs, but neat and clean say, "We do a good job, care about detail, and have ourselves and our work 'together.' "

If you want to say good things for your boss, start with how you look. It might even get you a raise. It couldn't hurt.

Looking good versus too good, and asceticism

Some people are so *nice* I'm not comfortable around them. I can't believe they are really that nice all the time, and I'm waiting for the big blowup. Or else I figure if they really are that nice, they won't bother with me for long because I know I'm not that nice. I dread the letdown when they discover it. There is also a type of person who *looks* too nice to be real. Sometimes they are both the same person. I keep wondering why they need to try so hard. Do they want attention? Or what?

I knew a lady, a pastor's wife, who was the picture of perfect fashion every time I ever saw her. She was eye-catching in a crowd, the only peacock in a flock of doves. She had the monochromatic color scheme down to perfection in several different colors. Her pink straw hat (usually in a congregation of hatless women) matched her pink purse and shoes, the pink gloves were just a shade lighter. And the outfit always had the requisite color emphasis of some item in a brighter shade. It was always that way. I had the distinct impression that she wasn't real, that somewhere under all that clothing was a plastic woman. That's what's really wrong with ostentation or out-of-place overdressing, it draws attention to the clothing. It makes the wearer seem only an accessory worn by the clothes.

But the woman who dresses so drably that she draws attention to herself is as far off the track as the peacock. Good dressing has something in common with driving with the traffic. If you go thirty miles an hour when everyone else is going fifty you are as likely to get a ticket as if you are going seventy. Maybe more likely, because you are a rarer bird, and so unexpected.

In some circles it is thought to be a mark of spiritual substance to look drab and be at least ten years out of style. I know that sounds catty, and I don't mean it to be. It is just an honest assessment of the reality of living as though women are to look old-fashioned, that somehow it is holy to do so. I went to a college where there were several representatives of this school of thought. I don't put them down for it. Someone taught them this, they didn't think it up themselves. But it doesn't work. If you look so out of step as all that, you draw as much attention to yourself as the woman with the wild-and-crazy outfit or the scanty one.

If you go to excess in either direction you are saying by your dress, "Look at me, I'm different." And you may also be saying, "Look at me, I'm a little weird." If you don't want to look weird, then don't do it, even if someone who looks and sounds important says you should. You should be deciding clothing for yourself.

Clothing as manipulator

I do not think manipulation is a good idea, no matter what you use to do it, whether it be your white boots or your Saran wrap, or your other "costumes." While clothes say things about you and you should make them say good things, you shouldn't use them to lie or steal.

If you package yourself as Sex Maniac of the Year when you are really Polly Fearful, that's a lie. You may be able to fool all the men some of the time, and some of the men all of the time. But when he finds out the truth (as he will) he isn't going to like it any of the time. Why lose a man's trust and your own self-respect by pretending to be someone you aren't? Why not just be you? If you really feel like wearing a certain kind of unusual clothing, or none at all (in an appropriately private place) sure, go ahead, but let it be you who decides. And do it because you want to, not to get something from someone else.

I don't know of a much more lonely feeling than the one that comes from being loved or accepted by someone else *under false pretenses.* You know that the love and acceptance aren't really yours, they belong to the façade you have built. You are the outsider, the love and the lover are going on without you. Don't do it.

The woman who is learning to be her own person, who is balancing herself and her life to have no hidden homeless parts of herself, cannot afford to manipulate others even with clothing.

Men are people, too. I feel very strongly that it is wrong to manipulate or deceive them sexually or any other way. I want the same wholeness for them that I want for myself. You can't manipulate and deceive the man in your life and still respect him. You probably can't respect yourself either.

I know it's easier, or it seems like it is, to smooth things a bit by just manipulating men a little, at least some men. They kind of ask you to, or force you to it. But in the long run it makes for a relationship that cannot be open and free between the two of you. When men and women have to pretend with each other, they cannot reach out and really touch. They never know who the other is, not really. It is better to stop that, or never let it happen.

Teaching others

Teach the children in your life to view clothing sensibly. Help them know how to look good. Don't send them to school looking sloppy, not like Little Lord Fauntleroy either. Send them off looking good and feeling confident.

In Shakespeare's *Hamlet* (Act I, Scene 1), Polonius gives his son, Laertes, some fatherly advice before he leaves to go abroad. Some of it has to do with clothes:

Costly thy habit as thy purse can buy,
But not expressed in fancy; rich, not gaudy,
For the apparel oft proclaims the man.

Good taste, is what he is saying. Good taste in clothing reflects good taste in other areas. At least, to the viewer it does. We can teach the children in our lives good taste and why it is important. We can teach them harmony in color and line. And we can teach them to care for those clothes. Not easy perhaps, but possible.

They may never loan their blouses to you, or remember where they stuffed the mates to their socks. But when you see them going out or coming in looking good and feeling good, it will be your reward.

Who and how are you?

Who do your clothes say you are? What do they say *to you?* Do they say that you are the martyr of the family, that your needs come last? Do they say you are afraid to look as good as you can, because you don't know how to handle friendship and closeness? Are clothes a barrier between you and others? Do you want your clothes to say what they do? Or would you rather change the message?

How about dressing to say both to yourself and to the world, "I'm okay, I'm neither so drab that I want everyone to feel sorry for me or not see me at all, nor do I want to say by my gaudy clothing, 'Hey look at me, I want lots of attention, I'm insecure.'"

Can you dress so that your clothes say, "I'm me, I'm happy about it. I wear what I feel good and happy in and comfortable in and about. I am free to be a whole person in this area, too"?

If you can't say that now, you can work toward it. How can you make one small or medium-sized change that will be more like the real you and the message you want to send to you and to others? Can you do it soon? Today?

CHAPTER 15

Fringe Benefits for Others

Known in the gates is her husband, when he sits among the elders of the land. (Prov. 31:23)

I've never liked the saying "Behind every great man there is a woman." I have been uncomfortable with that statement because it implies that woman's position is supportive only, that she cannot be the great one with a man behind her. And yet it is true that men who attain positions of power or major accomplishments often have women in their lives or a woman in their life who has helped make that attainment possible.

There seem to be two ways this happens. The woman may submerge her own life so totally in the man's that her life is but a satellite to his; she is purely supportive to him, with little left for herself. I am not comfortable with that kind of life for a woman, either for myself or for any other person, male or female. It seems to say that one of them is intrinsically worth more or is more important than the other. And I believe that everyone is important, that every life should have meaning in itself without relation to another.

But there is another way that a woman (it could just as well be a man) has a part in the greatness of a man. There are women who are *teachers* of men, whose learners go on to live out the teachings in a wider arena and become great because of what they have learned at their mother's knee or from another woman in their life. Abraham Lincoln talked about his mother in such terms. He said, "All that I am, or hope to be, I owe to my angel mother." Whether he was talking about his natural mother, Nancy Hanks, or his stepmother, who helped rear him after his mother's death, I do not know. But the woman his father married was a woman one could learn from.

Lincoln said that his father was not one to do things at home to better the place, but that his second wife had him at work doing that soon after her arrival. She took things in hand and made a home again where everything had fallen apart, both literally and figuratively. Lincoln reveals her as a woman of principle and determination who had the added asset of a pleasant disposition.

Mothers and wives make contributions to the lives of their family members. But positive contributions are not limited to those women who are wives and mothers. Sisters, aunts, teachers, friends, all have an impact on the lives of their close associates. In the case of the Proverbs woman, we are told that her husband had a part in the governing of the city or country. It is implied that she had something to do with it.

There are many ways this woman could have helped her husband in his activities. He may have been a representative of his tribe or city, or a businessman who closed deals "in the gates." Or he could have been somewhat like a judge, a member of the elders who listened to cases and were witnesses to legal contracts, as in the case of Boaz's declaration that he would marry Ruth in the book of the same name.

Whatever her husband did "in the gates," he was freed to do it by having a well-run establishment at home that could do without his constant attention. Women like our Proverbs woman ran the family enterprises and freed their men for military service and other duties. It was not that the women did the job as a second-rate man in emergencies, but that women were the home base managers, while men might range farther away of necessity. She, as we have had ample proof already, was an able manager and businesswoman as well as a compassionate neighbor. Who would not feel free to leave his concerns with her?

Sharon

When I first began thinking about the Proverbs 31 portrait of a strong, whole woman, I wondered if I knew anyone who met all the criteria, all the qualifications of this woman. As I mused on all her qualities, a name came to mind. Sure enough, I knew a Proverbs woman. I told her so. She was surprised (and smiled at the compliment).

No, she isn't perfect. I have even seen her make a couple of mistakes (no big ones yet). And she isn't trying to be superwoman that I can detect. She is busy trying to be Sharon, and doing it very well. She is happy, most of the time. She says it is probably because she has peaceful glands or something like that, but I suspect it is because she is a together woman, using all she is, and enjoying the process.

The thing about Sharon that I want to talk about right now, though, is her effect on her husband, Jim. He appreciates her, it is obvious that he does, but I feel sure he does not realize the full extent of the advantage he has in being able to rely on and live with a strong, whole woman the likes of Sharon. He himself is a man with roller-coaster emotions. He is an intense, hardworking, often uptight achiever. She is stability in his life. He travels often in his work but he need never fear, she manages very well.

Jim has a gifted hostess for any business entertaining he needs to do. They also like to entertain students from the college where he teaches.

Sharon is a trained nurse. She works part-time at her trade.

This man is free to do his work, to hold a position of responsibility within his organization, to do many of the things he does, because he has such a balanced, competent wife. But I do not see her doing what she does as service to him. She does what seems right to her. And it works well.

Not every woman would live her life as Sharon does. It is not necessary to pattern ourselves after another person. What is important is to use our resources, to discover them first if necessary, and to use them in such a way as to be a positive influence and contribution to others whose lives touch ours.

Lojan

I know another woman (a psychologist) whose husband is reaping fringe benefits from her competence and caring. I talked to her husband, Clark, also a psychologist, not long ago. He said he was taking a year off from teaching to think and get in touch with himself. He will see private clients two or three days a week, but the major support for their family will come from Lojan.

"She is encouraging me to do this," he said. "She would like to support me now and let me have time free to do what I want to." He said that he had been so work-oriented for so long that he felt a great desire to balance his life, to be more fully human and pull away from the workaholic life-style so many men have fallen into. Lojan is encouraging him to do so, and helping make it possible.

Other ways

Not everyone can do what Lojan is doing. Not everyone should. But there are so many ways people in our lives can reap fringe benefits from living with and near a woman who is balanced and strong, her own person.

"I'm proud of you." My husband said that to me after I wrote a book I wanted very much to do, went out to speak when I was terrified, and stood up under some pretty weighty brickbats thrown at me because I dared to challenge the second-class status of women in our evangelical churches. I believe he meant it.

In this case my husband said he was proud of me because of an ethical issue, because of a conviction I was not willing to let die, but he has said those words to me before for other reasons. Sometimes when I have accompanied him to some work-related social function, he has said that to me when we returned. I think he meant he felt good to be associated with me, that I didn't shame him. I'm not telling you this to make myself some kind of example for you to copy, but to illustrate the need of those in our lives to be able to be proud of us.

Now, I am fully aware that some men would not be proud of me for writing about equality for women, they would be ashamed. Fortunately I am not married to a man like that. So having someone close to you be proud of you has to be looked at judiciously. Some teenagers are not proud of you (so they say, or imply) for anything you could do, except stay home and keep a sack over your head. So one must take the opinions of others with a grain of reality. Even teens can be proud of you (they will even tell you so occasionally) for being a whole, balanced person, for having a sense of humor, being understanding, and admitting it when you are wrong.

You might ask yourself what kind of fringe benefits your family, spouse, business associates, roommate, employees, employers, or friends get from being associated with you. Do you operate as an asset in their lives? Can they learn from you by simply being around you? Can they say, and mean, "I'm proud of you, I'm richer for the association?"

Rather than take any negative answers to the above questions as reasons for discouragement and self-dislike, why not see them as opportunities yet untapped. I'm not advocating that you become a nuisance trying to brighten everybody's life or that you develop a missionary zeal for improving others by your shining example. Such people are a pain. What I'm advocating is *being aware* of the fringe benefits, good and bad, that can come from life with you, and tipping the scales in favor of the good. And more than that, do it by being more *you*, by using more of your genuine good qualities, qualities you may not have been letting out to the light of day.

A simple thing like how you look when with others can be an area for improvement. Are you someone you would like to be seen with? Would a different outfit (that you already have) look better? Why not do both of you a favor and look good for you *and* for the fringe benefit for the other person.

"I'm glad I don't have to worry about you." Muriel is twenty. She is potentially competent. She is even sporadically competent. But she is up and down about it. Her friends never know what kind of situation Muriel will get herself into. Her mother knows that she can expect Muriel to get in a pinch about once a month that she needs help getting out of. Mother is weary of solving Muriel's problems.

Why does Muriel do it? Probably because she needs to feel important, and somehow having others worry about her supplies that need. It isn't a very satisfying way to live. And it is not too satisfying for the people in Muriel's life either. Their fringe benefit is a negative one in this regard. They know they really can't count on Muriel. She is brilliant and supercompetent part of the time, but they never know when she will flake out on them, when she will start a job she cannot finish.

Muriel could decide to grow up and stop being a periodic incompetent. She could work to improve, perhaps being less of a perfectionist so she doesn't get snowed under so easily. She could make her family and friends happy to say, *"Muriel, I'm glad I don't have to worry about you anymore."* Do you know a Muriel? Are you one?

"I'm glad you're my mother, wife, teacher, friend." I'm not talking about someone being proud of you here. That may be involved in

the relationship from time to time. But the continuing result, the day-to-day fallout from good fringe benefits gives your family or friends the good feeling that they are lucky to be associated with you.

This cumulative fringe benefit probably cannot be contrived or arranged by manipulation. It might be possible to fake well enough for a while to make your associates feel good about living with you, but it can't last because it isn't built on a real person. When you aren't operating from your own real self, but pretending to be nice to get others to like you, the holes in your mask or armor begin to get larger as time goes on. Sooner or later it all crumbles.

The only way to a lasting fringe benefit for others of "I'm glad you're my ———" is to be the real you, the whole person. This isn't really easy at first, and maybe never easy all the time. But it's the good that is in you being allowed to surface that produces the cumulative experiences that make people glad you are in their lives.

That's not to say they will *always* think that. They will probably not like some of what you are, either because it is new to them and they don't know how to relate to your whole personality, or because you will do or say things that may be fine in the long run but not so fine in the short. Sometimes you have to do things that aren't pleasant at the time. Things like telling the truth that no amount of tact will make pleasant. It will not earn you smiles at the time, but someday may be a part of the reason someone is glad you are there.

Virtues can be catching

I'm suspicious of people who want to make other people better, or nicer, or prettier. It's probably because I have met too many improvers who were really out for power over other people. Their own particular righteous cause was merely an umbrella to operate under. They didn't care about the people they were supposedly trying to help, they only wanted to control them and feel superior.

But even though I'm suspicious, I am still of the opinion that you *can* help people. And it can be good for them and fun for you, or at least give you that warm good feeling someone calls a warm fuzzy. But the difference between those who want to control and those who want to help is that those who want to *help* don't push people around.

It may be necessary to push someone out of the way to keep them from being hit by a car. And it may even be necessary to use a certain amount of firmness to get your children to bed at night for their own good. But the giving of the kind of fringe benefits we're talking about in this chapter should not mean pushing people around or leaning on them to make them change.

Virtue, which is a good old word, if somewhat mistreated, should be caught.

The sign on the dashboard of my high school driver's ed. car said *Courtesy Is Contagious*. And our teacher, Moses Chavez, was himself courteously contagious. I think we all caught some of it from him that year. He, by being his own kind, considerate self, made us want to be like him.

When I look back in my life at the people whom I felt good about being around, it was because of the kind of people they were, and because they liked me. I don't remember so much that they tried to change me at all. They seemed to think I was all right already. They thought the same about themselves. And I admired them, and wanted to learn from them by observing their ways. They were contagious.

Parenting is like that. It *seems* easier to tell your children what to do and how to be. But *being* that way yourself will silently accomplish a large part of the job. And caring about them enough to let them know that you want the best for them will do most of the rest of it.

Being a good example

When I was a teen we memorized Bible verses in our youth meetings at church. One of the ones we learned was I Timothy 4:12, which says in part, *be thou an example of the believers*. We were given the impression that we were to be *examples* for other people to follow. This emphasis created a "no-no" attitude in many of us. We were told *what we could not do*, rather than encouraged to *be*.

Years later, I discovered that a truer meaning of that passage is that one should be a good *sample* of the believer. In other words, Timothy, a young man, is being encouraged to be a good sample of Christendom, not a bad one. The emphasis is on *being* the kind of person who is a positive representation of his faith. As a good sample he would draw others to his faith *because he would be attractive.* It's the same now.

We can infect others with ethics, with wholeness even, by being a good sample of a woman who is a whole person. It will involve *being* all we are. But it will result eventually in *actions* that spring from who we are. Those actions will then become fringe benefits for those around us.

CHAPTER 16

Manufacturer

She makes linen garments and sells them, and delivers sashes to the merchants. (Prov. 31:24)

Cottage industry is not dead. The Proverbs woman manufactured garments and sashes to sell for a profit to support her family and perhaps gain money for investments.

Recently we have seen a resurgence of that kind of female initiative. We women are beginning to use our ingenuity and creativity to break down the barrier the Industrial Revolution put between us and for-financial-profit business. We are finding more and more ways to be at home (where we either want to be or need to be) and also make a living with our own hands.

It seems strange that women would ever think that manufacturing was not a legitimate field for them, that women would be hesitant to enter "man's work." Historically, manufacturing has always been "woman's work." From earliest times, women have made necessary objects for their own use. Then, when time was available and times were prosperous, they expanded their manufacturing to provide excess products for sale.

Would you like to become a manufacturer or producer of a service for money? If you toy with the idea for any length of time, several questions and doubts probably come to mind. *I have enough to do already. I am overworked as it is, I need more to do? I don't know what I would do. Where would I get the know-how to run a business for myself? Where would I get the money to start out? It sounds like too big and new an idea for me.* But in spite of all the objections, there will often be a longing in the back of your mind that says, *Oh, if only I could!* Well, maybe you can.

A business of your own is not for everyone. And those who aren't inclined needn't feel pressured to become entrepreneurs. But more and more women are looking around them, evaluating their own personal resources, and saying, "Why not?" And they are being successful, too.

Let's look at some of the objections you may have or obstacles you see in your way, and then at some examples of businesses women have started, from simple ones at home to big businesses.

I am overworked already

Most of us are overworked already. And some of us are overworked for reasons over which we have little control. But most of us are overworked because of a maxim known as Parkinson's Law. It goes, "Work expands to fill the time available for its completion." And it does. It is so unnoticeable as to be unbelievable, but if you lie there thinking about it someday when you are sick in bed, you will see how so many things don't get done, and how little it matters with most of the undone jobs.

The laborsaving devices housewives enjoy today free them to do more work of the same kind. For example, with an automatic washer your family can change underwear every day and ditto outer clothes. They can also have a clean towel every time they take a bath, and you will probably not fuss too much, just resign yourself to washing those extra towels. We expand meal preparation by offering a larger variety of foods at each meal, cooking more complicated dishes, and making more trips to the market.

We ate simply on the farm of my childhood. Bread and butter made a good snack. Potato soup and bread made a decent supper. My own children think poverty is upon us if I suggest they eat bread and butter. And if their favorite instant food is not in the refrigerator they cry, "There is nothing to eat in the house! When are you going to the store?" No matter that the freezer is full, cupboards overflowing with things needing a little cooking or things that are never advertised on TV but that can be eaten without preparation (like raw oatmeal eaten out of a cup by sticking a wet tongue down to pick up the flakes, a favorite snack of my childhood). Work in the kitchen expands in spite of dishwashers. And going shopping expands to eat up time we saved by not canning our own fruit and vegetables.

If you decide you *want* to do something with your life that is different and requires your time and labor, you may very well find that you can reduce some of the time spent on work that has expanded to take the time you have.

You may find that you need to reeducate yourself about what is really important for you to do. And you may also need to (almost certainly will have to) reeducate your family or associates and friends to your changed priorities. But it *is* true that most of us *have* time for other pursuits, we are just using it for something else.

I don't know what I would do

Women are so well indoctrinated to be followers that they find it hard, at first, to lead themselves. They think in terms of: *What do others want me to do? What kind of job can I do with someone else directing me?* The first impulse, for many women, will be to work for someone else. They will think in terms of selling some product such as housewares, cosmetics, clothing on a party plan or door to door. And I am not in any way knocking that type of work or downplaying the ability it takes to do it. But when thinking about going into business for yourself, the reasonable first place to look is at yourself, not at others. What do *you* like to do? What are you good at? What *would* you like to do, if you could choose? Do you have skills that others would like to learn, or would pay you to use?

If you have worked at a job outside your home and now want to work within it, can you use the skills you have already sharpened on the job to work for yourself? Bonnie Cain was a crack secretary earning good money. But she wanted to quit her job and have some children. And she did not want to miss their babyhood and early childhood. She wanted to stay home and also pursue her own career. She and her husband, Bruce, started a business service company. They leased or bought office machines and photographic equipment. Bonnie types at home and does the bookwork. She works during the children's nap times and has trained them to respect her work by playing quietly during certain times of the day. She does not downgrade her work or allow her family to treat it lightly because she is at home and available to them. It is her business.

April Earle, my next-door neighbor, wanted a career in education. But she also wanted to stay home with her preschooler. She reasoned, "I'm going to be here anyway, I'm good with children, want to work with them." So she became a licensed day-care professional —at home.

April insisted the mothers of her charges treat her work as a business. She expected to have her working hours honored as theirs would be. And she required payment at the time agreed upon. She did not view caring for young children as "something no one else wants to do." She chose it and worked at it in a businesslike manner.

Many women who sit for children in their homes seem to feel it is a low-status job. Their own attitudes help make it that. They do not demand respect from those who hire them. But others view caring for small children as a job that is rewarding and professional while done in their home. Vi Gables is such a woman. She lives in a fashionable section of the city. Her beautiful home is well kept and pleasant throughout. Vi's profession is day care at home. She chose the house she has so that it would lend itself to this job. She has been in the business several years. It is obvious that Vi does not care for children because that is the only job she can get or that she must do it to make ends meet. She does it because that is the business she has chosen, and she likes it.

My point is that your attitude toward your own abilities and preferences has a lot to do with their successful execution. To make it in your job, whether self-employed at home or employed by others outside, you must respect your own abilities and needs. Do not sell yourself short.

Several women have opened beauty shops in their own homes. One woman, who had been a model years ago, started modeling and grooming classes for teenage girls. She covers the subjects of etiquette, clothing selection, makeup, exercise for figure improvement, and how to walk and sit gracefully.

But old skills revived or continued at home are only one possible source for at-home jobs. What, ask yourself, can you think of that would fill a need in your community? Sharon Mayer of Marshalltown, Iowa, decided it would be a good idea to compile a babysitting directory for her city.

She put signs up in neighborhood markets and other places asking for names of those who wanted to be listed. She charged each sitter one dollar for a listing in her projected directory. Then she went to merchants in town and asked them if they would like to buy advertising space. She concentrated on those who sold things parents would want to buy, such as children's clothing stores, shoe stores. Each advertiser paid ten dollars for an ad.

Sharon now had enough money to pay for the printing of 500 copies. The directory was sold to all the baby-sitters listed and those who had called asking for one before publication. Ads were placed in the local newspaper and copies were placed in the bookstores. The directory, an original idea to meet a perceived need, has become a business for Sharon, a successful one.

Where would I get the know-how to run a business for myself?

One of the good things about cottage industry, starting out small at home, is that you can learn as you go without risking large sums of money. Any costly mistakes will be smaller ones than they would be if you launched a large-scale undertaking. But you are not left up to trial and error as your only learning method.

The Small Business Administration, a government agency, has several services available to those starting out on their own. A list of publications can be obtained by writing to

U. S. Small Business Administration
1441 L Street, N.W.
Washington, D.C. 20416

You can also ask for the address and toll-free number of your nearest regional office. By contacting it directly you can find out which services it offers would be helpful to you.

There are many books available to help the new businessperson deal with all the ins and outs of getting a venture off the ground and keeping it in the air, or afloat. The resource section at the back of the book Wishcraft, by Barbara Sher, is loaded with recommendations for books and pamphlets that would be helpful to the new entrepreneur.

The library will be a good place to look, also your local bookstore. If you can get to a large mainline bookstore in a bigger city, you will find many titles on the subject. On a recent visit to a large bookstore in Chicago I found the following: How to Pick the Right Small Business Opportunity, by Kenneth J. Albert (McGraw-Hill, paperback); How to Succeed in Your Own Business, by William R. Park and Sue Chapin-Park (Wiley); *Up Your Own Organization*, by Donald M. Dible (The Entrepreneur Press Hawthorne Books); *Liberation Through the Marketplace*, by Helen Vanderberg (Graue Publications). Since new books are published on this subject constantly, you can go to your library and consult Books in Print or Paperback Books in Print, both of which should be in the reference section. They will contain listings for all books on the subject that are currently in print.

Don't hesitate to ask your reference librarians for help in locating books you need or want. They are very helpful people. Libraries will often purchase a book that is requested if they feel it has wide enough appeal to help several of their patrons. And books can often be borrowed from other libraries, even those across the country, through interlibrary loans. So ask for help; you may be surprised at how much you get for free.

Other possible aid to your education in starting your own business at home can come from a similar business in your area. If you are thinking of working in a field that is common enough to have businesses near you, you can go to the proprietor and ask for advice directly (I'm assuming you are not going to be in direct competition with your adviser). Most people are willing to help a beginner if asked.

Another possibility is getting a part-time job or temporary job helping in a business similar to the one you want to start. You can even ask to be treated as an apprentice, learning the business as you work.

Where would I get the money to start out?

Banks are not always helpful to women who want loans, business or otherwise. Chauvinism is a fact of banking life, I'm afraid. At least, that is what I hear from others, and I have enough experience with it myself to make me believe it. You may need to convince your banker that you mean business and will not tolerate any condescending treatment.

Don't be afraid to talk turkey to bankers. They are in the business of loaning money. They are not there to do favors for poor little women. Expect to be treated in a businesslike manner; refuse to deal with anyone who does not treat you that way. When you go for a loan interview, dress appropriately. Sit up straight. Be natural, but firm. If you are given the runaround or treated in a patronizing manner, ask to see another officer, preferably one in a supervisory position. And tell them why. If you are still not treated in a businesslike manner, go elsewhere.

The Small Business Administration also has some loan funds available. It even has a loan program specifically for woman-owned businesses at this time. Since programs and services are funded for an indefinite period of time, you will need to check with the SBA about what its currently available services are. You can do that by writing to the address mentioned earlier, or by calling a regional office.

It sounds like too big an idea to me

Most things that are new and different are a little, or a lot, scary. They sometimes, often even, turn out to be pleasant after you get the hang of it all. If starting your own business or cottage industry sounds big and too different, then let it simmer awhile in your head. Visualize yourself getting started. What would you do first? What kinds of work would you be doing? Picture yourself doing it, talking to people about it. Allow yourself to become comfortable with the idea before acting on it.

Maybe after a lot of thought you will change your mind and decide that you don't want to do it after all, or not now. Or you may decide that you want to think about a different business venture, that the first idea has led to another or several others that sound even better. Try them on for mental size too. Don't feel you have to push yourself. You can relax and be comfortable with an idea before you get into doing it. It's a macho myth that you have to push yourself and be uptight to get anywhere. Unless you must act soon because of pressing problems, it is to your advantage to wait and make yourself comfortable before acting.

But don't be dishonest with yourself either. It does take a bit of courage to step out of old patterns. It takes a little inner push to do something on your own after being told to be a good little follower all those years. But you can tell the difference between needing to simmer the thought a little longer and overcooking it, can't you?

Oh, if only I could!

Wayne Dyer says that the things people regret when they look back on their lives are not what they did but what they *did not do*. It's saying to yourself, "If only," that hurts. *If only I had done what I really wanted to when I got out of high school. If only I had done what I really wanted to ten years ago, twenty years ago, however long ago*. It will never be sooner than today.

You *can* choose what you want to do. And you can do it, almost certainly so. Don't let other people set the standard for what you want to do and be. You set it. Dare to dream. Be a realist, but be a realist who dares to dream of a reality that is possible.

The way to begin is to take the first step. You do not have to burn bridges, cut off routes of escape, or change your life now. All you have to do is take the first step toward deciding what you *might* like to do. When that step is taken, the next step will show itself to you. And the next. Until you arrive where you want to be.

Where it can lead

Gloria Pitzer wrote a column for a newspaper. She compiled some small cookbooks. Then she began toying around with recipes. She wondered if she could duplicate the flavor and texture of famous foods sold in fanchise chains and commercial bakeries. Could she duplicate Kentucky Fried Chicken, Arthur Treacher's Fish and Chips, Sara Lee Coffeecake? Well, yes, she could. Whether they are really made the way Gloria makes them, she doesn't know, but they taste that way.

At first she sold the recipes on cards and printed a cooking newsletter, working from her home. The newsletter and recipe sales grew to the point that her husband quit his job to work for Gloria's home business. Her recipes are now found in her cookbooks. And the cookbooks and newsletter are sent out from Pearl Beach, Michigan, by a business that has grown to the point that it is now a whole family affair. National exposure in magazine and newspaper articles has brought in even more business.

Mitzi Hands was a creative homemaker interested in crafts. She painted flowers and bouquets on small wood plaques. Then she got the idea, *why not sell them to gift stores?* So she took a few samples to gift stores in town and soon had more orders than she could fill. Two painting friends were then enlisted to paint plaques too.

Mitzi realized that crafts were becoming increasingly popular hobbies. She decided to open a craft supply store. The store was Hands' Crafts. It thrived. Next came an idea for manufacturing the raw materials for crafts. So she opened a shop to make wooden plaques used for painting. Mitzi's husband, Russ, like Gloria Pitzer's husband, decided to go into business with his wife. He took over operation of the manufacturing division.

Eventually Mitzi decided she wanted to sell real estate. She had guided her crafts business from its birth to full-grown self-sufficiency. Russ runs the manufacturing end of things; the store has been sold. Mitzi is now happily learning the real estate trade. She says she wanted to be at home when the plaque painting took off, but now her sons are almost grown and she feels free to go farther afield.

Mike McGrady, in his book *The Kitchen Sink Papers*, tells of his wife Corinne's home business that expanded. At first she designed and made plastic jewelry. Then she devised a cookbook stand made from plastic. She worked at home, enlisting her family to help with bending plastic and other manufacturing tasks. Through a series of wonderings what it would be like to have a year off from his job as a newspaper columnist to spend at home, and Corinne's desire to have a year to devote full time to her growing plastics business, Mike became "housewife" for a year and Corinne the breadwinner.

At the end of the year, Mike was wiser about the real job of home-maker and Corinne eager to continue her business. They wrote a family agreement that allows both adults to follow their own careers and to share equally the responsibilities at home. The eventual results of Corinne's cottage industry were the equalization of the whole family and the freeing of each member to be more his or her own person.

Writing is a cottage industry. I hadn't thought of it that way so much before beginning work on this book, but it is. My beginning efforts to go into the writing business have, after five years, led to contracts with three different book publishers, several magazine articles, speaking engagements, and satisfaction. I have had a chance to have a part in making changes in my Church and society for the benefit of women, and ultimately for men as well. I look forward to more opportunities and satisfaction in the future from my cottage industry.

Other writers who write at home have gotten rich in the process. Marilyn Durham, who wrote *The Man Who Loved Cat Dancing*, produced a best seller with her first attempt. She said she loved to read, had always wanted to write, but never did it. A housewife in Indiana, she says she thought about it for two years before she set out to write her own book. Since she had always been a voracious reader, she began to analyze the books she liked or didn't and determine why. Then she studied books on writing. Some were helpful, some not. Finally she began her own book. After trying to market it herself unsuccessfully, she wrote to agents until one agreed to read it. It was accepted and soon sold.

Whatever your yearnings or abilities, please be good enough to you to search them out. You may want to go into a business for a special purpose, to send your child to college, to have a home business while your children are small, to earn money for college later, or simply because you feel like it. Whatever your desire springs from, let it live and grow if it wants to. Who knows where it will lead.

Cottage industry and manufacturing, goods and services produced by women working for themselves or with their families, have a long and honorable history. There is no reason why women cannot continue it now.

If you aren't one who is inclined to go into business for yourself on a small or large scale, you can at least cheer on those who do. Encourage your sisters, whether they dance to the same music you do or not. We can affirm good qualities and abilities in each other and all profit from the pat on the back.

Whether you are a young woman in high school or a woman who has the years of experience to qualify her as a senior citizen, do not feel you need be hampered by your age. Look within, and look around you. What can you do, or learn to do? What needs doing?

Go to it!

CHAPTER 17

The Best Clothing

Strength and dignity clothe her . . . (Prov. 31:25)

Every woman needs both. Strength and dignity. Real strength and real dignity come from within. They cannot hinge on acquired material goods or a coercive pseudo-strength that comes from the ability to wield power over others. Nor can dignity be something one puts on for show to impress others. It must shine out as reflected light from an inner flame of self-respect.

The most vivid and poignant account of both strength and dignity that I remember reading is Maya Angelou's description of her grandmother Henderson in her autobiographical book *I Know Why the Caged Bird Sings*. Maya's black grandmother owned a country store in Stamps, Arkansas. I'm an Arkansan myself, from the northern part of the state, but even from my vantage point farther north I can remember the attitude toward black people among the general white population. It took courage to be a prosperous black woman.

But Grandma Henderson's strength went deep, deeper than merely making her way among her own people, surrounded by a potentially volatile and violent white population. And her dignity matched beautifully her strength.

Maya tells in the book of an incident in which her grandmother is taunted by three young white girls in front of her store. They stand on their heads to reveal pantyless bottoms, their means to insult her. The grandmother hums a hymn and goes on with her sweeping, neither giving an inch in submission nor returning insult for insult. When Maya is furious that her grandmother did not drive them away she receives a lesson in the realities of black Southern life and personal dignity at the same time.

Women are denied their own personal dignity in many ways in

our society. We are examined spread-eagled by male gynecologists who may insult, patronize, and hurt us at the same time. I well remember the experiences I have had on the doctors' examining tables. It came as a surprise to me when I encountered the first one who was kind and gentle and treated me with respect and consideration. I said, "You didn't hurt me." He said, "It isn't necessary to hurt anyone," as if he knew all too well what so many of his colleagues did.

Men know the discomfort of dignity-destroying impersonal treatment, I'm sure. But there are indignities that they never experience. Men don't have to walk down the street, as a general rule, knowing that those of the opposite sex watching them are mentally undressing them from crotch to bosom. They are not propositioned by drivers of passing trucks and cars. They do not have to try to get used to the physical eye exam women frequently undergo when being introduced to a male.

I began working at the telephone company soon after graduation from high school. The first day on the job, I was taken around the office and introduced to everyone. After a few male introductions I realized that their eyes started at my ankles and traveled up to my face and back down again. I began to watch their eyes. Every single one of them did it. They were assessing me physically as if I were a commodity to purchase, a side of beef, meat on the hoof.

It was a revelation to me. I had thought, before that, that I was just another *person* to my co-workers. Now I knew I was something else, something to be evaluated. Who I was, was not nearly as important as what I was.

Now, I'm *tempted* to counter that type of mental undressing with a pointed stare at the fly of the man's pants. I haven't done it yet, but am reserving the possibility for future encounters with the kind of blatant rudeness that I have experienced in the past from certain males.

And it's not always the "physical exam" that tries to strip us of our personal dignity either. There are other visual and verbal ways to make us feel that we are things, not persons. Like the way an administrator at my husband's school always checked my hemline when I came to a social function. There were rules for students and staff about hemlines (*far* longer than the short skirts that were in style). When I walked into a room where this man was, his eyes always moved immediately to my legs for evidence of code violation, even though as a faculty wife the code did not apply to me (and I wasn't given to wearing short, short skirts anyway). I've wondered how female students and staff felt about his assessments.

Then there was the fellow student, when my husband was still in school, who stared constantly at my protruding pregnant front throughout a conversation with us years ago. To this day, whenever I think of that man, or hear his name, I automatically associate him with his rude staring. In those days I did not know what to do about such encounters, so I stood silently, feeling embarrassed and uncomfortable. Being older and wiser now (or brassier, take your choice), I would stare back or walk away. Not to return evil for evil or rudeness for rudeness, but to maintain my own personal feeling of worth.

It is impossible to keep others from treating you in ways that would reduce your own dignity. Just as Maya Angelou's grandmother did not have an unlimited choice in her dealings with the "white trash" girls, we do not always have the ability to deal with rude and cruel people as we would like. We cannot always walk up to the college administrator who employs us or our husband and say, "Excuse me, sir, but I am uncomfortable with your staring at my legs. Please stop." We cannot do it because we aren't comfortable with doing it, or because we would be cruel to do so, or even endangered by doing so. There may be too much to lose by confrontation. And confrontation is not always the way to go for other reasons.

Since true personal dignity comes from within, not from without, we must cultivate an inner feeling of worth. Ultimately dignity is not something given to us by others who treat us respectfully. It is something we give ourselves by treating ourselves respectfully. I have personal dignity, not when I try to look or act dignified, but when I respect and care for my own personal self, when I care enough for the woman living within to want the best for her.

Sharing dignity

An interesting thing about personal dignity is that you can't have it for yourself unless you are willing for others to have it too. It's strange, but you can't have self-respect unless you respect the selves of others equally with your own. If you degrade others, it soils your soul too. If you lift others up as equals to you, it lifts you up too. That "I'm okay, you're okay" feeling goes hand in hand with personal dignity.

Strength

Most women are strong. They don't always know it, but they are. It comes as a surprise the first time you realize your own strength. My father was always one to encourage us to be strong. He wanted us to run faster and farther, cry less, know more, and not fuss about problems. I was sure he didn't know what a weakling I really was. I was afraid he would find out, that I would embarrass him with a daughter who was substandard material. As a result, I often went on gut, as they say. I ran with my skinny body after strength was gone. I would be light-headed, but I did not stop. Growing up, I was both proud of what I could do, and afraid I really couldn't because I knew I overextended myself regularly and sometimes it caught up with me.

Over the years I learned to live a little more reasonably, faced the fact that I couldn't do *everything*. But I also became a bit brainwashed by the female myths. I grew to think that men *were* stronger, both emotionally and physically. Then I had children, faced a few crises, saw how the world works and lives, and realized eventually that I *am* strong. I can work hard and feel good about it. I can survive difficult things. I can help others grow and mend. It's a good feeling.

I look about me and I see other women who are strong. But what disturbs me is that many of them do not know they are. Still other women are afraid of their own strength and try to hide it. They have an uncomfortable struggle within.

Jane is a giggler and a laugher. But it is not happy, funny laughter, it is what's known as a nervous laugh. The problem is that Jane is a competent woman masquerading as a dingbat. She pretends to be weak and dumb, but occasionally she accidentally reveals the real stuff she is made of. She works very hard draining off the tension generated by her masquerade. She is into sports with a vengeance that is more than pleasure. Something is chasing her. I think of her and I want to say, "Jane, why? Why not just dump the pose? Why not let all you are bloom and grow, why not use your resources?"

For some reason—maybe she thinks she will make her husband

feel inferior or that he won't like her if she shows her true colors—she cannot face her own strength and competence. So she goes on cutting up her legs while shaving them before a big event and losing the kids in her charge on school field trips.

Evelyn doesn't have the outlets for tension release that Jane does, so she has become a sniper. Years ago she was sold the idea that a wife must be less than her husband, that this was part of God's "Plan."

Evelyn would make a fine businesswoman, executive of a company, director of almost anything. She is a good leader, or would be. But leadership is closed to her because of her beliefs about "roles."

She had the misfortune to marry a man who is exactly right for her. He balances her perfectly. He is quiet and gentle, she is fiery and quick. He loves a peaceful life, she wants hustle and bustle. If Evelyn could let her strength surface and be guiltless in using it, she would be fine. But she thinks that it is wrong for women to be leaders. She is very active in her church, but not doing the leading she is so well fitted for. Instead she has become a force behind the scenes, manipulating and maneuvering others. She also has outlets in the form of destructive verbal sniping at women who do the things Evelyn would like to but does not dare do, or the women married to men Evelyn sees as dynamic and forceful. She feels that part of her problem is her husband, that he is too meek and spineless. But the problem is not him, he is fine; it is that she cannot admit her strength and use it.

I said all women are strong, or almost all are (I shrink from unnecessary generalizations, having been stung by them). Women are strong both biologically and emotionally. They have to be that way in order to survive life as it really is for them.

It is ironic that girls are taught that they are sugar and spice and boys snips and snails and puppy-dog tails when, in truth, it is the girls who will deal with the snips and snails and puppy-dog tails of life. Women have menstruation, a bloody mess, every month. We produce babies, a messy, hard job, which we do again and again and usually weather very well. Until recent times women were the healers caring for the sick and injured. They also prepared the dead for burial. Women cook the meat. Ever think of how revolting a piece of raw meat really looks? And women mop up the vomit from the family flu and change all those thousands of dirty diapers. I had a neighbor whose husband promptly threw up every time he saw a dirty diaper soaking in the toilet. How far would motherhood get if we all were afflicted with that? Women can't afford to be as squeamish as we are taught we are. Women *have* to be strong.

Inner strength can be present in all of us, whether physical strength is there or not. Inner strength involves personal respect and dignity, but there is much more to it than that. It also involves having the courage to know the truth about yourself and the world and making your peace with that truth. It is living in reality and being willing to deal with it, not shrinking back into neurosis or emotional dependence. We can all use our woman strength and our personal resources to become strong, stronger than we know, stronger than we are right now. The potential is there.

The counterfeits

There are fakes out there: people who pretend strength and dignity, but who don't have it. It isn't too hard to spot them. The identifying factor is often unwillingness to share with others, their lack of ability to allow you to have strength and dignity too.

All virtues are mirrored by a vice. Those who counterfeit strength and dignity actually possess the mirror vices of domination and imperiousness. They *demand* a certain kind of treatment from you, but they do not give the same consideration back.

Victoria considers herself a woman of culture. She does everything properly and carefully, and is disdainful of those who she feels are beneath her. She is the center of the world. Every person or event is evaluated in relation to its benefit to her. She sees nothing and no one as valuable in their own right, only in relation to their treatment of her or benefit to her.

Her air of imperiousness makes her a joke to her acquaintances, an embarrassment to her family. She manipulates others and pressures them with whatever leverage is necessary to get what she wants. If guilt will do it, she uses that; if money will do it, then money is the instrument.

The woman is self-deceptive. She cannot see that she is not strong. And she cannot see that she has no real dignity either. For she debases others with her imperious behavior.

Another example of this false dignity is Mrs. Phoebe Tyler on the soap opera "All My Children." Mrs. Tyler thinks she is an aristocrat, but her dignity does not extend to others, it is an illusion.

How does one get that way? How does one change? In Victoria's case, the behavior was learned from her mother. She was poor and trapped in a bad marriage. Her defense was to pretend that she was "better," better than her churlish husband, better than others in her town. She carried herself with a "queenly" grace and gave the small Victoria a false sense of personal values.

It would be possible for Victoria or any other person who lives by this fakery to change if they were willing to be honest with themselves. If they could bear to settle for the real world, a change could come. But unfortunately, most who carry on this pose occasionally reveal that they secretly, behind all the façade, think themselves of little value. If they truly valued their own selves, they would not need to pretend. So it comes to a matter of valuing one's self, of finding the good that is in you, the hidden abilities, the longings unfilled, and letting them out to the light and developing them to full use. It can be done. It takes some personal courage, however. But then, wouldn't real strength be better than fake strength?

How to keep your own dignity and strength

We have talked a lot about knowing who you are and finding out what you want to do. It is important to know the person who lives in your body—if you don't know the real you, how can you love her? And if you don't love her, how can she prosper? And how can she love others?

It isn't always easy to find out who you are. Many people are afraid to find out who they are. I was a member of a get-together group of Christians who met on Sunday nights for five years and shared problems and insight, studied the Bible and talked. We were all dissatisfied with the kind of non-help our churches were giving. We wanted something better, we weren't sure what. Maybe we wanted to start a different kind of church, we didn't know. The group eventually disbanded as some moved away and others found churches they could be comfortable in. But the group was a real help to its participants during the years we met. One of the areas we helped each other in was in finding out who we were and learning to love ourselves.

Many of the members of our group had grown up with feelings of worthlessness. They felt that, deep down, they were no good. One woman said that during her childhood she was taken to a church where hellfire and damnation were the main subjects preached on. She grew up with the fear that she could not please God, that she was evil to her very core. She said it was hard for her as an adult to really believe that God could accept her and love her. She was afraid he couldn't *really* love someone who was so bad. She knew with her *head* that God loved her, but in her heart she was not convinced.

One of the men had grown up in a home where he was spoiled on one hand and denounced with constant criticism on the other. He suffers periods of discouragement in which he feels that he is no good, that he can't win, that all is lost.

For both of these friends, and others in the group with similar stories, the key to freeing themselves of the hampering, binding effect of their past programming was in getting to know themselves, and in learning what God is really like. They had to dig down into their own hearts and minds to find out who they actually were. They had to do it often enough and long enough to override the bad and erroneous information fed into their emotional computers when they were children.

We probably all have erroneous material about ourselves in our mental data banks. We all need to know who we are, what our good points are, what we long for. We need to know that we are all right. God does not want us for friends because he has bad taste in companions. He loves people, knowing full well who and what we are.

If God loves you, you can't be all bad. And if you are worth that much, you can safely explore who you are and not fear it is all dark, evil, and full of wiggling squirmies down in your psyche.

I don't think we have to get compulsive about knowing ourselves. I expect to keep learning more about myself all my life. But I welcome the information. I want to be a good friend to me. After all, we are stuck together, Me, Myself, and I. We might as well be friends and accept each other.

To keep your own dignity and strength, or to gain more, find out who you are. Embark on a continuing education about you. When you find good things, own them. When you find areas that you want to cultivate for more return, help yourself grow to become all you can be.

Regardless of your outward circumstances, have personal strength and dignity within by regarding yourself with respect and honor, by loving yourself and being realistic about you at the same time. Being realistic involves both a true appraisal of the outward world and in the inward world. And that involves the positive good as well as the negative truth. You do not have to fear that you will become imperious and domineering, egotistical and vain if you love yourself and treat yourself well. If you are honest with yourself you will know when truth is turning to fiction and when you are about to sacrifice others' dignity to your own.

Contributing to the personal dignity of others

We can reach out and encourage strength and dignity in others or feed it to make it grow by affirming them as worthwhile persons. We can give them the gift of respect and honor for no other reason than because they are unique human beings. If we treat people as people and not as rich or poor, handicapped or unhandicapped, smart or slow, famous or unknown, we can feed their own sense of worth.

Everyone is someone, no one is nobody.

My father has one arm. I grew up seeing how other people relate to him. To us he was just Daddy. I never thought of him as being unusual. Well, I did think he was handsomer and stronger than other people's fathers because he *was* (and still is) handsome and strong. His one arm was as muscular as the one on the Arm & Hammer baking soda box. But it surprised me when other people acted as if he were *different*. Handicapped people aren't really handicapped—unless we treat them in a way that handicaps them.

During the Second World War we went to California to live, so my parents could work in the defense plants. Even though I was only six or seven years old at the time, I can still remember my father's discouragement and humiliation at being refused work because of having one arm. This was work he was completely capable of doing. It was just a prejudice. He was always an extremely competent worker, worked harder than others, probably partly to prove that he was a man who needed no quarter because of his lack of an arm, and probably also because he believes in doing a day's work for a day's pay. There was almost nothing he could not do except sharpen a pencil and roll up his shirt sleeve. But the prejudice was there.

People without arms or legs, or sight, or who are for some other reason termed handicapped, are *people*. They should be treated that way. We should never talk down to them or behave in a paternalistic manner. We should allow them the same dignity we want for ourselves.

The same consideration should be shown to children. "It isn't easy being green," sings Kermit the Frog on "Sesame Street." And the children in the audience know what he means. To black children it may also mean it isn't easy being black among some whites. But by and large, it isn't easy being a child. The real oppressed minority is children. It is true that some children are spoiled mascots. But who would choose that as a good life anyway? The vast majority of children are exposed to demoralizing, dignity-destroying treatment repeatedly during their growing-up years.

There is a grade school across from my house. And so I have seen a lot. And heard a lot. Years ago a certain teacher would daily put the children lined up to go in the front door through their paces. She would have made a very tough, ugly military drill sergeant. She yelled, "Get in line! All right, John! What do you think you are doing? We will stand here all day if you don't straighten that line!" It went on every morning and noon when she had the job of opening the doors.

Last month Richard Truitt, one of the teachers, retired. I went over to tell him good-bye. He said he had always tried to respect each child as a person. I told him that was one of the things I had always appreciated about him. Then he said, "You know, we had a teacher here years ago who I used to think just got up every morning so she could come over here and be mean and boss kids around." I thought of the drill sergeant and wondered if it was her.

I come from the upper South originally, and it seems to me that children are generally more highly valued in the South than in the North (I just now consulted Bobby Burchette, a southern child transplanted to the North, and he agrees). I regularly see some mother berating her child in a shopping mall or store here in the Chicago area. The poor kid will be verbally humiliated in public and often slapped as well. The offense usually appears to be minor and perfectly normal, especially for some overtired, hungry child. But since it is a child, the mother (or father) thinks nothing of the public abuse. I can't remember ever seeing that kind of thing in the South.

But Southerners have their own brand of dehumanizing and dignity-destructive badgering of children. Where I came from, teasing children was a popular sport. Children were told all kinds of lies for the entertainment of other adults. Joking can be funny if the child is not the butt of the joke and understands what is going on. Real jokes don't hurt. But teasing and baiting are only another way of saying, "You aren't important, I am."

People who are poor are also people whose dignity we need to protect. I have accompanied friends who were desperate and in need and went to the welfare office for help. Some of the welfare workers were kind. But there was a prevailing atmosphere of disdain and lack of care, as if to say, "These people are deadbeats, who cares about them."

Once I made phone calls for a young woman who was not able to recover her husband's child-support checks from the state welfare office where they had been sent by mistake. She could not get *any* action. I talked to one woman who called me "dear" but who would do nothing. Finally, after much switching to other departments and calling back, a real human being was reached. This woman was kind and sympathetic. She said, "I understand how she feels, I depend on child-support payments from my husband too, and I know what it means to need them and not get them." And she initiated action that brought the missing money. That woman was an oasis of kindness and respect in a sea of bureaucratic red tape and uncaring workers.

We can recognize, preserve, and nourish our own strength and dignity. And we can encourage it in others. It's good clothing to put on. And good clothing to share.

CHAPTER 18

Laughing at the Future

. . . and she laughs at the future. (Prov. 31:25)

The Proverbs woman has clothed herself with strength and dignity —and she laughs at the future. Why can this woman laugh at the future? Can you do that?

This thirty-first chapter in the Book of Proverbs shows evidence of being written relatively early in Israel's history. Later, the married woman's dowry protection was eroded away. Exceptions to the marriage document made it relatively easy to divorce a woman and avoid returning her marriage portion. But at this early date the dowry probably functioned as it was intended, as financial security for the married woman.

A certain amount of property and/or money from her own family's resources went with a woman into marriage. This portion remained hers. Her husband could legally, if he wished, keep the increase from its investment. But the original amount was hers and hers alone. If she was divorced, the dowry would be her means of support. She was not sent away from her marriage empty-handed, nor was she dependent upon the generosity of an ex-husband or court of law.

That vineyard the strong woman bought and planted may have been purchased by her with some of her dowry money. A woman thus endowed could invest and prosper with her own money.

In addition to financial security, the Proverbs woman enjoyed a respect in her old age that is more common in the East than in our culture. Age was respected for its wisdom. Experience was valued. Youth was not idealized and idolized as it is in our country. Respect and honor for parents are encouraged and commanded in many places in the Old Testament.

A woman could look ahead and laugh at the future, if she was a wise woman. The Proverbs woman was not like some other women of her time. She did not rely on her looks to bring her favor and security. She did not waste her personal resources. The combination of her own wisdom and practicality and the society she lived in made it possible for her to look to the future without dread.

What do you have to look forward to?

The largest group of people with incomes beneath the poverty level in the United States are older women. A lifetime of substandard wages with no retirement benefits, unequal Social Security benefits, and a life devoted to husband and family do not contribute to a sense of humor when a woman is old.

Divorced and deserted wives often find themselves out in the cold both figuratively and literally. Too many women have bought the dream of a house in the suburbs, a loving husband, and three children and found the payoff was being left for a younger woman, children who did not care to be bothered with Mother, and a home in the suburbs that was too expensive to maintain on her income.

We are told repeatedly that menopause makes us *unfemale*. Medical articles are often heart-chilling to the woman who reads that her breasts will shrivel, bones crumble, vagina dry up, and lip sprout a dark mustache. Fortunately those harbingers of doom seem to be male doctors who have never experienced menopause. I am glad to see more enlightened information surfacing now. Women are beginning to write about themselves. We are finding out that menopause is not a horrible monster that destroys our femininity and distorts our bodies. We are not even doomed to take estrogen, with its time-bomb fears of possible harm. Many women are finding that exercise, good nutrition, extra vitamin E, calcium, and even ginseng make menopause little more than a ripple in their lives.

Because of our practice of marrying men older than we are, most women can anticipate that they will be widows one day. We tend to outlive men by several years.

With all this bad news to anticipate, do American women have any reason to laugh at the future? Not if we approach our lives in the manner that we are encouraged to. Not if we are going to invest our lives as though only the first thirty years counted for anything.

Investing your life for the whole of it

The Proverbs woman has invested her life, she has not thrown it away. Too many young women, and not so young women, here and now do exactly that: they throw away their opportunities and their futures.

We are taught, many of us, to be empty-headed dolls. The media are full of images of women who are admired, wanted, loved, and sought after. They are blond, rounded, slim in the middle, not too bright, and soft and compliant. Beauty and youth—that is what a woman needs to succeed. At least, that is the message.

Now, we will, most of us, say we do not buy that image, that we are smarter than that. But our collective actions deny it. The cosmetics business in this country is a multibillion-dollar industry. The largest ads, full pages in shimmering color in all the magazines women routinely read, are devoted to making us, or promising us they can make us, look young, beautiful, and luscious. We may know that we will not look like that model, but it makes us *feel* we look more like her if we use the same cosmetics. We will at least feel beautiful.

What happens to a woman who invests her life in her youthfulness and beauty? I know one woman who is desperately clinging to the illusion that she can be twenty forever. I am sure Diane is an intelligent woman; I have talked with her and she doesn't sound like a woman who is only a decoration with no thought life beyond her lipstick.

But Diane somehow believed the myth that you must be young and beautiful. She is trim and slender, even attractive. But she has a frightened, forced gaiety that is punctuated by a nervous habit. She blinks her eyes compulsively.

Diane wears a long platinum wig all the time. She also wears leopard-skin-patterned underwear. Now, there is nothing wrong with either wigs or fancy underwear, but the composite picture Diane presents is of someone desperately trying to be Barbie Doll at somewhere plus forty-five, and it doesn't wear well. She runs in fear, it is in her eyes. I wonder if she knows what she is afraid of. Is it that she might lose her husband if she does not keep up the pose? Is she afraid to change and grow and mature as a person? Whatever the reason, Diane is stuck, thinking twenty is all the life there is.

Too many women do not know the difference between wine and grape juice. Maturity and experience can wear very well. A woman can get better with age. We are not over the hill when we stop having to worry about acne. We are just beginning. Life supposedly begins at forty, but we act as though it ends there. I frequently hear forty-year-olds talk about being "old." Baloney! No one is old unless they want to be. My grandma Dicy was not old at ninety. She was never *old*, she was always better. My husband's aunt Helen Hinshaw was not old at eighty-three when she went out like the bright spark she was. I saw Mamie Eisenhower on TV when she owned many years and I can't believe she was ever "old."

Just as the strength and dignity the Proverbs woman clothed herself with came from within, so also must our staying quality come from within. If we do not view ourselves as a disposable, as someone who is out of it when she is past a certain age, then we will not be. Women are people, not sexual aberrations who cease to be whole persons when they no longer have menstrual periods. We must stop buying the myths and believe what we know to be true inwardly: we are *us* all our lives.

But the inward security must work itself out in an outward action for our futures to be something we can laugh about. The hard cold facts are that if you do not do something about your future, probably no one else will either.

Preparing for the future

Young women starting out have beautiful opportunities. They are entering an era in which women will increasingly be able to stand tall and walk proud. It will take a while, I may not see it, but the day will come when women will be able to be equal persons before the law and in the job market, and in the home too. We do not need to build a society on forced or coerced inequality for any group of people.

If you are young in years you have longer to invest your life. You can profit from the mistakes of others. Your future can be fuller more easily than it will be for many who find themselves already in a situation that pinches. Let me encourage you to view your life as an investment for you and for others. Do not throw yourself away. Do not *give* yourself away. Expect, and make sure you receive, what is best for you and your future.

Financial security

Every woman needs a way to support herself financially. It doesn't matter if you are rich, beautiful, and charming and the world is at your feet. All that could change. You need to be self-sufficient financially. The greatest hardship women alone face is lack of money.

Any woman can find herself alone. We grow up thinking that will not happen, and I hope it will not happen to you. But it might. We buy insurance hoping we will never need it, but are wise enough to buy it anyway. Even if you intend to be a homemaker supported by a husband, get a trade for yourself.

If you are already married and without a trade, go get one. It is possible to go to school at night or by correspondence, to teach yourself, or persuade someone else to train you. Even if it takes you years of part-time work to learn your trade, do not neglect to start after it. Even if you never need or want to use it, please get it.

There is another reason besides financial security for you to be able to support yourself, several reasons in fact. One is that it is good for your own self-esteem. Housewifery calls for many skills. It is actually a job that demands the ability of a corporation executive with skills in all branches of the company. But our society and many of the families in it do not highly value the housewife's contributions. She is seen as the woman of all work, as the servant of the family. It is good for you to know that if you needed to or wanted to, you could go out and earn with the best of them.

Another reason it is important for you to have earning potential is that, men being human, they sometimes are heavy-handed with a woman who is dependent on them financially. Sometimes the heavy-handedness is subtle: you tend to feel bad about wanting more money for this or that, or you do a little extra for him that you do not expect for yourself because you don't bring in any money. With some men it isn't subtle at all. They will demand haughtily, "What did you spend it all on? You want more!" Some are glad to lord it over the dependent wife.

It's amazing what a little financial clout will do. You don't even have to flaunt it. If the people who live with you realize that you can make it very well without them, they definitely invest more effort in making sure you want to make it with them. This is nothing against men. It is merely the facts of financial life. Power corrupts, and financial power tends to corrupt the one who has it all. So equalize the possibilities.

While you are looking for a way to make sure you can support yourself, please be kind to yourself. Don't settle for what you know you can get without any hassle. Instead, go after what you really want. It may take longer, but it will wear much better with time. Ask yourself what you like to do so much that you would do it for free. Then get a job or qualifications for one in that field. Why not get paid for doing what you like?

Women who are already in a job or career field but not happy there should analyze the situation and see if they can switch to something they like better. Both men and women tend to stick with jobs they hate because they are already trained for them or have seniority or retirement benefits. Or they simply fear change. It's your life, and if you are not happy with your job, you are throwing away pieces of your life every time you go to work. Life is a day at a time, an hour at a time. Don't waste it piece by piece in a situation that you can change.

Educational opportunities are opening up for adults in colleges and other training institutions in ways that were unheard of a few years ago. We are going to become a nation of older, not younger, people in the future. Because of this, colleges will have to go to educating people who are out of their teens and twenties if they hope to stay in business. Go back to school, they will welcome you there. It is never too late.

Besides getting the skills to support yourself, project the future of those skills. Will you have to retire at a certain age? Are there auxiliary fields you can enter from the one you are interested in? Does the field you want to try for offer enough variety and opportunity that you will not be boxed in? We found that we, as a family, had less mobility than we would have liked because my husband's job is specialized to the point that he cannot work just anywhere he would like to live. So think about where your job will place you and if its restrictions are likely to bother you before you invest too heavily in it.

Investing in relationships

As my husband and I were on the way to buy groceries a few days ago we passed a hitchhiker. The young man was dirty and ill-kempt and wore dark glasses. He looked almost menacing. Thinking about the warnings of the danger of picking up hitchhikers, I said, "Who would give *that* man a ride?" My husband said he wondered why any girl would pick such a substandard-looking, scruffy fellow to go around with, to love. He had seen a clean, wholesome young woman with a similar man recently.

As we thought about it, we realized that our society's messages to young women as they grow up overwhelmingly condition them to link up with someone beneath their own capabilities. They are taught that boys are crude, girls are soft and sweet. Men are uncultured, women are tactful and healing. Men are domineering, women are submissive. So when a girl sees a fellow who is rough, rude, domineering, crass, and selfish, she thinks, "Oh, here's a *man!*" She does not know until she gets him home and lives with him that what she has is not a man but a little bratty boy.

We encourage immaturity in our men and a savior-mothering attitude in our women. A girl has to have enough insight to see the flaws in the reasoning behind those messages and enough experience or cold-eyed observation of others to know that the myths aren't true. A lot of girls don't make their way out into the truth soon enough.

We thought of several young women we know as we rode along that afternoon, young women who had fallen into marriages or liaisons with young men who were destructive to them. Donna married to escape a home where she felt she was not loved. Her father was dead, she wanted a man to love and care for her. Jack seemed strong. He would fight for her even if someone slightly insulted her. Though he drank and smoked pot, and his jobs didn't last, she married him anyway. He was protective.

Donna produced two babies in rapid succession. Jack did not like her to use birth control. And she found that his hair-trigger willingness to fight now focused on her. She was afraid even to mention birth control to him because sometimes when he was drunk he would remember it and beat her. Donna and her babies became caught in a downward spiral. She knew that she must leave him if she would save them and herself. They were often hungry and needed medical and dental care. But she was afraid of what he might do to her if she left.

With one last bit of courage, she escaped and went into hiding. She is now in the process of divorcing Jack, though she lives in fear that he will take the children away from her and hurt her for leaving him.

Lila married the young man who made her pregnant. She dropped out of high school because he made life difficult for her when she tried to continue. Soon she realized that he had impregnated her purposefully so she would be forced to marry him. He, feeling like a lonely outcast, had wanted someone who would belong to him. He was possessive toward her and alternated between totally ignoring her and dictatorially ordering her to serve him.

She began to get terrible headaches. To relieve the headaches she took Darvon. Soon she had to take it every day or she would have a headache the next day. Lila finally left her husband.

Anita has stayed. She has three children under the age of five and is pregnant with another. Fatigue is a constant companion. Her friends say she is a different person from the one they knew before the children came. She was alive and vibrant, now she is dull and plodding. Anita had thought marriage would solve all her problems. Instead, they have intensified.

None of the young women we thought of had wanted to *invest* their lives as individuals. They had viewed marriage or a relationship with a man as an escape. They felt that belonging to someone would make their lives full and satisfying. It didn't. As long as there are women who will look to marriage as escape and a man as rescuer there will be thrown-away lives or thrown-away years.

The relationships we women maintain and continue must be positive ones if we hope to invest our lives instead of depleting ourselves. We should look at our family relationships, our business relationships, and our friends realistically.

Ask yourself honestly: Does this relationship deplete me, or does it nourish me? Another question to ask yourself is: Where will this relationship lead? Is it *likely* that this person will improve because of his or her association with me?

What makes you so special that you can change someone who has

not been able to be changed by others or by their own efforts? Don't
overestimate your own power.

Ask yourself: Do they need me? If so, beware. They should be able
to survive very well without you. If they can't, then you will likely
have a parasite-host relationship. And they will be the parasite on
you. It may sound flattering now to be so needed, but it will not feel
good later. Relationships should be built on *liking* each other, not
needing each other. It takes two whole people to make a couple. One
and a half won't make a satisfying relationship.

Before we leave the subject, something should be said about the
woman who is the parasite in a relationship. We are not immune to
that either. Being an emotionally dependent person in a relationship
is a poor investment in your future, too. Not only will the partner
who carries more than his share of the load tire and wilt or rebel
under it, but you shrink your own personal horizons by being overly
dependent. We can share and care for each other, yes, but we must
do it as equals if the relationship is to remain healthy.

You might ask yourself if you play "female" games with men. Do
you pretend to be weak and helpless to manipulate them to get what
you want? Do you insist the man in your life make all the decisions
alone, do all the hard things? If so, you don't have an equal relationship. It isn't based on honesty and sharing.

Where are you?

Where are you in your own life-investment time line? Are you a
high school woman who is investing her energies in being cute and
cheerleaderish, with no thought to discovering your real resources?
Where will this land you in fifty years?

Are you a twenty-five-year-old secretary who longs for a home and
children? Have you thought of your life as a whole life investment?
Or are you drifting along to see what will happen? Are you Cin-
derella waiting for Prince Charming? That's a fairy tale, you know.
They aren't true.

Are you forty-two and wondering where all the time went, and the
children, and the color in your hair? Can you take stock and begin to
do what you really want to? Remember what you used to dream of
doing? Why not now?

Or are you sixty-plus, and younger people and some of your contemporaries, too, act as if the ball game is over? Does everyone want to stereotype you as a has-been, but the girl inside you is the same twelve-year-old who ran down the lane to the apple orchard to climb trees and eat secret green apples? Why not let her out? As one woman said, "I am seventy-four years old and I no longer care what people think of me. I do what I please." You may live to be a hundred and six. Do you want to waste all those good years? Why waste even one day? Why not begin where you are to get to where you want to be.

Laugh at the future

Our Proverbs woman could laugh at the future because she was a clear-eyed realist, not an empty-headed doll. She also had benefits we do not have. Financially, she was secure, as much as she could be in a land of famines and periodic war. Since we do not have her resources, we must use the ones we do have and can create for ourselves. We must provide for ourselves where our society and families do not.

We can look within and assess our resources, look without and assess our possibilities. Then we can get to work and make a future for ourselves that will bring a smile whenever we think of it.

CHAPTER 19

When She Opens Her Mouth

She opens her mouth with wisdom and gentle teaching is on her tongue. (Prov. 31:26)

Eyes may be the windows of the soul, but the mouth is the door that lets it all out. As the Bible says in another place, "from the abundance of the heart the mouth speaks" (Luke 6:45). This strong woman's speech both reveals what is within her and is also a means to reach out and help other people.

There is a negative stereotype to the effect that a woman who is strong and energetic is also likely to be domineering. I think this view reflects a prejudice against women being whole, well-balanced persons rather than the true state of things. This prejudicial attitude toward women who have strength and initiative is evident even in the footnotes of the Bible version I have been taking my quotations from to begin each chapter of this book. As I read the verse that heads this chapter I noticed a little footnote indicator and looked to the bottom of the page, hoping for some gem of information about the original language. No, what I found was this comment by one of the translators of the Modern Language Bible: "She is not domineering as such an energetic woman often is."

Here, in one of the most stirring and enthusiastic Bible passages about women, the man who has translated it cannot refrain from criticizing the very type of woman he has just escorted out of Hebrew into English. Is it any wonder women have been confused about their own possibilities and are hesitant to reach out and grow into their whole potentials?

There is nothing strange about a strong, whole woman also being wise and gentle in her teaching and speaking. We have no trouble imagining a strong, whole man who is also wise and gentle. But women have been discouraged from being strong and whole for so long that when we read about one we tend to misread the description. We cannot see how she can be other than unusual, unique, unlikely.

I'm not so sure this kind of woman is as unusual as the Bible translator thinks. He may not recognize one easily. Though such women are not nearly common enough, there are several around. More than one or two have made an impact on my own life. I know I had several schoolteachers who were like that, women who were strong, firm, but kind. Matey Davidson taught me in the fifth grade, Purna McClellan in the fourth grade, at a small school in Bergman, Arkansas. My eighth grade teacher there was another example of this kind of woman. I cannot remember her name but I can see her face, remember her voice, and the way she dealt with me. Where others had sometimes found me a nuisance who always knew the answers and couldn't bear not to share them, she affirmed and encouraged me. When I corrected her errors in class (as I was wont to do), rather than be insulted at my impertinence, she said graciously, "I stand corrected."

Miss Haas taught me eleventh grade English. She was a tiny woman. We were scared to death of her. We thought she was a tiger. But I found that inside she was a caring woman. She will have a share in any success I may ever have in life because she challenged me to *use* what I had. Few others did. I could go on and on naming such women. You must have met them too.

You *can* be strong and whole and also wise and gentle and kind.

Why the stereotype?

Like many stereotypes, though, there is a grain of truth behind the myth. Though it is not true that strong women are necessarily domineering, it is true that women tend to be better in general at tongue-to-tongue combat. There have certainly been enough silly comments to the effect that this is inborn and that women are more verbal by nature so they naturally have sharper tongues. And that supposedly sets us apart again. And, incidentally, tends to make any man who is verbally fluent have to carry the slight or more than slight stigma of effeminacy.

I think inborn nature has nothing to do with the incidence of shrewish or razor-tongued women. It's as simple as this: those who can't fight with their fists learn to fight with words. We develop skill with the weapons we have. We also pick up the skill by observing the skilled practitioners who precede us. It is often passed from mother to daughter with success.

Women tend to practice and gain skill on men who are vulnerable. Sometimes this involves practicing on male children, who are extremely defenseless. They grow up to be easy targets for other female verbal assaults.

I was horrified to discover myself contributing to this bad state of affairs. I have one son who was maddeningly impervious to being reasoned with as a child. All the others could, with some hope of success, be sat down and explained to how it was unprofitable and even unreasonable to hit little brother or hack up the sofa arm with one's little hammer.

Not this one. He sat there staring at the wall behind me and, when I was through, promptly went back to doing the same thing. He mentally turned me off. Why I don't know; maybe he didn't really understand. He used to mix his own sentences up pretty badly, maybe mine didn't register just right. I was forced to spank his little bottom. That worked better, but I always considered it a failure to have to do that. Eventually I resorted to throwing away the little hammer. That worked best of all, but the method was certainly limited in its use for solving the problem of beating up on little brother.

When the unlistening son got old enough that spanking was not the thing to do, I moved over, without realizing it, to verbal spanking. I would give him a tongue-lashing that was worse than the spankings it replaced. I kept at it because it worked. He was no match for me. So he said nothing. One day, after a particularly devastating recital of his shortcomings, I suddenly realized what I was doing. It was one of those awful moments of truth that break upon you when you instantaneously see yourself clearly after a long time of not realizing just exactly what you have been up to.

I realized that my verbal harangue was totally unfair to him. It was character destruction, assassination of his self-worth. And he had no defense. Verbally, he was neither fluent nor skilled. He had no way to rescue his pride or dignity. Now I try to cool off before I confront him with his misdeeds, and simply state firmly what I do not like and, if there is a consequence, what it is.

We women are too easily tempted to vent our anger on male children. I have seen it happen so often. A family who lived near us years ago went through a weekly cycle. Over the weekend the husband harassed his wife. On Monday she terrorized their oldest child, a boy (who looked like his father and had the same name) about a year older than my daughter. On Tuesday the boy was out for blood and my kids got it from him. If we had had a dog, it would have been in trouble on Wednesday, I suppose.

It is the old pecking-order sequence: we can't hit back at those who are stronger, so we find excuses to take out our anger on those who are weaker. I firmly believe that much male hostility to women is a result of this vicious circle. Women are repressed and put down by men or by a male-dominated system. Mothers sometimes take out their resentment on their young sons; and teachers and others over children, on little boys in their charge. Those little boys grow up with an accumulated load of unconscious resentment toward women that has been years in the making. They then pass it on to the women who become vulnerable to them. And on it goes.

A first step toward breaking this cycle is being aware of it. If we know the sequence, we can look for its tentacles on us and pry them off. You can find ways to rid yourself of your hostility without taking it out on a victim. You can even find ways to minimize your own victimization. Making yourself more self-reliant, less dependent, more able to find your own way in life, to protect yourself, and to find personal satisfaction and value within yourself, all work to reduce your victimization possibilities.

Children, little boys in particular, can be purposely viewed as *people*, not as the reincarnation of their father. You can train yourself not to pass along the universal thump.

The destructive power of words

Jack Webb, the actor, tells a story about his lively grandmother. When they were so poor that they could not afford enough blankets to keep them warm, she would cover her bed with layers of newspapers and say, "Sticks and stones may break my bones, but words will keep me warm." (Newspapers are very good insulation, though the words don't have anything to do with it.)

But the saying in its usual form, "Sticks and stones may break my bones, but words will never hurt me," just isn't true. Words may not break bones, but they can break hearts. And ruin careers, and separate friends, and besmirch character. Words can go with you all your life.

Louella was a neighbor of mine years ago. She was very attractive and pleasant to talk with, a good person to be around. One day she confided to me that she was unhappy with her husband. She said he was too mild-mannered and slow. She wanted him to be as enthusiastic and energetic as she was. I said, well, he was the way *he* was and she couldn't expect him to be like her. Then she said maybe the real problem was that she had married him not because she loved him but simply because he had asked her to. Then she explained.

When she was a small child, Louella's father liked to bounce her on his knee and say, "You are the ugliest little thing! You look like a little monkey." It was one of her earliest memories. He may have thought she was cute, but Louella, who believed his words (as children will), *knew* she was ugly.

"I married the first man who asked me," she said. "I would have married *anybody* who asked me. I thought I would never get another chance because I was ugly." Louella's fear of being unattractive made her put on her makeup flawlessly every morning before she did anything else. I never saw her other than in the best possible condition. Her clothing was always spotless and perfect. Actually she was very good-looking. But she still feared being ugly. Her father's words still lived within.

Jill sat at the family supper table listening to the conversation with half an ear. Suddenly she heard herself addressed. "Jill, when you are eighteen, I won't have you bumming off me. You will have to move out." This came from her father. She was stunned. At sixteen her mind was far from leaving home. This was the father who had loved her and protected her and taught her how to ride a horse and to drive the car.

What was wrong? Nothing was wrong. He had said it without thinking first. The family conversation had swung to the subject of growing up and leaving home. And he had come out with a foolish statement, one that he promptly forgot but that Jill never did.

She began to wonder if he did not want her there anymore. She wondered if he did not like her, if he was repulsed by her now that she was becoming a woman and not a child any longer. Years later she reconciled it as his just saying a dumb thing. But it had hurt her at a time when she needed to be reassured about belonging, not put in doubt.

The statements that caused Jill and Louella pain were not meant to hurt them. They were only careless, thoughtless statements by parents, parents who weren't being wise with their words. But destructive words are not limited to foolish usage. There is also gossip, and there are lies.

I have not been the victim of gossip too many times in my life, or at least not that I knew of. But one experience made me realize what a potentially damaging practice it can be. In my case I don't think it really hurt me at all, but it did make me angry.

Stan and I were planning to be married in August. But early the previous spring we "discovered" that we were getting married within a week, that it was so sudden my mother did not even have time to come for the wedding from the Midwest to California (where we were attending college). This was a surprise to us. Whatever had we done to give anyone the impression that we were suddenly getting married? (The inference was that I must be pregnant and a hasty wedding in order.) We were particularly amazed in the light of our practice of being very proper about following the dating rules of the strict school we attended. We had been the souls of propriety.

We decided to see if we could trace down the rumor to its source. So we asked the ones who asked us about it who had told them, then we went to those people and asked the same question. The story laced back and forth through the student body. Finally the gossip came to rest with two women. One was the wife of a professor, and the other a recently married ex–dorm mate of mine.

They had come to the conclusion of our emergency marriage with the aid of the following data: Stan and I had gone to talk to a man living across the street from the women's dorm. He had a big old house and was in the habit of renting the upstairs apartment to a married student couple in exchange for yard work and occasional cleaning of his apartment. We knew that the couple living there then were leaving after graduation and we wanted to live there after our marriage in the fall. Someone had seen us talking to the man. That was all. Those two gossips had manufactured the story out of their own imaginings.

Gossips often think theirs is a harmless pastime. I'm not so sure it is. It too often hurts someone. And the one who passes it along often does not know of the hurt or the lengths to which it grows. It is better for both the gossip and the gossipee that the juicy details do not get passed on at all.

If you want to stop listening to gossip, there is one way that never fails to stop others from bending your ear with it. Don't tell them any. If you don't have something to share, soon no one wants to share with you.

Having been stung by gossip, and never admiring the practice too much anyway, I have tried to avoid passing on personal information for some time now. I find that I am often the last one to know who is pregnant, and whose marriage is failing, and a lot of other things. But it hasn't hurt me any. I am pleasantly surprised when a new baby appears that I did not suspect. And I don't have to give the look to the unfortunate one that says, "I know all about what you are trying to hide." I usually *don't* know.

Then there are lies. It would be simpler if lies were obviously meant to be destructive and motivated by evil impulse. But the trouble is that many people tell lies for what they think are good reasons. The damage is just as great, however. I personally have been victimized by lies.

Last spring I was asked to speak at a local chapter meeting of the organization Housewives for ERA (now called Homemakers Equal Rights Association) on the subject of my first book, biblical feminism. I was not asked there to speak on the Equal Rights Amendment, nor did I go there for that purpose. But as a result of my appearance there a campaign was begun against me by four or five anti-ERA women who attended. Seeing the incidental mention of my husband's employment in a newspaper announcement of the forthcoming meeting, they came in order to get ammunition they hoped would force my husband's employer, Moody Bible Institute, to make a political statement against the Equal Rights Amendment.

Slanderous and lying letters were written to the president and two other administrators at the school where my husband taught. The letter writers complained about my speech and appearance at the meeting, and questioned whether my husband should be allowed to keep his job.

A right-wing political activist pastor in this area who was given a copy of one of the letters made copies and distributed them at his church and at a religious schools meeting, and broadcast most of the contents over a radio program. People were urged to write to my husband's employer to object to the awful things I supposedly said and believed.

Within a few weeks another religious activist was at work and the same slanders and lies appeared in a paper called the *Blu Print*. Readers were also encouraged to write to Moody Bible Institute to object to my husband's employment there.

Many letters were received by the institute. At no time did any of the spreaders of slander bother to call me or write me to ask if the information they were spreading was true. Instead, they wrote to ask for the firing of a man they did not know and they denounced a woman they had no knowledge of. In fact, if any of them had even bothered to consult a copy of my book *Woman Be Free!* they would have known that those accounts could not be true.

The women involved were so frightened by the stories they had been told by others about the possibilities of damage to their own homes, churches, and country if ERA became part of the Constitution that they justified any lying and unfair tactics they might use on me and my husband. The broadcasting pastor and the publisher of the *Blu Print* did not care enough about the harm lies could do even to check their facts.

The moral of the story is: When in doubt, don't. And the end does not justify the means. Words can hurt.

My husband lost his job.

The constructive power of words

The Book of Proverbs has more to say about words. I marked this poetic picture of the use of words in my Bible long ago:

A *word fitly spoken is like apples of gold in pictures of silver.* (Prov. 25:11–KJV)

Writers and speakers are aware of the power words have. I am awed by their power. Though words are only the poorest symbols for the real feelings and events of the world, they can make you laugh and cry. And they can make you act, or change your opinion. They can wound and they can heal.

But, I wonder, does the average woman realize the value and potential power of her words for *good?* Do you know what your words can do?

We women have access to people when they are most vulnerable and thus most impressionable. Children are with us more than with men. We wake children, put them to bed, care for them when they are sick, feed and bathe them. We see their naked souls when they are sad and hurt and lonely and scared. We can share their joys and sorrows. We have opportunities to build and teach with words that most men do not have. Women are also the vast majority in the caring professions of nursing and care for the disabled and infirm.

Milton Freed wrote a book called *TA for Tots,* in which he talks about how children are born "prinzes," but with the disappointments and frustrations of life come to think of themselves as "frozes" (frogs). He shows how to help turn people back to prinzes by means of "warm fuzzies." I like the term "warm fuzzy." It is anything that makes you feel safe and good. It can be a hug, a loving or caring look, a touch, a smile, a word.

Since reading *TA for Tots* I have been more aware of the good that can be done by giving verbal warm fuzzies. I used to *think* a lot of good things about others but not necessarily express them. I try to let them out more now. And I can see the results before my eyes.

I look at my child across the room and he says to me, "What are you thinking?" And I say, "You are beautiful. That is what I was thinking, really beautiful." And because he knows I am being totally honest, he is not embarrassed, but smiles from his innermost self. I have given him joy and confidence by sharing my thought. Eleven-year-olds sometimes wonder if they are anything but dirt, torn pants, skinny legs, and trouble to the teacher.

I try to tell my children the good things I see in them. I don't make things up. And I don't tell them the next day that *they* are bad. I may say the shirt is dirty, or the pants torn and go change them, or take a shower for goodness' sake. But the child remains beautiful.

Have you ever stopped a woman on the street or in a store and told her you love her dress, and where did she buy it? Most people are extremely pleased at your affirmation of their good taste. Few are insulted.

For three years, as I saw my son's fourth grade teacher, Barbara Smith, come and go from the parking lot across the street, I admired her taste in clothing. I thought of telling her I did and asking her where she bought her clothes so I could go there too. But the opportunity to do so never seemed to present itself.

But this spring, near the end of school, I met her on the sidewalk at the annual school fund-raising event. Suddenly I blurted out, "I have been admiring your taste in clothes ever since you came here. Please tell me where you buy them."

She said, "Wherever I can. I make a lot of them." She also smiled with delight and said, "You just made my day!"

As I walked on, I thought, *what a small investment from me to give her a good feeling that will last all day and perhaps come back whenever she thinks of me or her taste in clothing.* Why not give warm fuzzies to everyone you can? Words may be cheap, but they are a good investment.

Teaching words

Words have limitations in teaching. They have to be backed up by example. They must be timed properly and in the right amount. One of the most common mistakes parents make in teaching their children is thinking that telling a child is the way to make him or her know something. Usually showing is better than telling.

But the right words at the right time can teach very well. I remember something my father taught me long ago after I had been asking question after question, pestering him to give me answers to things I couldn't understand. I said finally, "Daddy, you are a grownup, why can't you answer all my questions, I'm only a child?"

He said, "A fool can ask questions a wise man can't answer." Those words startled me with a new view of reality. *Everything did not make sense to adults.* I had thought they knew everything, could do anything. It was the beginning of my realization that they were human and limited. The world was bigger and more complex than even they could always deal with. I lost some of my childhood security then, and some of my naïveté. Nothing would be so "cut and dried" ever again.

Some teaching areas are closed to women. Others appear to allow women in, but actual entrance and success are very difficult. If we want to become pastors, priests, or rabbis and teach about God we find that many obstacles are put in our path, some of them impassable at this time. College and even high school administrators prejudicially resist hiring women to teach certain subjects. Many churches bar women from teaching adult males.

But women *can* write. It is ironic that many of the same people who will exclaim against women teaching men in churches or colleges appreciate women writers who are doing the identical job on paper. What is the difference between preaching from a pulpit and writing a book with the same message? What is the difference between sharing the Communion rite and sharing Christ on paper? Until those avenues of service are open to us all—and I am convinced they will be one day—we can write.

The written word can teach, it can encourage, and it can do anything the spoken word can do. You can write to help those you know and those you do not know. During his imprisonment after Watergate, John Erlichman regularly received letters from a woman in Michigan whom he had never met urging him to begin again. I have received encouraging letters from readers at precisely the time I needed them.

Perhaps you are someone who should write. You want to. But you wonder if it is a silly, impractical idea. You are not good at it? Hardly anyone is in the beginning. Or you have doubts about what you write and its possibilities for success? Most writers do, even highly successful ones. Arthur Hailey still fears that each book will not make it.

My encouragement to you is: Don't be afraid to give it a try. Give yourself some time to learn and practice. Read a few copies of *The Writer*, a magazine you can find at your library. See what you think and where it leads. Maybe you have things to share, to tell, to teach, that only you can do in the way that is needed.

I'll end this chapter with one more quotation from the Book of Proverbs:

> . . . *the tongue of the wise heals.* (12:18)

Let your tongue be like that.

CHAPTER 20

Minding Your P's and Q's

She looks well to the ways of her household and eats no bread of idleness. (Prov. 31:27)

Have you, like me, found that it is much easier to solve other people's problems than your own? And doesn't it often seem easier to go afield for satisfaction and a feeling of accomplishment than to find them in one's own job and home? At least, that is what we imagine when we daydream about "what if." *What if I weren't still at home with these parents, but were out on my own? What if I had a husband like ——— instead of the one I have? What if I were young and beautiful? What if I . . . ?* And we think *if* our lives were so, then things would not be the way they are with us here and now in our own "business." It would all automatically be better.

Daydreaming and musing and wishing are not bad occupations in themselves: they help us know what we want. They give us mental clues to who we are, and who we might become. But when those activities are used as a substitute for action, or reality, then they are not good. I find that being realistic about my own daily situation is sometimes the hardest thing to do. I am tempted to look at the past and the future, but not give adequate attention to the present. One can get into the habit of thinking, *Oh, this will not last long, and so why get out of joint about it.* But our lives are made up of continuous *nows.* And the work of minding our own *p*'s and *q*'s is the most important work of all.

An important foundation to build on

We need a sound base from which to venture out into a wider world. If our home base is shaky, we cannot build a life that does not threaten to cave in from time to time.

On one level it is purely practical to have your own house in order before you venture out into a wider experience and tackle bigger things. Taking care of our personal business provides experience in solving problems and finding out what we can do and how much is reasonable.

But beyond the purely practical, there is another reason why taking care of the home front, the basic business of our lives, is important for us: that is the feeling of security and confidence it gives us. It is a bit like knowing your underwear is clean and sturdy with no rips or safety pins holding it together.

I am a person who has many varied interests. It is easy for me to become immersed in one or more of those interests without making sure that my basic work is well in hand. Sooner or later, it usually catches up with me and I find myself trying to juggle an impossible number of activities. And then I feel inadequate and foolish. I somehow have the idea that if I spend the time and effort to take care of my basic responsibilities there will be nothing, or not enough, left over for other things I need to do and want to do. So I run fast and try not to think about the work piling up. Now, that isn't realistic.

Part of the problem with me is perfectionism, I am sure. I have trouble doing a reasonable amount of work on a project or responsibility and then letting go and turning to something else. Maybe I also have the problem some children have, which is that they find changing from one activity to another unsettling. These children are upset by sudden demands to stop what they are doing to do something entirely different. They need to experience completion of the task at hand. It helps to warn them before you want them to change activities so they can bring what they are doing to a close painlessly.

But since I am no longer a child, I am responsible for dealing with my peculiarities, whether it be perfectionism or difficulty stopping before I am ready. I know there are times I avoid starting something I want to do because I am afraid of interruptions and cannot bear to have to leave it hanging.

You may be like me in some ways, or you may have your own reasons for avoiding looking at your own business and being realistic about it.

The Proverbs woman's business

Our lady was a woman of many occupations. She was a businesswoman buying and selling land and merchandise. She was a producer of materials for her household's use and for sale. Manager of a staff of workers was also one of her job titles.

It is interesting to me that this woman reached out to others and was involved outside her own business, but she was definitely one who minded her *p*'s and *q*'s too. Her business was well taken care of. I don't see her running off to a committee meeting with wet clothes turning sour in the washer because she had forgotten for three days to put them in the dryer.

It is important to look at this woman in a reasonable way. We do neither ourselves nor God a favor when we take something in his word to us and idealize it to the point of making it totally useless to us. We must not look on this woman as a superwoman whom we cannot expect to emulate at all and still be our own human selves. No, she was a regular, normal, sensible woman. Her work was possible without spreading herself too thin. It was varied, but it did not devour her. We can learn from her in a reasonable way. We do not have to sentimentalize or canonize her. She was a *real* woman.

Household then and now

This woman looked well to the ways of her household. Her household included husband and children and servants, that we know from the account. We know she had woman servants and can probably assume she had menservants working for her too, because of the vineyard and because of the fact that most households of any size would have had both.

So her business consisted of producing necessities and work for her family and servants. In other words, she was the family manager. This involved being able to *assess* needs and resources, *decide* what needed to be done, *supervise* work, and *evaluate* the results when it was done. She also had to be able to *delegate* work and some supervisory jobs to others. She did not do all the work all by herself.

The first step toward getting your own business by the tail is defining exactly what it is. What does your household consist of? What are your basic responsibilities and work? (Not the peripheral things that you choose to do but that are not really necessary or basic.)

Try this: get out a pencil and paper and list the areas of responsibility you have and the work description and tasks under each area.

I did that once, and two things impressed me immediately. First, I do a tremendous amount of work and hold a huge load of responsibility in my "household." The other insight was that I was trying to do too much all by myself, that I should delegate many jobs and learn to supervise others better. I also decided that I should feel better about myself because I had so many skills that no one ever gave me much credit for.

Being a homemaker is not a high-status job in our society. It is commonly assumed that it is nothing at all to be nursemaid, child psychologist, fix-it woman, cook, marketing analyst, housecleaner, laundry maid, tutor, adviser to the lovelorn, home-school liaison officer, diplomat—and I could go on. But the skills needed and the effort that can be expended are staggering.

Assessing needs

Let me encourage you to use paper and pencil when problem-solving and analyzing your needs. I'm a firm believer in the value of writing things down.

First of all, if you haven't done it already, you can make a list of what your business actually is. Put it all down. Now *assess* your information. What are the problem areas? Are you trying to do too much, making it impossible for you to do it as well as you would like to? Look over your list for places you can make changes.

For example, are you the best person to do all these jobs? Do you need help? Where? Who might help?

Put down all possibilities under a new heading: *Possible Changes.* You may find that ideas will spring to your mind and solutions present themselves immediately. If not, put the list away and let it simmer for a few days on your mental back burner. Then pull it out and try again.

Deciding on action to take

I have often thought up good changes to make, usually too many at once to be successful with any of them. After finding all those solutions I went away feeling good, but that's all I did. I did not *do* any of them, or if I did, I didn't do them for very long.

I remember such sessions with myself in college and high school. I would list all the things about me and my life that I wanted to change. Then I would make a list of everything I wanted to do differently and say to myself, *Beginning right now (or Monday), I will do all this.* Inevitably I found it impossible to make all those wonderful changes at once, became discouraged at my loathsome incapability for improvement, and sank back into the comfort of old familiar ways.

Once I read Benjamin Franklin's autobiography and made myself a chart like his on the virtues he wanted to cultivate in himself. I was discouraged to find that I did not seem to improve at the rate he did. I suspected I would never reach Franklin's level of virtue accomplishment.

I eventually learned that if I wanted to make changes I had to be realistic about my ability to change. First I had to decide on something specific. And I must not make sweeping changes all at once. I could successfully make one or two at a time, and the smaller the better for first tries. That worked. I have not reached perfection, I'm afraid, but I have tasted improvement.

So look over your list of possible improvements in getting your business in hand and decide on *one* to begin with. Then actually begin.

Supervising work

You need to be able to supervise your own work as well as the work you choose to delegate to others. It might not seem necessary to learn to supervise yourself, but if you have not been doing your own work well or as well as you would like, then you may need better supervision.

Again, be realistic about your capabilities. You may not be able to work effectively for long stretches of time without a break. Or you may be one of those people who do best by setting aside a large block of time free from interruptions and getting the task done in one fell swoop. *Know thyself.* Ask yourself, "What kind of worker am I? How do I function at my best? What do I need to be efficient and enjoy my work at the same time?" Perhaps you have been trying to work in the work patterns of someone else. Try looking at yourself as the unique person you are and fitting the work to you, not bending yourself to the work.

You may want to experiment with different ways to do your work until you hit on the one, or ones, that fit you. Getting your own work done is usually not so much a matter of *making* yourself do it as discovering how you can do it willingly.

Now we come to supervising others. I should first say that it is possible, even likely, that you are doing things or trying to do things you should not be doing. Work expands to fill the time available. People around you will usually willingly let their work expand into your time and out of theirs.

Humans being what they are, we tend to go the way of least resistance. And that means doing nothing instead of doing something. Those in your family, dorm, or work surroundings may have felt you were someone who was more willing to work than they were.

Wives and mothers, especially, may find that a creeping work load stacks up on them. Or that work which was theirs temporarily because of an unusual or short-term situation has become theirs permanently.

My children have often had the impression that all work in the family was really mine and that they only did a little to be indulgent with me. I have had to explain repeatedly that when they were babies I washed them and their clothes because they could do neither. Also I did things like cooking, washing floors, picking up, dusting, vacuuming because they could not do it. But since they can now, it is no longer work that I should necessarily do.

You need to ask yourself if your work is family work, household work, company work, or your work. For example, washing your hair is probably your work. Washing the sink may be family or household work.

When you decide which work is necessarily yours and which is not, then you can ask another question. Is there an equal work load in this household? We are talking about reasonable equalization, not splitting everything precisely among all participants. Some people should have more free time because they are children or for other reasons. But is the work split fairly? Fairly in the sense of equality of persons, no one being the scullery maid for everyone else.

If there is an unequal work distribution you can get the other people together and discuss it. They may be willing, and then they may not be. If not, you can decide on strategy to ease them gradually into a more equal share. Or if you are feeling confrontationish, you can just announce that you aren't doing it all anymore and this can be their job starting whenever.

It helps to know who you are dealing with. It is no victory to confront unsuccessfully and alienate them in the process. You may feel better for a while, but you have really gotten nowhere. So think over how you want to go about it. And if your first attempts have less than ideal success, don't give up. Try another tack until you find one that does work.

Supervising work done by others is a job that needs some clarifying. Personally, I have trouble supervising my children. I do well the first few days. They work and all seems to be going smoothly. Then, hating to tell them what to do and check up on them, I assume they will continue their good work unsupervised.

After a few more days or weeks I notice suddenly that the work is no longer getting done. My inquiries are met with the most imaginative excuses possible. If I'm not convinced, the nonworking workers then become angry with me. I have insulted them. They aren't sure they want to work for someone who doubts their good intentions.

I need to learn to keep on supervising (by quietly checking to see if the work is actually being done) after my initial success. I need to find a maintenance level that is both effective and easygoing. I'm working on it.

Supervision should be done with a light touch. My husband tends to go in the opposite direction and be a bit heavy-handed about it. He often has rebellions and uprisings among his charges. One needs to steer a middle course, being firm enough to see that the work is done, but not forgetting to treat the workers like people of equal humanity instead of slaves owned body and soul.

I find that I tend to forget that supervision is necessary at all. I like doing what I want when the mood strikes me. And since I love freedom for myself, and like to share that freedom with my children (and if I had employees I would probably do the same thing), I tend to forget that everyone doing their own thing may leave some important work undone.

The same kind of doing-my-own-thing attitude got me into jams in college. I love to learn—about things that interest me. So I worked on the subjects I liked, and the ones I did not like, or that had boring teachers, I let slide. As a result I had to deal with a grade or two that I *did not* like. I had to reevaluate my work habits. I decided that even though I wanted to study what I liked, I also wanted to get respectable grades in other classes as well. So I supervised myself to get them.

Help for minding your P's and Q's

Two very good books have helped me mind my own business better than ever before. *How to Get Control of Your Time and Your Life*, by Alan Lakein (Wyden), is so important a book that I think it should be given to all college students the minute they walk on campus. Actually, it should be given to students before they finish high school.

The book contains the nuts-and-bolts techniques necessary to help you determine priorities in your work and then get all the work done.

Items to do are written down and evaluated with an A, B, or C rating, with A being more important, B less so, and C even less. Then you look at the A's and determine which one should be done first. Reevaluation of the work list is done daily. Some items that were B's become A's as the time for their completion approaches. For example, buying a birthday gift may be a C a month before the date but is a B later and eventually an urgent A.

Lakein helps the reader decide which work needs to be done at all. For the paper-weary, he advises a drawer or box for C paper, things you don't need but can't stand to throw away yet. He suggests letting it sit for a space of time and then throwing it all away at the end of that time if you haven't used any of it.

There are also methods for getting work done that you tend to put off. He suggests giving yourself a time limit to work on a job that needs doing, but that you are avoiding. Work only ten minutes at a time on it. Divide the job into small manageable pieces. Then your work list would read, instead of "Write Article," or "Clean Basement," "write *outline* of article," or "work on *five-foot area* in south corner of basement." By cutting jobs down to size and giving yourself a small time segment to begin them, you overcome the "too big to do" hesitation you feel.

The other book I like on the subject is *Getting Organized*, by Stephanie Winston (Warner Books). This paperback explains why many of us are disorganized—because we are still listening to and rebelling against a voice from childhood that said, "Clean your

room. Do what you *should!*" The book also tells you how to organize
your finances, work, home, and clothing.

I liked its gentle "take me by the hand" instructions about money.
Her simple instruction on finances helped me go gather up all the as-
sorted folders, loose checks, and box of mishmosh that was my financial system and make order out of it. Winston recommends doing
your financial work once a month on the same day each time, paying
all bills and bringing your bank book up to date. She has a more
complicated system for those who want it.

I also profited from her way of dealing with paper work and mail.
She suggests taking all mail directly to your desk to open it, sorting
it there into a *to do* folder, a *consultation* folder for those things that
you need to talk to your spouse about (if you have one), and a *file*
folder for material that merely needs to be filed. Read and throw the
rest away. She also adds a *pending* folder for things that need attention later or are waiting for responses.

Winston also has a *to do* notebook in her getting-organized
scheme. You carry this little notebook with you all the time and
write down everything you think of that you need to do or have to
do. Then you don't have to worry about forgetting something. And
you don't have to carry it all in your head. You check with this notebook before writing your list of things to do each day. I tried using
her method and it works very well.

Setting priorities

Both of these books help you set priorities so you can spend your
time and effort on the things in your life and work that are the most
important to you. Their point is often that we are disorganized and
ineffectual because we spend so much of our time doing things that
we do not need to do, or that someone else should be doing. It is not
that we don't work enough, but that we don't work wisely enough.
Actually, by using some of these techniques you will find that you
are doing more work with less effort and definitely enjoying it more.

You will need to have enough self-confidence to promote yourself
to manager of your own personal business instead of only being the
worker. Good management doesn't mean being rigid and work-
controlled. It means being realistic about the work and about yourself
and your own values.

Just doin' nothin'

By not being realistic and reasonable with ourselves we women waste a lot of our own precious time. Some of us seem to drift through our lives, every day doing what seems to need doing, or what others think we should be doing. That is a waste of our time as surely as the more obvious ways of wasting time. But before we talk about wasting time too seriously, we should look at the value of "just doin' nothin'."

When I was a child I loved to just do nothin'. I think all children enjoy that, or at least those who do not have a TV umbilical cord do. It is a time when your soul grows and your imagination exercises. Maybe your bones even grow then, too. Children need to be able to live in their own personal world and lie in the grass and look at the clouds or the ants and think nothing. It has bothered me to see my own children overprogrammed by their schools and allowed so little recess time to spend as they liked.

I'm convinced that adults also need this open free time to muse and imagine. We are as fully human as when we were children. We still need the peaceful doin'-nothin' time. People take up Transcendental Meditation and learn to systematically do nothin'. I wonder why they can't just *do* nothin'. Probably because they have forgotten how.

In all the organizing and being wise about the use of your time, don't restrict yourself when it comes to the doin'-nothin' habit. We all need that. We need to be able to lie on the sofa with a book in our hands and not read it at all. And we need those staring-into-space times wherever we are.

No one should be able successfully to shame us for them either. If you are surrounded by one or more of those human creatures who want an explanation for your every move or lack of movement, you have my sympathy. You will have to reeducate them to leave you be. No one should have to explain every move.

This doin' nothin' is not just rest or relaxation, it is the essential activity of a creative mind. Your child is innovative and imaginative precisely because she does not have to give account for her time and thoughts. She can be free to let her mind take her where it will. You need that freedom too.

Time wasters

Anything that you don't *want* to be doing (when it isn't something that definitely should be done by you right now) is wasting your time. You are wasting your time when you go to the store three times this week because you didn't bother to think about what you might need before you went the first time. You are wasting your time when you sit in front of the TV watching something you think is mediocre but you don't want to bother thinking about what you would rather do.

You usually waste your time when you don't use your head first. Be willing to think about your work and your life. Be courageous, make choices. Try them out. Evaluate and try another way if that seems better.

It's your own precious time. And it's your business.

Mind your own business.

CHAPTER 21

Praise

Her children rise up and call her blessed; her husband, too, and he praises her: "Many daughters have done nobly,[1] but you transcend them all." (Prov. 31:28,29)

As Wayne Dyer says in his book *Your Erroneous Zones*, your family members are experts on your behavior. They know the real you.

It's not unusual for adults (children, too) to put on a benevolent and benign appearance for the rest of the world and be hell on wheels at home. I remember all too well the pressures on a minister and his family to be, like Mary Poppins, practically perfect in every way. And too many ministers and their wives try to accommodate that expectation. They put on an act for the outside world that they cannot maintain at home.

Ministers' families aren't the only ones who have to live with this dichotomy. Executives and workers at all levels are prone to suppress the hostilities and resentments they experience on their jobs and turn them loose at home.

Coerced praise

Because our family members know us so well, their genuine praise is worth more than that of anyone else. I say genuine praise because all praise from family members is not necessarily authentic.

Some fathers and mothers have a game they play on their children and each other. It could be called "Praise Me or Else." Or else I will cry, get depressed, get sick, or get even with you if you don't praise me. I know a woman who coerces praise by setting people up like this: She says, "Do you like my new hat?" If you try to be diplomatic and say, "Well, it is not exactly my style or preference, but I can see why you like it. And it is attractive in [some way you can honestly praise]," she will say, crestfallen, "You *don't* like it, *do you?*" And she will coerce you further until you either praise her or allow her to feel insulted. If you say, "No, actually I don't care for it," she is *really* insulted. This woman's family has learned to let her manipulate their emotional responses in all manner of situations in order to prevent her from crying, pouting, and making life generally uncomfortable for them.

If you have a sneaking suspicion that you are somewhat afflicted with her habit, do not go and ask your poor family if you do it. Because if you are like that, they will probably be afraid to tell you. If they do, they fear they will be in for another bout with you. Watch yourself instead. You can catch yourself, and you can stop. Make it a continuing effort not to coerce or manipulate people in *any* way. Then eventually the praise you receive can be believed.

Another way praise can be coerced is by heaping it on others in excessive amounts and then waiting puppy-dog-like for them to return the favor, being profusely grateful when they do. The recipients of your excessive praise will feel guilty if they do not praise you constantly, whether it is completely genuine or not.

It isn't fair to your praisees to heap it on until it runs off and makes an embarrassingly large puddle on the floor.

Family priorities

To receive praise that is real, one must earn it. There are many obstacles to earning genuine praise from families just now. It's too easy for families to get lost in the shuffle, to get squeezed out, forgotten, or short-changed.

Just as minding your own business should take top priority in your work life, minding your own family relationships and concerns should come first in your relational life. Unfortunately, at this time and in this society many pressures converge to make it difficult for us to give the attention and priority to our families that they need and deserve.

Too busy

Today there is some sort of mystique about being too busy. We hear of women who are "on the go." They are presented to us in commercials as sleek, well-coiffed, well-dressed, bright women. Looking at them makes you think being "on the go" is exciting—living life to the full. A certain beer is advertised for those who want to "grab all the gusto" they can.

Advertising aims to meet us where our insecurities lie, paint them over in a positive way, and then sell us something that will make us feel better about them. So when you see your TV commercials presenting the woman on the go as the ideal, attractive woman, you might want to check and see if they are trading on your insecurity at trying to live too fast and too shallow. Maybe being on the go and grabbing gusto is not the best way to live. And maybe a certain kind of car, beer, panty hose, or hair spray is not the way to deal with the problem of life-style overload.

Families and people get lost in a too-busy life. At least, they do in my life and in the lives of some others I have known.

Charlie's mother was on the go. He let himself in at home for lunch alone during the second grade when I first knew him. After school he often came to our house and stayed until five or six o'clock. He said it was all right because his mom didn't get home until then and she wouldn't wonder where he was.

Charlie was an angel child. He had, by his mother's own unsolicited admission, raised himself. He was no trouble, he was beautiful and kind. And he was lonely.

Charlie will graduate from high school this year, I think. He may not if being present in mind makes a difference. He has been high on pot since he discovered it in junior high school. He's not lonely anymore.

I have known more fathers and mothers who were too busy to listen and care for their children and spouses than I care to think about. And they didn't really know it. Not that they weren't told. I have to believe that sometimes those children and wives and husbands objected. But it was always discounted, or promises were made, or things were substituted for meaningful relationships. They were too busy to do more, maybe someday things would be different. Someday is too late.

Too preoccupied

Sometimes being too busy and too preoccupied go together. Some people never unwind from work or away-from-home activities. Even when they are there, they aren't *there*. There is nothing quite like playing Monopoly with someone who is elsewhere in mind, or watching a child listen to a bedtime story read by a parent who isn't there in spirit.

The homelife of the preoccupied person is a long, arid wasteland. There is always semi-touching and semi-loving. And semi is not enough. It never is.

But there is another kind of preoccupied that people can be in a family. There is the preoccupation of concern or personal pain. When a family member has a problem that they cannot lay down, their attention is always partly preempted by that problem. They cannot quite be there either.

I think it was Charlie Shedd who said the greatest gift a man could give his children was a happy and contented mother. He was on target in the matter of preoccupation. A woman who is miserable in her marriage can have so much of her emotional resources tied up in the unresolved conflicts with her husband that she cannot give her children all the love and attention she would like to. She always carries a double load, struggling to free her mind and loving heart to reach out to her children when it is bound up in pain because she cannot also reach out to their father.

This situation makes "staying together for the children's sake" somewhat of a contradictory statement. Often the children are the greatest losers of all, because they have never been able to live with a happy, relaxed mother.

What can you do about it? For the ordinary too-busy preoccupation, you can write on your calendar (otherwise you will be too busy or too tired to do it) a date with yourself every month to reassess your personal priorities, your human priorities.

You can ask yourself what the rush is all for anyway. And who is being lost in the shuffle? And is this what you really want from life? Do your family people have a right to a better situation than this?

You can also write down concrete steps you can take to change. You can begin a process of daily effort, with results you can measure, to stop your overbusy life-style. You can leave work at work.

Ask your family to tell you when you "aren't there." Ask them what they want in human contact from you that they are not getting. But be sure you do not set them up to tell you what you want to hear. They may not feel free to tell you how they feel. Try to look at the situation through their eyes.

You might also ask yourself what you are running from. Maybe you should face it and do something about it. You can change.

For those who are preoccupied because of problems or emotional pain: I am not going to pretend that you can easily solve your problem. It may not be as hard as you think, because you are so close to it that you cannot see it in perspective. But it may be every bit as bad as you think. And I am not going to be so unfair to you as to assume that it is not.

But even if the worst is true, that you are for the moment stuck in it, I want you to know that you do not have to give up. People in prisons made with bars and stones have found ways to keep their own selves alive and alert and whole. And you can too, though your prison seems invisible to others.

One woman was kept in solitary confinement, a political prisoner, for several years. She was given only black bread and water and soup to eat, allowed no writing materials or books. She determined that she must not let her mind or her body stagnate and she must not lose hope. So she decided to do the best she could with what she had —not much, you must admit.

Saving a part of her bread ration each day, she kneaded it into a kind of dough that she could form into letters of the alphabet. These were hidden and allowed to dry. When enough bread-dough letters had accumulated she constructed poems with them. Knowing that she must have exercise and that writing what she could was not enough stimulation for her mind, she formulated a plan to walk to all the cities she had ever visited.

She paced off the space in her cell and computed how many trips it would take back and forth to walk a kilometer. As she walked she imagined and remembered in her mind's eye the scenery and buildings along the way. She could see them inwardly, feel the breeze and the sun, smell the dust and the grass. As she visited towns and cities, she remembered the friends who lived there and greeted them again in her imagination.

This woman traversed most of Europe from her cell and kept her mind and body healthy. When she was released, she was stronger and wiser. She had not been beaten.

Other stories have come out of concentration camps. One woman wrote notes on scraps of paper that she stuffed into her son's teddy bear so she could write about her experiences when she got out. Another set about organizing the cleaning and necessary work to make the compound neat and orderly. People who have survived such confinements have testified that it was those who immediately set to work to *do* something constructive, who did not dwell on the impossible but did what they could to better their circumstances, who kept healthy and made it through.

I have been talking as though you *are* trapped in your problem. But almost always there is a way to improve or remove the situation. Ask yourself what *can* be done. Get help. Try. Don't give up.

Often when we are demoralized and depleted by a difficult personal situation all our escape and help routes seem blocked. But when you are thinking this way, ask yourself if it is *absolutely* true. Is there *some way* to reclaim your own life?

Above all, do not let your situation make you think that you are less important or worthless, or this would not have happened to you. Your own value is tremendous. It is not conditional upon the value some other people may put on you. God sees you as someone of great value. If he loves you, can you conscientiously and realistically do less?

Sometimes the past imprisons and preoccupies us. A problem from the past can produce a mind-set within you that preoccupies you and deflects you from giving your full attention to the people you love. A habit has been formed of reliving old hurts. Or we cannot forgive ourselves for past failures. Or we cannot forgive someone else for past injustices or cruelties. You may not even realize that the past is supplanting the present in your thinking, or that it is squeezing out genuine open relationships or time with people in your family.

Is this happening to you? If so, let me encourage you to reassess your mental attitudes and begin leaving the past behind. If it actually *is* past and cannot be changed, do you need to allow it to feed upon you now? You *can* leave the past behind. Not all at once perhaps, but at least a little more each day. You can consciously substitute pleasures and full attention *now* for those preoccupying thoughts when they come again. Keep identifying them and substitute. A new habit can be formed over the old one by repetition of the desired one. I am not advocating a suppression of your feelings. If you need to express these fears and feelings, you should do so.

Find someone who will listen, and talk about them. Or write them down, over and over again if necessary. But if the past is merely intruding because of habit, you can change that relatively easily, and you should. Do not allow the past to use up the present.

Too easy

Sometimes too-easy parents are also too-busy or too-preoccupied parents. But sometimes they are not. There are parents who are too easy because they are afraid their children won't love them if they are firm. And there are others who are too easy because they have followed bad advice on child rearing.

I am reminded of a young man I knew when I was a teenager. He was the most jumpy and indecisive person I knew. He did not know what he wanted to do about anything. He was a likable fellow, but just kind of made of Jell-O.

Once he talked about his childhood. An only child, he said his mother had raised him alone. And that when he was born she had decided to use "psychology" on him. At that time the prevailing view on child psychology was to let the child do whatever he wanted and not bend him in any way, so as not to give him hostile feelings and hang-ups. So if he wanted to go to bed, he went to bed; if he wanted a new wagon, he got one; if he wanted to wash, he washed; if not—he was dirty.

My friend said the result was that he never knew which way to go or what to do.

His mother loved him, but she had no certainties in her life and there were none in his. He lacked the security of knowing that Mom knew what was right and wrong, what was good for him and what was not.

A kid should not have to learn *everything* by experience.

Too strict

A kid should not have to live in a punitive atmosphere either. There seem to be two kinds of parents who are too strict: those who are almost always distant and stern, and those who alternate between affection and anger.

Many reasons exist for too-strict parenting, all the way from repeating the bad treatment your parents gave you to wanting to impress other adults. But whatever your reason—which you can find out by a little honest soul-searching—you should face the fact that being too strict is as bad as, if not worse than, being too easy.

Childhood is not as pleasant and fun-filled as most adults tell kids it is. Growing up can be painful and lonely and frightening. Children need the loving support of their parents, not the added burden of stern taskmasters or hot-tempered punishers.

It hurts me to remember a neighbor child whose mother was a harsh and even cruel taskmaster to him. I watched him struggle to please her, and never succeed. He loved her dearly and longed for her to love him in return, but he received so little back.

She did not understand his childish ways and determined to stamp all folly out of him. I talked to her about it once (the only time I ever did a thing like that) and gave her my copy of Gesell and Ilg's book on child behavior, hoping that somehow it would help her allow him to be a little boy, that I could save him some pain by that small act. It was all that I could do.

Though you need to set some limits for your children, they also need room to grow and experience childhood—and the freedom to make mistakes too. Most of all, they need to be loved. Don't be so afraid you will be too lenient that you cannot be flexible and loving with your children.

Working at relationships

I've been talking as though this chapter is only about parents and children and wives and husbands. But it isn't. Other similar relationships can be as satisfying and productive or wearisome and stagnant as those in families, and for the same reasons.

Roommates in a dormitory or apartment relate to each other somewhat as family members. Since your roommates get to know the real you, their praise is valuable too. If you are a strong, whole person, your close associates will profit as well as you.

The way to get along with roommates and apartment mates is much the same as getting along within a healthy family. You treat others the way you would like to be treated *if you were them*. And you treat yourself just as well.

For example, suppose you prefer to stay up late and cram for exams, but your roommate would rather get a good night's sleep before a big test. If you treat her the way *you* enjoy being treated, you will make a pot of coffee large enough for both of you and keep the lights burning brightly.

But if you want to give her the consideration you would like *if you were her*, then you will quietly take your coffee to the room of someone else who likes to stay up and cram. And leave her to sleep without the light and the maddening sound of slowly turning pages to keep her awake.

If you sacrifice your needs and desires and go to bed when she does in order not to bother her, you are not treating yourself as well as her. You will eventually resent it. And she will either feel guilty about it or become a bit selfish from practice at accepting such sacrifices.

The most important thing to remember in living within family relationships or family-like relationships is that *whole persons treat other people like whole persons*. You do not either give unreasonable and unfair advantages or take them.

Being the greatest to your husband

The praise from our strong woman's husband can be summed up by "You're the greatest!" If you have a husband, or had one, or might have one someday, you probably have an opinion about what could make that man say, "You're the greatest." Our culture also has much to tell us about how to make the man in our life say to himself, if not to us, that we are the greatest. Unfortunately some of it is misleading, even false.

Early in life women are taught to be passive and compliant and men are taught to tell us what to do. But being a yes-woman is not a way to be the greatest. Being a yes-woman puts you in a doormat position that encourages people to walk on you.

Those who are easily walked on are not generally thought of as "the greatest." Oh, you may have an affection for them, and even love them, and do nice things for them from time to time. But the *greatest?* No, not really.

Our Proverbs woman was the greatest because she was all the person she really was. She did not hide facets of her strength or love or capabilities or sensitivities under a cloak of compliance. She could be kind and firm, and she could be loving and honest. She was herself.

I want to make a plea that in order to be the greatest to your husband you must be the best *you* that you can be.

I don't know if you have ever thought about this, but have you had the feeling that you have given up the person you were before you married the man, that parts of you have eroded away, even from pressures applied by him? Unfortunately it can be true that each one destroys the things he loves. A man, for any number of good and bad reasons, can distort and maim the woman he loved and make her into someone else.

It happens slowly, giving in here and adapting there, until you aren't you anymore. And unfailingly, he doesn't like his creation as well as the real woman. But since it has happened slowly, both of you may not realize that that is the problem.

You can reclaim the original woman who is you. You can reach back and bring her forward in time and give her health and freedom again. It can even be done diplomatically. That is not to say that there will be no opposition, but that it need not be a destructive process.

It is surprising when you find that people eventually like you better for being your own self, even though they will at first oppose and object. But they will come to appreciate the change, because who you are is always better than who you pretend to be.

What being the greatest is and is not

Being the greatest, excelling them all, is not looking more beautiful than everyone else, having the cleanest house or the best-behaved children, doing the most volunteer work, being the sensuous woman, and having your hair neatly in place as you do your gourmet-cook thing. That way lies magazine ads and emotional and physical collapse.

We have been a bit brainwashed by advertising's image of the housewife who does her work in high heels and a spotless shirtwaist dress. Ring-around-the-collar is *not* a major problem a woman needs concern herself with. And a husband who loves you for getting rid of it is not the kind of man you probably have (or want) either.

The trouble is that women have been taking suggestions about how to run their lives for so long and are so isolated from each other in their work and lives that they fall prey to the image builders. We are exhorted by parents, church, and school to be the nicest, most giving, cleanest, and most efficient creature humanly possible. The trouble with that is that it is not *humanly* possible to be that nice. We lose part of our humanity in the process of being Polly Perfect.

Being the greatest and excelling them all is being the *whole* woman we *are* and doing it with quality and class. Then you are the greatest you that you can be.

And strangely enough, those who live with and love you will think so too.

CHAPTER 22

The Key Ingredient

Charm is deceitful and beauty is passing, but a woman who reveres the Lord will be praised. (Prov. 31:30)

There is no doubt in my mind that beauty and charm open doors for women. After reading a book called *Guide to Glamour*, by Eleanor King, several years ago, I decided, in a mischievous and curious moment, to put its principles and techniques to the test with a scientific experiment. I dressed up in a simple black dress that showed off what attractiveness I possessed and made myself up to look my best.

Then I went shopping at a stationer's and office supply store and proceeded to use on a salesman all the charm techniques I had discovered. The book's suggestions worked so well that I was shocked and uncomfortable with my sudden power. I felt I had discovered a dangerous new secret weapon. It didn't seem right for the man to fall over himself helping me because I looked at him a certain way, or walked and talked a certain way. I felt a bit dishonest, too, because I am not naturally *that* charming and was totally unaccustomed to such adoring attention.

I went away and thought about it, and though I can admit to having taken more care about how I looked and behaved from then on, and about relating in a pleasing manner to others, I never repeated the experiment. I was uncomfortable about it because I felt that not only was it not me, but the man saw me more as a creature to admire and fantasize about than as a regular human being. I felt too much like an object to be comfortable.

And that's the problem: beauty and charm are too often roads toward becoming an object. Long ago, women were bought and sold. It was a mark of status for a man to have beautiful women and lots of them. Kings had harems full of concubines and wives. A politically powerless woman could, by using her beauty and charm, gain a measure of power impossible by direct means. Witness the success of Salome's dance of the seven veils, which brought her the head of John the Baptist on a platter. But she still remained more of an object to be possessed than a person.

Being regarded as an object, or as someone whose most important assets are beauty and charm, can create a profound loneliness in a woman. Many beautiful women have stated that they feel insecure in their personal relationships because they are never sure whether others love and appreciate them for their own selves or for their ornamental value. It must be something like being very rich and wondering if your family and friends love you or are hanging around waiting for you to give them something or die and leave it all to them.

What it was like then

Beauty and charm were the stock in trade for a woman wanting to be a queen. You may remember the story of Queen Vashti in the Book of Esther. She was beautiful, probably had been chosen partly, if not entirely, for her beauty. When summoned by the king so he could show her off during a drunken banquet, she refused to come, and unleashed a barrage of male outrage and concern throughout the kingdom.

So it was decided that she must step down and another queen be found, a beautiful one, of course, but one who would not refuse to do the king's bidding. It is obvious from the story that the only thing the woman need do was be beautiful and ready for display.

Esther, the replacement for Vashti, was chosen by means of the biggest, most outlandish beauty pageant imaginable. The contestants were prepared for a full year before each spent the night with the "panel of one." Win or lose, each woman was one of his objects from then on. Even if he did not desire further contact with her, the woman was added to his harem.

Esther had to walk a fine line to be more than just a pretty face in the court of Ahasuerus. By exquisite diplomatic skill she was able to save her people, the Jews, from destruction. She even gained some political power afterward. But in the beginning it was beauty and charm that got her the job.

What a striking contrast to the usual royal attitude for King Lemuel's mother to recommend that he be realistic about the limitations of beauty and charm.

How it is now

Nowadays we have beauty contests, which have always seemed rather obscene to me. I have watched them on television with growing distaste, yet unable to turn the thing off. Two messages continually come across to me, contradictory ones.

On one level everything is respectable and honorable. The MC and commentators behind the scenes tell us about the contestants and events of the previous week with tones and attitudes that say, "This is a wonderful opportunity for these young women, these are wholesome girls in a wholesome event."

On another level I am picking up the sexually suggestive comment, the inferences and looks that tell me the wholesome part is a joke, that what I am really seeing here is flesh on parade, some kind of sexually voyeuristic ritual performed to satisfy the unhealthy needs of millions of viewers. But I cannot tie it down and be certain that is what is behind it all.

Though the conversations with women who place high are often inane and silly, and the production numbers like graceful cattle performances, I can still almost convince myself that it is all honorable and decent, a contest to find the most accomplished, talented, bright, beautiful woman—until the bathing suit competition. That does it. When I see those young women marching down that ramp symbolically nude and the men in dark suits looking up at them, I feel sick inside.

It is the slave parade all over again. "Which one looks good to you, Al? Which one do you want to take to bed?" And if you want to insist they are only judging line and configuration, then that reduces the woman to an animal. High school agriculture students are taught to judge cows and pigs that way, hindquarters and all.

Elizabeth Ray was a beauty contest winner who went on to Washington, D.C., and became an "employee" of a certain senator. She said that being intimate with powerful men, being sought after by them, gave her a sense of importance and value. She said she also felt she was vicariously taking part in their power through her close association with government leaders.

Unfortunately for Elizabeth and others like her, those men viewed her more as a provider of a service than as a sharer of power or coequal human being. She is an example of a woman who had beauty and charm and was regarded as an object to possess and use rather than as a fully human person.

Other beauty contest winners have not fared so badly. Jinx Falkenburg became a radio personality; Polly Bergen, an actress, among other accomplishments. Anita Bryant used her singing talent to forge a career in music and then wrote personality-based books for the religious market. But those who went on to better and bigger things did it with abilities they had *in addition* to their beauty and charm. The beauty and charm merely opened the door to a wider audience and larger opportunities.

Then are beauty and charm bad?

There is a sour-grapes attitude toward beautiful and charming women that is sometimes present in those who either do not possess the same assets or do not feel they have a chance to possess the women with the assets. It's "If I can't have it, it isn't any good anyway." They will say that beauty and brains or beauty and character do not coexist.

But that neither makes sense nor is very gracious. Beauty and charm are not bad at all, they are good. *But they are inadequate to base your life on.* They are assets that, like most assets, also have disadvantages built in. What one needs to do is be realistic about beauty and charm.

Beauty is good because, as Ralph Waldo Emerson said in "The Rhodora," a poem we were required to memorize in high school,

Tell them, dear, that if eyes were made for seeing,
Then Beauty is its own excuse for being.

Beauty is but harmony in visual form. And harmony is pleasing in all things. But harmony and beauty are only *parts* of anything. We must not make them the *whole* thing for us. And this goes for both the beautiful and the nonbeautiful. It is as easy to become obsessed with our lack of beauty (or imagined lack of it) as with its presence.

How charm is deceitful

True charm is only good manners taken a step further. And no one should object to good manners and a pleasing personality. But when charm or beauty is used to manipulate people or substitute for honest emotions like love and concern, then it *is* wrong, and destructive to both the charmer and the object of her wiles.

Charm can deceive its possessor as much as those it is used on. Repeated success with charm can lead you to believe it will never fail to get the desired result. But ultimately most people realize they are being had, and the manipulator loses. Or you meet someone who sees through you from the beginning and you wish you had started out honest because you want them to believe you and you know they never will.

I know a man who is charming and attractive and uses it to manipulate and get things from people. The sad thing to me is that he does not know that I and others see through his ploys. He goes merrily on, making a fool of himself, thinking he has everyone else fooled. Actually they feel sorry for him and cannot bear to tell him it isn't working because they do not want to humiliate him.

Beauty that is passing

Beauty that is purely youth and firm, nicely arranged flesh is passing. That is the hardest thing to face for the beautiful woman whose whole identity is based upon her looks.

I remember reading about a chance encounter between a Prince of Wales (not the present one) and one of his past mistresses. The writer praised the prince because he had been kind and attentive toward his ex-mistress in spite of, as he put it, "her ruined face."

I thought the statement profound. The prince was as valuable as ever, but the woman was used, discarded (however touchingly) for another human glove fresher and more starched.

The beautiful woman who relies on her beauty for *everything* knows what the future may hold, and it haunts her. She can either live fast and merry and "grab all the gusto" she can since she only goes around once, or she can treat her face and form with aseptic and meticulous care to stay every line and wrinkle until the very last moment.

There is another option for a beautiful woman. She can build a beauty that ages well. Such a woman will know, as the French do, that an older woman has a beauty and charm that is superior in some ways to that of a young woman. Experience and wisdom can blend well with a body that has seen years. In fact, many women who have not felt they were beautiful when young have found that they become more attractive later, that they "age" well.

We do not need to have a discard mentality about ourselves. Even if our society is ready to toss everything out from the newspaper to the new car after it has been used a bit, we do not have to go along.

Beauty from within

Women who are beautiful on the outside sometimes do neglect beauty within. Some of them see inner beauty of spirit as something of a compensation by those who do not have it on the outside. But after knowing women who are beautiful both within and without, I can say that anyone who can have both should never settle for only one.

And it's not that you can have only one kind. You can often have both kinds of beauty, even when you think not. If you are pretty confident about your looks, let me encourage you to look beneath your surface now and work on your inner person. Find out who the real person is who lives in your body. What are her assets, good qualities, talents, desires, kindnesses, longings? Feed that inner person and let her grow so you will not be a pretty package empty inside, but solidly beautiful like a good sand painting in a glass.

Beauty on the outside

And if you think you have a bit of beauty from within but can't get very optimistic about the outward kind, let me encourage you too. Most people don't use all their resources when it comes to looking good. So often I see women who have great potential but are making nothing of it.

A lot of women just give up on their looks. They try to look good enough not to be stared at, and that's about all. They should not do that. Looking good makes you feel good, and it even makes you act better, happier, more positive. Besides, others around you look at you all day. Why not give them a treat instead of a dull view.

I'm not going to become a beauty advice giver here, but there are two areas that I want to say something about—the top and the bottom.

Hair

Improving the looks of your hair, though relatively easy and simple, can do more to change your image and looks for the better than anything else I know of (except possibly looking pleasant instead of sour). Women do not do as much as they can with their hair.

Hair may not seem like much, only strings stuck to your scalp that need to be washed once in a while and fussed over when you go to something special. But hair is important. Do something good to your hair and you will look better all over.

I suspect women give up on their hair because they don't know what looks good on them and/or they hate to fix it and don't want to curl and set and sleep on gadgets. Well, I hate that too. But I found that I can go to a hairdresser and ask for a style that is attractive and can be washed, blow-dried, and either left at that, or, if I'm wanting to be fancy, set with an electric curling brush. I found a good hairdresser by asking people whose hair looked good where they went. If I didn't like the results on me, I tried another one.

When my hair looks good, I *feel* I look better. The next time you are down, try washing your hair and see if you don't feel better already. And if you want to feel *really* good, go and have a beautician do it.

If you doubt my claim that clean, neat, attractive hair is a key to looking good, try this: the next time you see someone who looks a little frumpy or obviously awful, ask yourself, "How would she look if her hair was pretty?"

Now for the bottom. No, not your hips. Some people in some places think large hips are very attractive. You may not be so fortunate as to be around those people, but big hips aren't so bad. The painter Renoir always painted nicely rounded women. I am talking about feet as the bottom area that can make you look good or spoil an otherwise pretty picture.

Feet

It sounds funny to concentrate on hair and feet to be beautiful. And of course it takes much more than that to look terrific. But my point is that you can do so much more with what you have most of the time, that just pointing out two easy areas for emphasis will help you begin to look at your looks in a way that could motivate you to action.

Oh yes, feet. Well, dirty feet in sandals would not seem to need mentioning. But they do, because they can ruin an otherwise attractive look. As can scruffy, dirty, or run-down shoes. Take a look at your feet. Could they look better? And it would be so easy to do something about them, wouldn't it? Why not.

I guess hair and feet frame the picture. They give that final touch to an otherwise good outfit. And if they aren't in good shape, they can ruin the nice effect too.

The rest of it

You really should make the most of what you have. It isn't vain to give attention to your outer beauty. It is merely wrapping a fine present with the paper and ribbon it deserves.

The library is well stocked with books about how to do it. And bookstores have more. But you probably don't even need outside advice to begin improving your looks. You can ask yourself what your best features are and then emphasize them; what your worst features are and distract attention from them, or camouflage them.

Don't be afraid to invest in your looks, for the sake of the rest of humanity as well as yourself. As one woman said about her face-lift, "It wasn't for me, I only look in the mirror when I put on my lipstick. But the rest of the world has to look at me all day." Incidentally, *Miss Craig's Face-saving Exercises,* by Majorie Craig, is a book that will show you how to keep your face in shape or bring it back into shape without a face-lift.

A woman who reveres the Lord shall be praised

Why does it say that in our quotation for this chapter? Is it some kind of magic, that God will give a woman a gift of praise if she reveres him? I don't think so. God says things because they are reasonable and work for us, not because he wants us to be mindless automatons who sit and wait for him to reward our unthinking compliance. There are good reasons why a woman who revered the Lord then would be praised. And good reasons why she will be now.

The woman who reveres the Lord has the best guide for her life. She has access to information and assistance that will help her build her life and invest herself in ways that will bring solid results.

She has the Bible to help her decide on values, teach her how to relate to others, and show her how to determine her priorities.

For the Proverbs woman, revering the Lord would have involved living by God's commandments and seeking to live the spirit, not only the letter, of those commandments. That would produce the kind of wise living taught in the rest of the Book of Proverbs.

Christians believe that when you begin your family relationship with God, when you accept Jesus' provision that makes a new relationship possible, a new element is added to your life. We believe that God gives us a permanent live-in part of himself in the form of the Holy Spirit to help us know how to live. So we would say that the woman who reveres the Lord nowadays could also have God within in the form of the Holy Spirit to help her live a life that generates praise.

We can base our own lives on solid ground by a real living relationship with God. The Bible is there for us to read and study. And God is there to give us personal encouragement and love.

Being a woman is no disadvantage with God. Throughout the Bible God treats women as fully human and fully included in his broad spectrum of provision. He used women to do all manner of things from being prophetess to army commander.

Ezer and neged

I'll give you one example of how God sees us, contrary to the way the Church has historically seen us. Genesis 2:18 says,

And the Lord God said, It is not good that the man should be alone; I will make him an help meet for him. (KJV)

This verse has been traditionally understood to mean that God created woman as a kind of glorified girl Friday for Adam. A nice girl, but slightly substandard and needing a man to supervise her work. The words *help* and *meet* have been condensed by common usage into *helpmeet*. We have been taught that this means woman should be a helper to man, not his equal.

But in Hebrew, the original language, the words *ezer* and *neged* do not have the connotations we have given them. *Ezer* means "help" all right, but not secondary help or assistant, as in assistant to the president. It means help in the way God helped Israel. The word is used in the Old Testament to refer to help by a superior force, such as help by God, as in Psalm 121:1,2:

I raise my eyes toward the hills.
Whence shall my help come?
My help comes from the Lord, who made heaven and earth.

The word *ezer* is never used elsewhere in the Old Testament to refer to subordinate or inferior help.

Neged ("meet") is a preposition in Hebrew and cannot be translated as a preposition in English and still retain the sense. It means "corresponding to," "fit for," "meet for." In other words, God created woman as a *real help* to Adam, someone who was like him, suitable in every way. There is nó hint of inferiority for woman in the original account.

Adam recognized woman's true nature and God's intent at once as he cried out, "Ah, at last! Bone of my bone and flesh of my flesh."

Not only are you as woman created both *ezer* and *neged*, but you are not flawed in the creating. God looked back over his creation work at the end of the seven days and said that everything he had created was good. Woman was included.

Praiseworthy women in the Bible

One way we can lay to rest the idea that women are created for decoration and subordination (and little else) is by looking at some

of the women in the Bible who built their lives on reverence for the
Lord and not on their good looks.

Jochebed—Without this woman's foresight and courage, there
would have been no Moses to lead his people out of bondage in
Egypt.

Deborah—Was a judge in Israel to whom people came voluntarily
to have her settle disputes. She was also a prophetess and an army
commander.

Jael—Capable, courageous, gutsy, and ingenious, she captured Sis-
era, the commander of the forces opposing Deborah and Barak, and
executed him in her tent.

Abigail—Her quick thinking and diplomacy saved her whole
household from destruction.

Mary—The mother of Jesus was willing to risk losing her be-
trothed husband-to-be, her good reputation, and the understanding
of her family to comply with God's request of her.

Mary of Bethany—Stepped out of "woman's place" to sit at Jesus'
feet and learn theology, an act so outrageous her sister was sure Jesus
would send her back to the kitchen.

Phoebe—A deacon of the church at Cenchreae.

Euodia and Syntyche—Were leaders in the Church at a time
when women were almost universally not expected or permitted to
lead men.

Priscilla—Was a tentmaker by trade and a Bible scholar on the
side. She helped instruct Apollos in the faith.

These are only a few of the women in the Bible. Did you notice
how many *strong* women there are in this list? It's ironic that
churches encourage us to be submissive and weak, and hold "Total
Woman" classes for us to teach us how to do it, when the Bible presents us with all these strong, dynamic women.

I think I like God's kind of woman better than the kind of woman
my church has encouraged me to be. God's women are whole, capable people. I want to be a whole person too.

Who will praise her?

Not everyone will praise a Proverbs-type woman. Some people
won't like their stereotypes violated. They may admire a bit from a
distance, but they will feel threatened.

If you are going to be a strong, whole woman you will find that some men will see you as a threat to their power over you and over the women in their lives. To some women your wholeness will threaten their feeling of security. You cast doubts on the rightness of their life-style, the necessity of giving up so much of themselves to fit a "role."

To others you will be a threat to presuppositions they do not feel comfortable about reassessing. And they will possibly see you as a threat to their theological system, which they will equate with truth itself and defend it as if it were God's word intact.

But you *will* be praised. Other whole people will praise you. Those who learn from you, or profit from your wholeness in other ways, will praise you. Some of it you may never hear, but it will happen. And the praise you do hear will be so good on your ear that it will be worth losing all the false praise of all the others. It will be very gratifying. I can tell you that; I have tasted a little bit already. And I want more.

How about you?

CHAPTER 23

Works Endure

Acknowledge the product of her hands; let her works praise her in the gates. (Prov. 31:31)

This is the last verse in the Proverbs chapter we have been thinking about. And it ends with solid force. This woman does not have to hide away and hope someone will remember what she has done. And she does not have to give up the ambitions she had, for a life of quietly living in someone else's shadow. Her works are a living monument to her. What she has produced and done makes words unnecessary for praise.

I have gained a new appreciation for the women in my life who have been strong and productive and self-determining like our Proverbs woman. I didn't realize how many there were until now. And my new appreciation is balanced by an increased sense of outrage at all the lost women who have seen their dreams fade and their works crumble or go unnoticed because of our treatment of women, treatment that makes too many of us get less from life and give less to it.

I don't want there to be any more women who are afraid to use their abilities. I don't want there to be any more women who struggle against impossible odds to use what they have. I want all my sisters to be free to use all they have and be all they can be.

Look at this woman's affirmation. She is a real person. She produced real results, real products. *And she gets recognition for it.* Let's have no more false humility from us. We need to acknowledge each other's works and contributions. Women must stop seeing each other as competitors and begin caring about each other as sisters. Let's praise our own sister's work, acknowledge her hand's products in the gates of our homes, our schools, our cities, government, professions, art galleries, and world.

Works endure

Vincent van Gogh killed himself. The only thing in Van Gogh's life that was a success was his painting. But he did not know it. He thought he was a failure all the way.

He wanted to be a missionary and went out to help the poor. His mission sent him home. He wanted to marry a girl he loved. She wouldn't have him. He *had* to paint. No one would buy the paintings. People thought they were odd, with the paint loaded on thickly and those black lines around everything. No thanks, they didn't want any.

Vincent poured all his soul into his paintings. While his life was dull and oppressive, he painted brilliantly colorful, vibrantly alive canvases. He was laboring to bring happiness to life, to compensate for his failure to live successfully and happily with others.

Now those paintings are worth millions of dollars. And art critics stand in awe of his work. Only his work endures.

Your work may not be valued by those around you yet. They may not acknowledge its value. But be assured, if you do good work, it will endure. Do not allow a lack of acknowledgment or praise to stop you or discourage you.

Human works endure

Not all good, enduring work can be signed. Much of it lives on in the lives and works of other people whose lives have touched ours.

Aunt Agnes brought me books when I was a small child. She and my mother and father who read to me are responsible in part for these words on this page. And if any of the words in this book make an impact on your life, they have a part in that change.

I learned about efficiency from my aunt Ila, about simplifying work and doing it without a lot of fussing around.

My grandma Dicy was a free spirit. She loved life, never lost her childhood joy and love of fun. I either inherited it or caught it from her. She shares in my joy and my life, and she will share in the joy my children have learned from me.

My mother's thoughtfulness, love, and loyalty will pass on down in my life and the lives of others in this family and elsewhere. When my daughter, Ann, stopped her car not long ago to pull a bully off a child in a schoolyard I recognized my mother's fierce sense of outrage at cruelty and injustice. My mother's work will endure.

Aunt Clema is pleasant and loving and hospitable. You always come away from her home feeling wanted and appreciated. I have to believe she learned that from my grandmother Alta Price, who died when I was only five years old. But I remember her loving pleasure in the company of others.

So many things endure, even when we do not know it. Whether they are openly recognized in the gates or not, they endure.

I hope you will invest more consciously in quality work, for your expression and satisfaction; and also that you will invest in the lives of others the good qualities that are in you or that you can cultivate and develop.

I think there is yet much that is good within you that you don't know about. Some of it you have been investing in an enduring way all along and did not know it. Other qualities and abilities are in embryo form and you either only suspect they are there or are totally ignorant of their existence.

Let me encourage you again to look within and find out what you can be as well as what and who you already are. Make that which endures from your hand and spirit quality work that will gleam and shine forever—in lives, and in the gates.

CHAPTER 24

Who Is She?

This book begins with a question: Who can find the strong woman, the one who is more valuable than jewels? I am ending with another question: Who is she? Who is this strong woman here and now? Where is she?

But before I ask the final question, I want to ask you this one: Who are you?

Who are you?

Who you are is determined by several factors. To some extent, you are who your genetic makeup says you will be. You may not like everything you have inherited, or you may be pleased to have come out so well. But regardless, you are who you began to be long before you were born.

But even though our heredity limits us some, we limit ourselves so much more that we do not even know the true bounds of that heredity. There is so much more to almost everyone than they use that we are all treasure chests whose many compartments are only opened partway, or not at all.

I said who you are began before you were born. My daughter, Ann, was a kicker. Her personality made itself known before I ever saw her. She was a person with drive and determination from the very beginning. During labor at her birth, she struggled against the contractions that were pushing her out into the world. With that determination and initiative put to good use, Ann can do a great deal with her life.

But who you are, assets and strong points, always has a reverse side. Ann's flip side is that she is easily frustrated and impatient at having to wait. As I tell her, she wants everything yesterday. You, like Ann, must be aware of all you are, both positive potential and negative possibilities. You have to be able to harness your own power, so to speak, without diminishing it or taking the joy out of it.

Who are you? Sometime when you are in the proper frame of mind, sit down and think about who you are. What are your earliest memories? What kind of little girl were you? What were you curious about? What did you like to do?

I loved to make mud pies and cakes. Jar lids were pans and twigs were candles. And my dolls dutifully ate what I cooked (at least, they pretended to). When I got older, I loved to bake. Then I collected cookbooks. Someday I will probably write some.

I can look back and see how who I am surfaced and developed into who I have become. It is interesting and profitable to look back for other clues to what my potential could become now. I also made "houses." When several children were together, we often lined up rocks and sticks to outline rooms of all sizes and shapes, doorways here and windows there. Does that mean I would have liked architecture? Or that I still would?

Try it. Who were you? The person you still are, but who may be hidden away within?

Who were you? Are you the child who was loved and cared for? Or are you the child who was not? If you were loved and now feel that you are not, why not love yourself. You are still you. And you are still as fine as ever.

If by chance you were not loved and cared for, can you parent yourself now as you should have been parented? All children deserve love and care. If you have not received yours yet, make up for lost time. Be kind to you now. Nourish all you were until you become wholly you, full-grown and flourishing.

Who are you? What is important to you? If you had a year left of your life, how would you spend it? If you had to write your obituary, what would you say? Is that the one you want, or do you want to change your way of living so that it could read the way you would like it to? Try writing one as it would be now, and then another one as you would like it to be at the end of a long life. What are your true values? Does your life reflect them?

Who are you becoming?

We are all constantly in the process of becoming. No one is ever static. We are either becoming something better and more to our liking, or moving backward, or solidifying. Even if you are engaged in a peaceful occupation that does not demand much from you, you are still becoming. Perhaps you are becoming more tranquil and that is good for you, a positive step. And if you grow restless with that life and are forced to continue it without any changes, then you may grow angry, or embittered, or stagnant.

Who you are becoming is a continuum. It is a long line of events and choices. Mostly it is choices. Things happen to us that we cannot control, true. But most of what we become has to do with the choices we make ourselves.

It does not seem that way at first glance. You can look at your life and see no way you could have avoided certain pitfalls that have determined its course. I know the feeling. I have looked backward at my own life and thought, *There is no way I could have known what that step would mean for my future.* And it is true, I could not have known. But what I *did*, the choices I made *after* the fateful step, were what actually determined *who* I became.

It is impossible to foresee every turning point and know which fork in the road to take. We should be as wise as we possibly can in taking those major steps. But we must face the fact that we cannot always know enough to take the right one. As important as major steps are, it is still the day-to-day choices that make us who we are.

If we say to ourselves that because of whom we married, or didn't marry, or the education we have or do not have, or the physical problems we were born with or acquired later, we must give up our hopes for becoming the kind of person we *could have been*, we are deceiving ourselves. Who you become is who you choose to become daily.

Darien is becoming a slow, dirty, slovenly gossip. She isn't there yet, but she is on the way. When Darien married Bill, she thought that two children would be the right amount. She planned on that. After one came, she found that she was not too eager to do all the extra work, but still wanted another one. When the second child came, her housework overwhelmed her. So she let it go.

Darien seemed gradually to give up on living her own life. She accidentally became pregnant again. Now, with three children, she has grown thick and slow. She lives in the world of the soap operas she watches all afternoon, and the gossip she gathers on long phone conversations with a few friends. She is *waiting*, waiting for things to get better for her, waiting for her children to grow up. Waiting her life away. Darien is becoming someone she does not want to be.

Janelle had a terrible experience. She was raped at knifepoint near her home. Since that traumatic experience, her humiliation at being questioned by police, and the embarrassment of going back to school where everyone knew, she has begun becoming someone else. She acts tough to cover her hurt. Frequently late to class and absent from school, she is drifting toward a drug-oriented group of students in her high school.

She thinks her bad experience caused all her problems, that something dirty happened that she cannot change. But Janelle is choosing every day whether she will become a truant or not, whether she will dress neatly or not, whether she will live her own life.

Karin has a husband who is demanding. He wants his wife at home when he comes for lunch. And he wants her to do his bidding.

She had been at home while her children were growing up. A capable woman who enjoyed being there, who had hobbies and interests that contributed to her happiness, she was surprised and troubled when she found herself changing. Her pleasant personality was becoming negative. She continually complained about injustices that happened at her children's school and in the neighborhood.

One day she suddenly heard herself clearly. *What is happening to me?* she thought. *This isn't like me.* For several days she thought about the way her life had been and how it was changing. She thought, *I am becoming a dissatisfied person, one who cannot see good in anything.*

Karin determined to change. She realized that though she had enjoyed staying at home and caring for her children, the youngest one would be out of high school in a short time and they did not need as much care and attention as she had to give. Her resources and abilities were not finding adequate use, as they had been. She also realized that her husband would be an increasingly larger irritant to her if she allowed him to set the perimeters of her life. It had been possible to endure his ways while she had the children as allies. But she

could see that in the future there would be only the two of them together.

She set out to make changes. First she got a small part-time job
close to her home. Gradually she stopped being home at lunchtime,
leaving food already prepared for her husband. Next she began to
project her future, and is making plans to qualify for a job that she
will enjoy. Karin has changed her direction, she is becoming who she
wants to be instead of who her surroundings would create if she let
them.

Balanced living versus perfectionism

Who would you like to become? In order to become the person
you want to be, the person you are inside and can be, you must aim
for a balanced life. When we think of making changes to become
who we want to be, we run the risk of trying to do too much too
soon, or of making sweeping changes that we cannot maintain. The
resulting striving for a perfectionistic goal can deplete us and ruin
our pleasure in the change-making, even doom it to failure.

You need to be able to spot perfectionism when it rears its head.
And you need to be able to tell the difference between perfectionism
and balanced living.

Perfectionism says, "I *have* to do this!" Balanced living says, "I
will try." And when it doesn't work, the perfectionist says, "It's no
good," or "I'm no good," or "It will never work," or "I can't." The
balanced-living person says, "It didn't work this time," or "It didn't
work yet," or "Maybe I had better change my tactics," or "I will
reassess the situation."

Balanced living is relaxed; perfectionistic living is uptight. Balanced living is flexible; perfectionism is win-lose. Perfectionists are
miserable much of the time. People who aim for a balanced life are
miserable a small amount of the time. The main trouble with perfectionism is that it is impossible to live up to, thus unrealistic.

But if you are a card-carrying perfectionist and highly trained at it,
merely identifying the condition will not make you stop it. What
will? *Living a day at a time.* If you face the reality of your hu-
manness a day or an hour at a time, you can beat perfectionism.
When you catch yourself making perfectionist demands on yourself,
stop where you are and say, *I'm doing it again. I will not do it for*

the next hour. If that is too hard, *I can be realistic for ten minutes, then ten more, and ten more.*

Making choices

The way to keep on becoming who you want to be, to make yourself the complete person you potentially are, is to:

1. make daily choices that send you in the direction you want to go.
2. begin again when you find you have made a poor choice, or developed an attitude you don't want, or gotten in a pinch that sends you in the direction you do not want to go. Stop where you are and begin again.

Who is this strong, whole woman?

We began this book talking about the feeling of incompleteness so many women experience now. And we looked at efforts to help us feel more fulfilled, more whole and complete. Some books for women encourage them to want less for their lives in order to be satisfied and fulfilled through an auxiliary relationship with a man. I do not believe that will ever work.

It is not that relationships with men are not good and satisfying, they are. It is that there is so much more to us than that, just as there is more to a man than that. Hardly anyone would tell men to be happy and content with simply having a wife and serving her, that they should seek nothing further to do with their lives. It is no more reasonable for us to limit our lives that way either.

I believe that to be whole and complete as a woman, to be *fulfilled,* if you want to put it that way, you must use all your resources. I also believe God knew this when he made us. And that is why he created us fully human, put all those fine, strong women in the Bible, and had this thirty-first chapter included in the Book of Proverbs. More than that, I believe that to do less with the great gift that God gives you than use it and enjoy it is to insult the greatest giver and most loving person who exists.

Remember what being a strong woman means. It doesn't mean being tough in a negative sense. It doesn't mean being unfeminine.

If you are born female, you never need to worry about that. What society calls feminine is only acquired behaviors. Feminine comes with the body. You can't lose it.

Being strong the way the Proverbs woman is strong is being a quality person through and through. It is being who you are, all the good things, all the positive things, letting none of them slip away or remain unborn. Any woman can be this kind of strong, because we all have the potential.

Who is this strong woman? If you want her to be, she's you.

NOTES

Chapter 1
1. Biblical quotations are from the Modern Language Bible (Grand Rapids, Mich.: Zondervan, 1969; unless otherwise indicated by name or initials (as, KJV for King James Version).

Chapter 2
1. Aileen S. Kraditor, ed., *Up from the Pedestal* (Chicago: Quadrangle, 1968), p. 29.
2. Paula C. Saunders, "Judy Blume As Herself," *Writer's Digest* (Feb. 1979), p. 19.
3. Ibid.
4. Augustine, *De Trinitate* 7.7,10.

Chapter 3
1. Jo Coudert, *Advice from a Failure* (New York: Dell, 1965), p. 124.
2. Ibid.
3. La Leche League International, 9616 Minneapolis Avenue, Franklin Park, Illinois 60131, encourages women who want to breast-feed their babies. It has local chapters and publishes a newsletter. A very helpful organization.

Chapter 5
1. Franz Delitzsch, *Biblical Commentary on the Proverbs of Solomon*, Vol. II (Grand Rapids: Eerdmans, n.d.), pp. 328, 329.
2. Dorothy L. Sayers, *Are Women Human?* (Downers Grove, Ill.: Inter-Varsity Press, 1971).

Chapter 6
1. Gerri Hirshey, "Now Save 15% on Everything You Buy," *Family Circle* (Feb. 1, 1979), pp. 53 ff.

Chapter 7
1. Billy B. Sharp with Claire Cox, *Choose Success* (New York: Hawthorn Books, 1970), pp. 41 ff.

Chapter 8
1. Estelle Fuchs, Ph.D., *The Second Season* (Garden City, N.Y.: Anchor Press/Doubleday, 1977), p. 244.
2. Paula Nelson, *The Joy of Money* (New York: Bantam, 1977), pp. 183, 184.

Chapter 21
1. strongly. Again the translator tries to express the composite meaning of the Hebrew word and comes up with "nobly" this time.

FOR FURTHER READING

Adams, Linda, and Lenz, Elinor. *Effectiveness Training for Women.* New York: Wyden Books, 1979.

Auerbach, Sylvia. *A Woman's Book of Money: A Guide to Financial Independence.* Garden City, N.Y.: Doubleday/Dolphin, 1976.

Baer, Jean. *How to Be an Assertive (Not Aggressive) Woman in Life, in Love, and on the Job.* New York: New American Library/Signet, 1976.

Bird, Caroline. *Everything a Woman Needs to Know to Get Paid What She's Worth.* New York: McKay, 1973.

Bolles, Richard N. *The Three Boxes of Life.* Berkeley: Ten Speed Press, 1978.

Brothers, Dr. Joyce. *How to Get What You Want Out of Life.* New York: Simon & Schuster, 1978.

Chesler, Phyllis, and Goodman, Emily Jane. *Women, Money and Power.* New York: Morrow, 1976; Bantam, 1976.

Craig, Marjorie. *Miss Craig's Face-saving Exercises.* New York: Random House, 1970.

——. *Miss Craig's 21-Day Shape-up Program for Men and Women.* New York: Random House, 1968.

Davis, Adelle. *Let's Eat Right to Keep Fit.* New York: New American Library/Signet, 1970.

Dudley, Dr. Donald L., and Welke, Elton. *How to Survive Being Alive.* Garden City, N.Y.: Doubleday, 1977; New York: New American Library/Signet, 1979.

Dyer, Wayne. *Pulling Your Own Strings.* New York: Funk & Wagnalls, 1978; Avon, 1979.

——. *Your Erroneous Zones.* New York: Funk & Wagnalls, 1976; Avon, 1977.

Ellis, Iris. *Save on Shopping Directory.* 7th ed. Ottawa, Ill.: Caroline House Publishers, 1979.

Evans, Glen. *The Family Circle Guide to Self-Help.* New York: Ballantine, 1979.

Fuchs, Estelle, Ph.D. *The Second Season*. Garden City, N.Y.: Anchor Press/Doubleday, 1977.

Gundry, Patricia. *Woman Be Free!* Grand Rapids, Mich.: Zondervan, 1977.

Jongeward, Dorothy, and Scott, Dru. *Women As Winners*. Reading, Mass.: Addison-Wesley, 1976.

Lakein, Alan. *How to Get Control of Your Time and Your Life*. New York: Wyden Books, 1973.

Lumb, Fred A. *What Every Woman Should Know About Finances*. Rockville Centre, N.Y.: Farnsworth, 1978; New York: Berkley, 1979.

McCullough, Bonnie Runyan. *Bonnie's Household Organizer*. New York: St. Martin's Press, 1980.

McGrady, Mike. *The Kitchen Sink Papers*. Garden City, N.Y.: Doubleday, 1975.

Miller, Lowell. *The Wholesale-by-Mail Catalog*. New York: St. Martin's Press, 1979.

Moldafsky, Annie. *The Good Buy Book*. Chicago: Rand McNally, 1980.

Molloy, John T. *The Woman's Dress for Success Book*. Chicago: Follett, 1977; New York: Warner, 1978.

Morehouse, Laurence E., and Gross, Leonard. *Maximum Performance*. New York: Simon & Schuster, 1977; Pocket Books, 1978.

Nelson, Paula. *The Joy of Money: A Contemporary Woman's Guide to Financial Freedom*. Briarcliff Manor, N.Y.: Stein & Day, 1975; New York: Bantam, 1977.

Pogrebin, Letty Cottin. *Getting Yours*. New York: Avon, 1976.

Sayers, Dorothy L. *Are Women Human?* Downers Grove, Ill.: InterVarsity Press, 1971. (This book is now out of print, as is the original collection of essays it was excerpted from, *Unpopular Opinions* [1947]. But it is good reading if you can locate a copy.)

Seaman, Barbara, and Seaman, Gideon. *Women and the Crisis in Sex Hormones*. New York: Rawson, Wade, 1977; Bantam, 1978.

Sharp, Billy B., with Cox, Claire. *Choose Success*. New York: Hawthorn Books, 1970.

Sher, Barbara, with Gottlieb, Annie. *Wishcraft: How to Get What You Really Want*. New York: Viking, 1979.

Stout, Ruth. *How to Have a Green Thumb Without an Aching Back*. New York: Exposition Press, 1955.

Stout, Ruth, and Clemence, Richard. *The Ruth Stout No-Work Garden Book*. Emmaus, Pa.: Rodale Press, 1971.

Tobias, Andrew. *The Only Investment Guide You'll Ever Need*. New York: Harcourt Brace Jovanovich, 1978; Bantam, 1979.

Verkuyl, Gerrit, ed. *Modern Language Bible*. rev. ed. Grand Rapids, Mich.: Zondervan, 1969.

Weinberg, Dr. George. *Self Creation*. New York: St. Martin's Press, 1978; Avon, 1979.

Winston, Stephanie. *Getting Organized*. New York: Norton, 1978; Warner, 1979.